'This wonderful book – a history, guide and manual in one – is well-titled. It promises us adventures, and delivers them. Well-armed actors should make rhetoric part of their arsenal. *Dramatic Adventures in Rhetoric* will train your eyes, your mouth, and (perhaps most usefully for actors) your ears. I like this book extremely. I'll use it. Fun but never foolish, precise but never pedantic, exhaustive but never exhausting, it deserves a place on every actor's, director's and playwright's shelf.'
Samuel West, *actor and director*

'A hugely enjoyable and, most importantly, a brilliantly user-friendly resource for writers, actors, directors, and teachers – politicians and protestors too. Rhetoric was always something I felt intuitively without properly understanding it. To be made more conscious of its rules and principles can only help me as a writer. A remarkably informative and entertaining companion.'
James Graham, *playwright*

'This is an incredibly revealing and insightful book, through which the authors guide us with generosity and wit. Surprisingly entertaining, it is packed full of funny and moving examples of the best dramatic writing, both classical and contemporary. Naming and explaining the devices that playwrights use (consciously or otherwise) can further our understanding of dramatic writing, and our confidence when working with it. I can imagine having it on my desk in rehearsal for problem-solving, or dipping into it lazily for amusement and inspiration.'
Jeremy Herrin, *director*

'We don't always know why we say what we say, or write what we write – but invariably, the Greeks have a word for it. Packed with memorable and quotable examples from sources ancient and modern, this witty and well-organised handbook offers a lexicon for our efforts, terms for our art. For any teacher, actor or writer, a useful and fascinating guide.'
Hilary Mantel, *writer*

'An exciting, useful and thoroughly entertaining book, which opens up whole new directions for text rehearsals. I am so looking forward to tackling a new script – I have never felt so prepared. Don't go into rehearsals without it!'
Nathaniel Parker, *actor*

GILES TAYLOR & PHILIP WILSON

DRAMATIC ADVENTURES IN RHETORIC

A Guide for Actors, Directors and Playwrights

OBERON BOOKS
LONDON

WWW.OBERONBOOKS.COM

First published in 2015 by Oberon Books Ltd
521 Caledonian Road, London N7 9RH
Tel: +44 (0) 20 7607 3637 / Fax: +44 (0) 20 7607 3629
e-mail: info@oberonbooks.com
www.oberonbooks.com

A catalogue record for this book is available from the British Library.

PB ISBN: 9781849434911
E ISBN: 9781783198177

Cover design by James Illman
Text layout by Konstantinos Vasdekis

Printed, bound and converted
by CPI Group (UK) Ltd, Croydon, CR0 4YY.

Visit www.oberonbooks.com to read more about all our books and to buy them. You will also find features, author interviews and news of any author events, and you can sign up for e-newsletters so that you're always first to hear about our new releases.

Thanks

We would like to thank:

James Hogan, Charles Glanville, George Spender, Melina Theocharidou, Andrew Walby, Lewis Morgan, James Illman, Konstantinos Vasdekis, Tia Begum, Emma Hall, Matthew Urwin and Ainé Ryan at Oberon Books.

James Graham, Jeremy Herrin, Hilary Mantel, Nathaniel Parker and Samuel West, for their kind words of endorsement.

Dr Catherine Henstridge at OED, for clarifying numerous definitions; Francis Matthews, for various title suggestions; Xavier Mascarell, for his support and encouragement; students at GSA and MTA, and directors on the Genesis Programme, for allowing Giles to practice what he preaches; Oscar Pearce, John Ramm, Matthew Pidgeon and Nicholas Boulton in the RSC *Wolf Hall* dressing room, for their suggestions; Simon Robinson, for drawing our attention to the device Reductio ad Hitlerum. And last but very much not least, the cast of the double-bill of *The Importance of Being Earnest* and *Travesties* at Birmingham Rep that inspired this book – Emily Bowker, Nick Caldecott, Tom Davey, Matthew Douglas, Abigail McKern, Emerald O'Hanrahan and Roger Ringrose, along with Associate Director Louise Hill.

Emma Anacootee-Parmar at Samuel French Ltd; Marigold Atkey at David Higham Associates; Tom Atkins at The Random House Group Penguin Random House UK; Sarah Baxter at The Society of Authors; Valerie Borchardt and Samantha Shea at Georges Borchardt, Inc; Kate Brower and Victoria Williams at Alan Brodie Representation Ltd; Michael Callahan at Josef Weinberger Ltd; Emma Cheshire at Faber & Faber Ltd; Rose Cobbe, Sean Gascoine, Christian Ogunbanjo, Giles Smart, Nicki Stoddart, Ilaria Tarasconi and Charles Walker at United Agents; Gordon Dickerson; Janet Glass at Eric Glass Ltd; Katie Haines, Julia Kreitman and Leah Schmidt at The Agency; Ben Hall and Lily Williams at Curtis Brown Group Ltd; Nick Hern at Nick Hern Books Ltd; Georgia Ingles at Wylie Agency; Mel Kenyon and Ginny Sennett at Casarotto Ramsay & Associates Ltd, Joyce Kelay at The Gersh Agency; George Lane and Elizabeth Grobel at Creative Artists Agency; Christine Lee at Simon & Schuster; Rupert Lord and Helen Mumby at Macnaughton Lord Representation; Jennie Miller at Independent Talent Group Ltd; Keelan Pacot at Grove/Atlantic, Inc; Imogen Sarre at Knight Hall Agency Ltd; Judith Scott at Amber Lane Press; Christopher Wait at New Directions Publishing; Claire Weatherhead at Bloomsbury Publishing Plc, and Jared Weber at ICM Partners – for their generous assistance in securing and granting permission for quotations.

Contents

Introduction

HENRY: Words... They're innocent, neutral, precise, standing for this, describing that, meaning the other, so if you look after them you can build bridges across incomprehension and chaos.

Tom Stoppard, *The Real Thing* (1982)

How This Book Came About

Back in 2011, the two of us were working on a double-bill of Oscar Wilde's *The Importance of Being Earnest* and Tom Stoppard's *Travesties* at Birmingham Rep. Initial round-the-table discussions included mention of how both plays drew heavily on rhetorical devices. One speech of Stoppard's play was only truly 'unlocked' once we spotted that it involved an extended PAROMOIOSIS.

The cast were fascinated by how many rhetorical devices were present in each play, but – understandably and not unusually – were unaware of their names and their effects. We compiled a comprehensive list, and a tea-break conversation led to the idea that we might be able to help other theatre practitioners to deepen their appreciation of the form and content of the plays they are working on, and in doing so to enrich their understanding of how best to communicate them.

What is Rhetoric?

The *Oxford English Dictionary* defines rhetoric in two ways: as 'the art of effective or persuasive speaking or writing', and as 'language designed to persuade or impress'. Aristotle's famous definition claims rhetoric to be 'the art of seeing the available means of persuasion'. Our core aim in this book is that, by identifying the *means* used, and by understanding fully the effect these devices can have on listeners – both on stage and in the audience – a character can be all the more persuasive, both in terms of what they say and the motivation behind it.

The word rhetoric comes from the Ancient Greek *rhetor*, meaning an orator or public speaker. Rhetoric has always been indelibly linked with oratory, but far from being the preserve of politicians and soap-box public speakers, it is in fact something each of us uses daily – it is simply *how* we communicate. Rhetoric is, to draw on Brian Vickers' beautifully succinct description, 'the formalizing of humanity's innate ability to communicate using language'.

We all use PROVERBS and MAXIMS; they play a huge part in society's common lore. We often compare things using SIMILES and METAPHORS, and we deploy our sense of humour well-honed by IRONY and SARCASM. These are all everyday rhetorical devices – and there are many more besides.

There are two kinds of rhetorical devices: the Dionysian and the Apollonian. The Dionysian is organic, colloquial, instinctive – such as those mentioned above. These are commonly used and have developed over centuries out of our need to convey our thoughts to each other with clarity. Is it any wonder that playwrights reach for such techniques? They provide a natural realism to dialogue, and we recognize in them the way we speak ourselves.

The Apollonian devices, on the other hand, are far more deliberate and constructed. These must be consciously and carefully created by a writer, and they say a lot about the style of a play and the characters within it. Look up the extraordinary PAROMOIOSIS or the beautiful SYNAESTHESIA, the excesses of PARIMION or the structured ascent of GRADATIO. Such devices are a pleasurable challenge.

As actors, directors and playwrights, it is vital to examine the *way* characters speak, and to discover – by how they express themselves – what clues there are to their wants, fears and motives. What specific words do they use, and why? What grammatical structures? What images do they reach for?

Dramatists of all periods (at least until the mid-20th century) were well-versed in rhetoric from their education. They appreciated that a well-structured thought could underpin and bolster the words and ideas they propounded. To adapt the architectural maxim *form follows function* – here, *form supports content*.

While we admit that the use of a device may not have been intentional by a writer, it remains relevant that it is there – both to the actor and to their character. Also, there is a key distinction between a playwright's voice and a character's voice: the former will *know* the effect of their words, the latter may not. This question opens up a worthwhile discussion of possibilities – integral to any rehearsal process.

How To Use This Book

Any brief search on the internet will reveal thousands of articles, books and discussions on rhetoric, covering the realms of writing, philosophy and politics. Our intention is not to summarize this vast scholarship (an impossible task), but rather to introduce you to how playwrights in particular draw on rhetorical devices, and how a greater understanding of these will assist you as a theatre practitioner.

Most of the terms we will introduce you to have classical origins, extraordinary names and are sometimes complex to understand. In an effort to demystify these often unfamiliar terms, each device is followed by how it is commonly pronounced, with italics to show stressed syllables. What you will discover is that behind these bizarre names are usually quite simple verbal effects. We demonstrate these through our many examples, drawn from almost 300 plays by 140 playwrights, from the Renaissance to the modern day.

As you explore this book, think of the sound of the words, the structure of the thoughts, and the images and ideas these engender. Above all, think of their *effect* on the listener. Plays are made to be enacted, the words lifted from the page and into the theatrical arena. Take the plunge, put your reading into practice, and *always* try it out loud.

Dramatic Adventures in Rhetoric is both a reference aid and a tool for textual analysis. There are several ways to approach the book: it may be read from cover to cover or just dipped into. The **Contents** page at the front – with its list of chapters and their sub-headings – will help you to narrow your search if you are trying to *identify* a device. In the **Glossary of Rhetorical Devices** on page 211, meanwhile, you can look up the *name* of a device – whether familiar or unfamiliar – and find a succinct definition. From there you can follow the page reference to find usage and examples. Any device listed there will appear in the book in small capitals. Alternatively, you can plunge into the **Index of Plays and Playwrights Quoted** on page 221, look up your favourite plays or playwrights, and start your journey in their company.

It is hoped that this book will inspire anyone connected with theatre to investigate rhetoric further, and to read dramatic texts more closely. Above all, it is a celebration of the spoken word, the performed word – the word in action.

> GEORGE: If words were only their meaning. Well then... *(He stops, smiling.)* But words are their effect also.
>
> David Hare, *The Absence of War* (1993)

Chapter 1 A Brief History of Rhetoric

TATTLE: Thou art a pretty fellow, and canst carry a message to a lady,
in a pretty soft kind of phrase, and with a good persuading accent.
JEREMY: Sir, I have the seeds of rhetoric and oratory in my head.

William Congreve, *Love for Love* (1695)

In order to understand how rhetoric filtered into – and helped to shape – drama, it is necessary to take a whistle-stop tour through the key elements of the history of rhetoric, predominantly in classical times. It is not essential to read this section first, or indeed at all – you may want simply to plunge straight into the individual terms in Chapter 2 onwards. Here, though, we will introduce you to some of the main building blocks of rhetoric, as identified by classical practitioners in particular. Inevitably we will refer to the Greek and Latin words for things that relate to speech and speaking. We hope you will relish such words, but please do not be put off by them – they are, after all, only names.

Following this introduction, we will fast-forward through the centuries until we reach the Renaissance: a key era, and the true starting point of our linguistic adventure. For it was during this time that scholars began to rediscover classical texts and to translate them into English. Concurrently, we see drama begin to surface as an *entertainment*, rather than as an enactment of religious parables in morality plays.

First, though, let us rewind to:

The Origins of Classical Rhetoric

The story starts in ancient times, insofar as both the Mesopotamians and the Egyptians valued the ability to speak wisely and eloquently. Aristotle, amongst others, references poets such as Homer and Hesiod, who were creating poetry as early as the 9th century BC, as well as the great playwrights of the 5th and 6th centuries BC – Aeschylus, Sophocles and Euripides. They are cited as using clear stylistic techniques of logical, ethical and emotional appeal. These predominantly oral cultures remind us that rhetoric is, first and foremost, a spoken art.

While exact dates are difficult to pin down, it is generally accepted that it was not until the Greeks, and in particular the rise of the city-state of Athens in the 6th century BC, that rhetoric came to be seen as an art, worthy of study and systematic development.

Ancient Greece: The Sophists

Our first 'cast' (as it were) are **The Sophists**. Their name comes from *sophia*, the Greek word for wisdom – from which we derive our word philosophy, a lover (*philos*) of wisdom. Athenian law decreed, as part of its democracy, that *any* man could be called upon to speak in the Assembly, and to persuade his fellow countrymen on the merits, or otherwise, of a particular piece of legislation. In response to this new need for orators, and therefore for rhetorical skill, groups such as the Sophists began to emerge around the 5th century BC.

Like a troupe of travelling players, the Sophists were originally a group of itinerant teachers and poets from Sicily, where formal rhetoric is said to have been started by **Corax of Syracuse** and his pupil **Tisias**. The Sophists – for a small fee – would offer their expertise on democracy, the law, and even culture. While not in any way an organized movement, some groups did rise to prominence; especially those led by **Gorgias** (known as 'the Nihilist') and **Protagoras** (credited with the statement 'Man is the measure of all things').

In time, the focus of the Sophists' work shifted to helping others to be eloquent in speech (not dissimilar to companies nowadays which draw on performance techniques to aid businessmen and women with their presentations). Their fees increased, too. Travelling from city to city, these orators would set up a shop in public arenas and teach young men the intricacies of public speaking by defining parts of speech, detailing styles of argument, and studying poetry. In short, these are the beginnings of what we understand as rhetoric.

Sophists proudly declared that they could win any argument on any subject – even without having prior knowledge of the topic. They famously drew on techniques that enabled speakers to undermine strong arguments and underpin weak ones. Overall, to them, the *manner* of speech was more important than its *meaning*.

Ancient Greece: Socrates and Plato

The Sophists' lofty claims that they could answer any question, and have the upper hand in any debate, brought them into conflict with philosophers such as **Socrates** and **Plato**, who dismissed the Sophists as money-grabbing conmen who used language falsely to conceal and to deceive. These philosophers condemned Sophists for their reliance on emotion, and for their manipulation of the truth: what Shakespeare later referred to, in *Love's Labour's Lost* (c.1595), as 'the sweet smoke of rhetoric'.

Here, a key fault-line opens up – as to whether rhetoric was a wise and honest skill, or a false and divisive art. The pejorative sense of a 'sophist' as someone whose arguments are elaborate but essentially devious comes from this time (and from it arises the word sophisticated – although the derogatory sense has since been lost).

In addition, **Aristotle** drew an important distinction between philosophy and rhetoric. He appreciated that rhetoric was valuable as a way of describing things truthfully, but only if it were based on reason. He determined, therefore, to regulate the elements of speaking, which he did in *The Art of Rhetoric* (4th century BC) – perhaps the first manual of our subject. In it, he defined rhetoric, as we mention in our Introduction, as 'the art of seeing the available means of persuasion'. This is crucial.

One cannot underestimate the impact and influence of *The Art of Rhetoric*. For the next 2,000 years, it was a key text for those wanting to study rhetoric, and it remained on the curriculum at universities until the 19th century. Aristotle goes into great detail about many aspects of rhetoric, but for our purposes it is necessary only to understand about proofs and genres.

First, proofs. Aristotle identified three key means of persuasion, based on a trio of appeals: *logos*, *ethos* and *pathos*. Although these terms may seem familiar, it is worth taking a brief look at their core values.

Logos is taken from the Greek for 'word', and represents persuasion through reason. This approach centres on the argument, and draws on logic and rational explanation. Often, this was through the use of SYLLOGISMS and ENTHYMEMES. Key elements here are the clarity of the proposition, the logic inherent in its reasoning, and the effectiveness of the supporting evidence. Unsurprisingly, given Aristotle's focus on truth, this was his favoured approach. Thinking of our own lives, don't we tend to believe people whom we trust? While, conversely, if we don't trust someone, do we not find it hard to accept their point of view? In terms of drama, it is interesting to consider the relationship not only between characters, but also between audience and actor in this regard.

Ethos is from the Greek for 'character' or 'habit', and means persuasion through the credibility of the speaker. Hence our word ethics – the study of concepts of right and wrong. Where *logos* concentrates on the facts and figures, *ethos* is concerned more with the style and tone of delivery. The speaker is not neutral in the telling: their knowledge of the subject and expertise in the relevant field, along with their personal integrity, reputation and good character, come into play here.

Pathos is the third proof, and comes from the Greek word that means both 'experience' and 'suffering'. It appeals to the emotions of the listener, and arouses their interest and imagination, as well as their sympathy and desire to respond. Choice of words is critical here. Advertising would barely exist without the emotional appeals that are at the heart of the *pathos* approach.

Alongside these proofs or appeals, Aristotle set out three genres of rhetoric, based on the aim of the speech, the function of the audience, and on the viewpoint of time. This trio is: *dikanikon*, *epideiktikon* and *symbouleutikon*. We said we'd be introducing some Greek and Latin words! These three relate to different arenas of examination, and also to the past, the present and the future.

Dikanikon (dee-*kan*-ee-con – meaning 'like a lawyer') to determine what is just, based on what has happened in *the past*; this is judicial or forensic.

Epideiktikon (*ep*-ee-*dayk*-tee-con – meaning 'showy') to apportion praise or blame, based on how people should feel in *the present*; this is demonstrative.

Symbouleutikon (*sim*-bool-*yoo*-tee-con – meaning 'counsel') to consider what is expedient – a guide for *the future*; this pertains to debate.

Classical Rome: Cicero and Quintilian

In time, the Romans conquered the Greeks, and while they subsumed their new subjects into their empire, they also assimilated aspects of Greek culture – including rhetoric. As with many retellings of stories, the Romans both adopted and adapted Grecian rhetoric. Most notably, they put less emphasis on Aristotelian logic, and favoured instead a greater dependence on stories that were exciting and adventurous, told with great stylistic flourishes and drawing on striking metaphors. More theatrical, one might say.

In Rome, the great statesman **Cicero** wrote a number of crucial documents, including *De Inventione* (*On Invention*, 84BC), *De Oratore* (*On Oration*, 55BC) and *Topica* (*Topics*, 44BC). As with Aristotle before him, he went into great detail. However, perhaps the most important aspect is that he stated that a man, in order to be persuasive, must be knowledgeable in the law, ethics, politics, history, medicine, art and literature. Good for pub quizzes then!

There is also an important work entitled *Rhetorica Ad Herennium* (*Rhetoric For Herennius*, 1st century BC), which may or may not have been by Cicero. This focuses on *elocutio* (style of delivery), and sets up six steps in the structure of any argument.

The Six Steps of an Argument

1) **Exordium** A preamble to engage the audience and establish your credentials.
2) **Narratio** A succinct statement of the facts and the key argument to be made.
3) **Divisio** A point-by-point setting out of the argument.
4) **Confirmatio** The evidence to back up the argument.
5) **Confutatio** A consideration of the opposing viewpoint to bolster one's own.
6) **Conclusio** A summary and conclusion.

Another key player in this Roman act of our story is **Quintilian**. Initially, he worked in the field of law and, like an experienced barrister, he honed and perfected his rhetorical skills in the courts. Later, he set up a school for teaching rhetoric, and wrote his masterwork *Institutio Oratoria* (*Instruction of the Orator*, c.95AD). This twelve-volume compendium covers all aspects of rhetoric, in considerable detail.

Quintilian developed and extended the five canons of rhetoric, first propounded by Cicero in *On Invention*, as a guide to creating and delivering a speech convincingly. Although, with regard to drama, we will be looking at the *effects* of word-shaping more than the source of the argument, it is useful to give a brief explanation of this.

The Five Canons of Rhetoric

1) **Inventio** Although the word suggests invention, this is less about 'making up' an argument and more about the search for the best way to *persuade*. Before formulating an argument, a speaker must define what information needs to be conveyed and how best to present it. Aristotle's three proofs – *logos*, *ethos* and *pathos* (outlined above) – are critical here. Setting is important, too: is it a formal or an informal occasion? The timing of the argument is also crucial – not only the length of the speech, but the optimum moment in which to deliver it. Last, but very much not least, the audience must be considered – who they are, and what their hopes, fears, interests and needs are. Only once all this is mapped out can the argument be developed and refined.

2) **Dispositio** The arrangement of the elements of the argument into a coherent structure for maximum effect. The sections of this are drawn from the Six Steps of an Argument (outlined above).

3) **Elocutio** This word suggests elocution – that is, clarity of speech – but originally it was more about the *style* of delivery. This stage involves determining how best to present the argument, drawing on figures of speech and other rhetorical techniques. Also considered is how the emotions might be stirred, in presenting the argument.

Once again, there is a trio – here, relating to levels of style, chosen according to the subject matter and the audience:

> Plain: *attentuata* (engaging, economical) or *subtile* (precise, simple)
> Middle: *mediocris* (moderate, ordinary) or *robusta* (solid, strong)
> High: *florida* (flowery, ornate) or *gravis* (weighty, severe)

4) **Memoria** This is the process of learning and memorizing your speech so that you can deliver it without the use of notes (sound familiar, actors?). It also consisted of building up a store of suitable quotes and other references which would enable the speaker to extemporize if the mood took him.

5) **Actio** This is the rehearsal of the speech, playing with gesture and tone of voice to ensure the most dynamic and persuasive delivery.

Building on Aristotle's Proofs and Genres of Rhetoric, Cicero's Six Steps of an Argument, and Quintilian's Five Canons, the **Progymnasmata** (*proh*-jim-*naz*-mah-tah) – from the Greek for 'preliminary exercises' – were developed. These were an established series of rhetorical exercises that began in Greece and subsequently became popular in Rome as well. Students would practise various forms of distilled rhetoric, including reasoning for and against an argument, praise and attack, comparison and description, as well as making up maxims, fables and other narratives.

So, as we have seen, the key foundations and building blocks of rhetoric were comprehensively laid down in Classical times – and have been drawn upon, in many fields, ever since.

From the Classical Era to Medieval Times: 5th to 15th Century

This period saw a shift, whereby rhetoric was seen not only in the political arena, but also in the realm of religion. Early Christian authorities were immensely concerned about pagan practices – including rhetoric – and in 391AD Emperor Theodosius issued laws to make pagan worship illegal. Later, Emperor Justinian (483-565AD) cut off support to the study of rhetoric.

Here our journey might have ended, were it not for influential thinkers led by St Augustine (354-430AD), who realized that although rhetoric was developed in a pagan age, its techniques could be used in the teaching of the scriptures, and for ongoing efforts in the conversion of non-believers. In the fourth book of his *De Doctrina Christiana* (*On Christian Teaching*, 397-426AD), Augustine quotes Cicero: 'He who is eloquent should speak in such a way that he teaches, delights and moves.'

This was a sentiment echoed centuries later by Sir Philip Sidney, who declared in his *Defence of Poesy* (1583) that poesy (that is, both poetry and drama) 'is an art of imitation, for so Aristotle terms it in his word *mimesis*, that is to say, a representing, counterfeiting, or figuring forth; to speak metaphorically, a speaking picture, with this end – to teach and delight.'

Rhetoric made up a major proportion – along with grammar and logic – of education at this time and for centuries to come, drawing on manuals such as Boethius' (480-524) *Overview of the Structure of Rhetoric*. Overall, however, it is generally accepted that during this period rhetoric was practised, rather than expanded.

The Renaissance

This means, as you no doubt know, rebirth – and this period, generally said to span from the 14th to 17th centuries, certainly saw a resurgence of interest in rhetoric. It was the theories propounded by Greek rhetoricians, rather than by Roman writers, that were adopted by scholars at this time. Also, crucially, the proliferation of texts that were increasingly being written in English, rather than in Latin or Greek, led to a far greater readership.

This was a time in which English was developing exponentially, and playwrights used this linguistic plasticity in their work. Shakespeare, for instance, is attributed as having contributed over 1,700 words to the language. His work exemplifies how playwrights were inspired by rhetoric. Yes, Marlowe led the way, and other writers, such as Ben Jonson, Beaumont and Fletcher, Webster and the like were prolific, but Shakespeare capitalized most on this burgeoning of the English language. Perhaps they drew on the many rhetorical manuals that were in circulation at this time, with such marvellously baroque titles as *The Art or Crafte of Rhetoryke* by Leonard Cox (c.1530), Richard Rainolde's *A Booke Called the Foundacion of Rhetorike* (1563), *The Garden of Eloquence* by Henry Peacham (1577), and George Puttenham's *The Arte of English Poesie* (1589). Even if they didn't, Shakespeare and his contemporaries certainly knew how to shape a phrase to maximum effect.

The Restoration, the Victorians and Beyond

Thereafter, in every age, there appear playwrights who clearly relish the use of rhetoric for dramatic effect. In the Restoration, these included George Etherege, Aphra Behn, William Wycherley and George Farquhar. Bridging into the **18th century**, William Congreve continued the tradition, as did the likes of John Vanbrugh and Oliver Goldsmith.

Richard Brinsley Sheridan led the way triumphantly into the **19th century** along with such playwrights as Edward Bulwer-Lytton and Dion Boucicault, but no discussion of the Victorian age would be complete without mentioning Oscar Wilde. His mother read poetry to him from an early age, and he developed a fascination with all aspects of neoclassicism, including rhetoric. Wilde went on to study Greats (Latin, Greek and Philosophy) at Trinity College, Dublin and Magdalen College, Oxford, and later lectured on the Italian Renaissance. Thus he was exposed to the two wellsprings of rhetoric. He found in rhetoric a code through which he might hide his unconventional feelings, and satirize the strait-laced mores of Victorian society. These double-meanings, which conceal as much as they reveal, were to come to a peak in his plays, which are packed with rhetorical trickery, invention and quips.

George Bernard Shaw picked up the rhetorical mantle and carried its popularity deftly into the **20th century**, opening the way for such luminary wordsmiths as Noël Coward, Terence Rattigan, John Osborne and August Wilson. We have been led into the **21st century** by such writers as Tom Stoppard, Alan Bennett, Caryl Churchill, Timberlake Wertenbaker and Bryony Lavery, who in turn have paved the way for such leading young playwrights as Laura Wade, Mike Bartlett, Lucy Prebble and James Graham. You will find works by these and many other playwrights cited in the chapters that follow.

So, armed with a few classical terms and an understanding of the origins and structure of rhetoric, let us proceed. Relish the adventure!

Chapter 2 Sound

HIGGINS: Mere alliteration, Mrs Pearce, natural to a poet.

George Bernard Shaw, *Pygmalion* (1912)

We lower you into the tantalizing depths of rhetoric with a selection of devices that have an acoustic effect, some of which will already be familiar. Who does not remember ALLITERATION from studying poetry at school? And the notoriously unspellable ONOMATOPOEIA? Perhaps you even recall ASSONANCE and SIBILANCE too.

We are all brought up with nursery rhymes and songs that utilize such devices to playful effect. Books for children invariably reach for these devices to introduce them to the musicality and fun of language. Those of you who are familiar with the Dr Seuss series will know what we mean.

In adult life we are no less bombarded with these devices, usually from the realm of advertising. Such repeated sounds are invaluable in making tag-lines and jingles catchy, thereby ensuring the product is remembered. Think of the ALLITERATION of 'P-p-p-pick up a Penguin' for the biscuits of that name, the overt ASSONANCE of Typhoo Tea's 'You only get an OO with Typhoo', or the mischievous HOMOIOTELEUTON or rhyme of Puffin Books' motto: 'There's nuffin' like a Puffin'.

These devices – and other less familiar ones in this chapter – have also been popularly used by playwrights throughout the ages. Shakespeare and other writers of the Renaissance were particular advocates. They made plays for thrust stages with a wrap-around audience, usually out of doors. Such theatres require a terrific muscularity of language and diction in order for the texts, and therefore the stories, to be conveyed dynamically to the audience. If a playwright laces a particular line, idea or joke with ALLITERATION or PARACHESIS, it will 'ping out' and lodge itself in the minds of the audience all the more effectively.

These devices easily made the transition into the High Comedies of the Restoration, and on into plays of the same tradition in the 19th and early-20th centuries. From the second half of the 20th century to our own time, such devices have become more sparingly, though no less effectively, used. Playwrights choose carefully when to unleash a pithy ALLITERATIVE PAIR or a robust HOMOIOTELEUTON, and to maximum effect.

Delve into the following pages to reacquaint yourself with some old friends – and meet some rather extraordinary new ones. Enjoy the examples we have found and always try saying them out loud to appreciate their full effect.

THE ALLITERATIVE FAMILY

It is generally acknowledged that consonants carry the energy of our thoughts, which in turn translates into our communication. In writing or performing plays we must always consider the sounds we are making, and use them to their optimum to help clarify character and the telling of the story.

ALLITERATION from the Latin meaning 'to the letter'.
When neighbouring or key words begin with the same single sound and, in most cases, the same letter. ALLITERATION is, in fact, the most simple and common form of PARACHESIS (see below).

> MRS CHEVELEY: Nowadays, with our modern mania for morality, everyone has to pose as a paragon of purity.
> Oscar Wilde, *An Ideal Husband* (1895)

In this quotation Mrs Cheveley's cynical viewpoint is punched home by the two clusters of alliterative words, the repeated 'M's and 'P's achieving a brilliant balance.

The acoustic effect of ALLITERATION is not confined to the first letters of words alone. It can also be the first letter of the **Stressed Syllable** of a word, as when Adriana in Shakespeare's *The Comedy of Errors* (1594) says 'I'll weep what's left away, and weeping die' – the 'W' in 'away' is just as active as the other 'W's.

Plosive Consonants – that is, T, D, K or hard C, G, P and B – are particularly emphatic. Martin in John Osborne's play *Luther* (1961) considers the imminent end of time with 'There can't be anything left but the black bottom of the bucket'; the repeated 'B's accentuate the bald, nihilistic image. Similarly, the Victorian *pater familias* Clive in Caryl Churchill's *Cloud Nine* (1979) describes effeminacy as 'A disease more dangerous than diphtheria'; an actor might be inspired to use those three 'D's to create a particularly derisive effect. And consider the 'K' and hard 'C's accenting this observation about the radio:

> KATE: D'you know what that thing has done? Killed all Christian conversation in this country.
> Brian Friel, *Dancing at Lughnasa* (1990)

Labial Plosives – B and P – are particularly used when a pejorative effect is required. Benedick in Shakespeare's *Much Ado About Nothing* (c.1598) mocks Don Pedro and Claudio with 'You break breasts as braggarts do their blades'; the 'B's are unavoidably active, and gloriously so. Leantio in Thomas Middleton's *Women Beware Women* (1621) describes 'Base Lust / With all her powders, paintings and best pride'; the combination of 'B's and 'P's is clearly indicative of his mistrustful attitude towards this particular sin. And look at this embittered example:

FAULKLAND: Sir Anthony's presence prevented my proposed expostulations.
Richard Brinsley Sheridan, *The Rivals* (1775)

'M's are employed to achieve a wide range of effects. In Edward Bulwer-Lytton's *Money* (1840) Sir John Vesey – about to meet the executor of his brother-in-law's will – proclaims 'This is a most melancholy meeting'; the repeated 'M's create a suitably sombre tone, whether sincere or not. Whereas Grace in Dion Boucicault's *London Assurance* (1841) uses 'M's to disdainful effect when she remarks that 'Marriage matters are conducted nowadays in a most mercantile manner'. And the torrent of 'M's in this example – to pronounce them the lips must be very active, almost pouty – suggest a flirtatious manner:

ALGERNON: I want you to reform me. You might make it your mission,
if you don't mind.
Oscar Wilde, *The Importance of Being Earnest* (1895)

'W's are used in several ways too. In *4.48 Psychosis* Sarah Kane includes the autobiographically prescient line: 'This is not a world in which I wish to live'; the mournful ALLITERATION of the 'W's – combined with the ASSONANCE of the short 'I' sounds – makes this sentence pleasing to the ear, in direct opposition to the character's bleak, suicidal statement. Conversely, when Van Swieten in Peter Shaffer's *Amadeus* (1979) suggests that Mozart should join their Brotherhood of Masons, he adds 'We would welcome you very warmly'; there is indeed a persuasive warmth in the repetition of the 'W' sound. And how about this pugnacious example:

TROY: What you watching where I'm walking for? I ain't watching after you.
August Wilson, *Fences* (1985)

Other effects commonly employ ALLITERATION, though are not drawn to any particular letter:

Comedy Daniel in Kevin Elyot's *My Night with Reg* (1994) proclaims 'You are looking at a new man: Monica Monogamy, that's moi'; a classic piece of camp humour, accentuated by the profusion of 'M's. The porn actor Colin in Alan Bennett's play *People* (2012), while filming in a chilly stately home, complains that 'Hypothermia and a hard on don't go hand in hand'; quite apart from being very funny, the 'H's rather breathily get his point across.

Affectation Staying with Bennett, Lady Rumpers in *Habeas Corpus* (1973) refers to a sexual indiscretion during an air raid (which resulted in her daughter Felicity) as 'one mad magenta moment'; her self-conscious choice of words tells us a lot about her character. And Lord Are in Edward Bond's *Restoration* (1981, revised 2006) claims that his 'figure sets a fashion few could follow'; the 'F's delicately heighten his foppish bragging.

Sound Echoing Sense In an effusive moment after her betrothal to Bassanio, Portia in Shakespeare's *The Merchant of Venice* (c.1597) says that for him she 'would be trebled twenty times' herself; the three 'T's brilliantly echo the trebling.

ALLITERATIVE 'KNITTING'

This is what we term the practice of using ALLITERATION to point up crucial words for stress and sense. If you only say the alliterative words, you have the whole meaning.

Barabas in Marlowe's *The Jew of Malta* (c.1592) sums up his trade with 'This is the ware wherein consists my wealth'; the alliterative words – ware-wherein-wealth – hold the nub of the sense. More playfully, when Ehmke in Michael Frayn's *Democracy* (2003) is angry with his colleagues, he vows to 'give them both the most colossal boot up the backside'; both-boot-backside – the sense is clear! And here's a glorious example:

> JOHNNY: I've been here since before all you bent busybody bastards
> were born.
> Jez Butterworth, Jerusalem (2009)

ALLITERATIVE PAIR

This is what we call two alliterated words deployed together to 'ping out' an image or idea.

Think of Tony Blair's rhetorical masterstroke on the death of Princess Diana, when he referred to her as the 'People's Princess'. Think too of such common phrases as 'bad blood', 'cold comfort' or 'find fault'. Pairs really serve up an idea. As a performer, one has to decide whether a character is conscious of using these – and, if so, what effect it will have, both on the audience and on the other characters.

In Arthur Miller's *Death of a Salesman* (1949) the character of Happy belittles his penchant for sleeping with his boss' fiancées as a 'crummy characteristic'. Prince Hal in Shakespeare's *Henry IV Part Two* (c.1598) examines the crown resting on the pillow beside the dying king, his father, and proclaims it a 'polished perturbation'. And here's a pleasingly punchy example:

> FAUSTUS: This soul should fly from me, and I be changed
> Unto some brutish beast.
> Christopher Marlowe, Doctor Faustus (c.1589)

Stressed Syllables Once again, the effect need not rely on the first letter of words, but can be the first letter of the stressed syllable of a word, as when Harriet in George Etherege's *The Man of Mode* (1676) complains of her maid's attempts to do her hair, saying 'How I do daily suffer under thy officious fingers!' – the 'F's in 'officious' are just as potent as the 'F' in 'fingers'.

Insults These are greatly boosted by ALLITERATIVE PAIRS, such as when the hapless Mrs Fainall calls the scheming Mrs Marwood a 'treacherous trull' in Congreve's *The Way Of The World* (1700), or when Max in Pinter's *The Homecoming* (1965) calls his younger brother, Sam, a 'paralysed prat'!

Disdain The INVECTIVE of insults can soften into mere disdain. Note how the arms manufacturer Undershaft in Shaw's *Major Barbara* (1905) dismisses his critic, Professor of Greek Adolphus Cusins, with 'You tire me, Euripides, with your morality mongering'. Or when Gordon in J.B. Priestley's *Dangerous Corner* (1932) berates his wife for allowing their friends 'to talk about your husband in this fulsome fashion'. It is easy for an actor to invest in these repeated sounds, and to good effect.

Wit The natural playfulness of ALLITERATION readily lends itself to witty characters, such as Septimus in Tom Stoppard's *Arcadia* (1993) who refers to an indiscretion in the grounds of a stately home as a 'perpendicular poke in a gazebo'. Or this observation by a master of his butler, in which the ALLITERATION deftly points up the PARADOX:

> ALGERNON: Lane, you're a perfect pessimist.
>
> Oscar Wilde, *The Importance of Being Earnest* (1895)

Affectation Pairs also work winningly for more affected characters, such as Brandt in Michael Frayn's *Democracy* (2003), who describes mushroom picking as the 'mycological mysteries'. His choice of words tells us a lot about his intellect, education and playful sense of pretension. Conversely, Eddie in Arthur Miller's *A View From The Bridge* (1956) complains that his beloved niece, Catherine, is inviting male attention by 'walkin' wavy'. He may think he is belittling her sexy walk, but it will appear to the audience that this slightly absurd turn of phrase points to his inability to come to terms with his niece growing up. The dichotomy between what effect a character thinks his words have and how the audience perceive them is always worth examining.

Lust From the Medieval Morality Plays onwards, the letter 'L' is often used where sexual matters are concerned. This, we think, must be because of the *visible* activity of the tongue when pronouncing the letter. Ben Jonson refers to 'lust's labyrinth' in *Volpone* (1605-6), and in William Wycherley's *The Country Wife* (1675) Sir Jasper Fidget thinks his wife has been unfaithful to him and addresses her as 'thou libidinous lady!'

Character Trait Timberlake Wertenbaker – In *Our Country's Good* (1988) – gives Major Ross a plethora of ALLITERATIVE PAIRS: he describes Australia as 'this possumy place', and decries the criminals he is overseeing as 'contumelious convicts' and 'vice-ridden vermin', and, when they take part in a play, as a 'caterwauling cast'. An actor must investigate why his character has this foible and how best to use it.

SIBILANCE from the Latin meaning 'hissing'.
A form of ALLITERATION using only 'S' sounds.

It is traditionally equated with the hissing of the serpent in the Garden of Eden and therefore with Original Sin, and by extension **Evil** in general (not for nothing is the baddies' house in the *Harry Potter* books called Slitherin).

Here's a classic example from Shakespeare: Don John, the villain of *Much Ado About Nothing* (c.1598), has tricked his brother and Claudio into believing that Claudio's fiancée is being unfaithful. Don Pedro and Claudio thank him, to which he responds:

> DON JOHN: O plague right well prevented! So will you say when you
> have seen the sequel.

It is not uncommon for an audience to boo Don John at this point, so eminently villainous does he come across – almost like a pantomime baddy.

In a more modern example, John Proctor, the doomed protagonist of Arthur Miller's *The Crucible* (1953), tells how the supposedly demonically possessed Abigail is tormenting him: 'Now she'll suck a scream to stab me with' – a surprising image, made all the more visceral by the SIBILANCE.

There can be a real hissing **Viciousness** to a heavily sibilant line. Katherine in David Hare's *The Secret Rapture* (1988) derides power-crazed, vodka-fuelled business executives, saying that they 'smile their stupid shiny smiles'.

SIBILANCE is also often deployed to depict **Mockery**, **Disdain** or – as in the following example – **Revulsion**:

> EDWARD: There are times the sight and sound of you disgust me.
> I can feel a smell off you. Sickening. The sight of you sickens me.
> The sound of you. I find your smell sickening.
>
> Frank McGuinness, *Someone Who'll Watch Over Me* (1992)

SIBILANT 'KNITTING'

This is our term for when SIBILANCE is used to point up crucial words for stress and sense.

Melinda in George Farquhar's *The Recruiting Officer* (1706) says 'You are a servant, and a secret would make you saucy'. Here, the key words – servant-secret-saucy – give us a sense of the meaning. Whereas when King Henry in Shakespeare's *Henry V* (c.1599) describes a soldier who, in the future, will 'strip his sleeve and show his scars', the sense is wholly expressed in the sibilant words: strip-sleeve-show-scars. In the following example (the lack of inverted commas is Shaw's own), note how the SIBILANCE emphasizes the REPETITION of the word 'same' – same-sort-sinner-same-salvation:

BARBARA: Theyre all just the same sort of sinner; and theres the same salvation ready for them all.

George Bernard Shaw, *Major Barbara* (1905)

SIBILANT PAIR

This is what we call two sibilant words deployed together to 'ping out' an image or idea, often in a belittling or pejorative way.

Lady Macbeth in Shakespeare's *Macbeth* (1606) speaks of the 'swinish sleep' of the two guards whom she intends to blame for the murder of Duncan. Tom Stoppard, in *Travesties* (1993 edition), has Nadya recall her husband Lenin's irritation at the 'saccharine sentimentality' of Charles Dickens' *Cricket On The Hearth*. And Alison in John Osborne's *Look Back In Anger* (1956) describes her and Jimmy's cloyingly childish game of Bear and Squirrel as:

ALISON: A silly symphony for people who couldn't bear the pain of being human beings any longer.

CONSONANCE from the Latin meaning 'sounding together'.

The repetition of the same consonants within successive words, and not just at the beginning.

Consider the lush, flirtatious advances of Charles Courtly towards his intended, Grace, in Dion Boucicault's *London Assurance* (1841): 'Meditating upon matrimony, madam?' – the savouring of the 'M' sounds requires particularly active lips. Or the belittlement of Elyot by Amanda in Noël Coward's *Private Lives* (1930) when she calls him a 'Chivalrous little love'; the effect achieved by the combination of 'L's and short assonant 'I's.

The use of the same sound repeatedly is often employed to create an effect of resolute **Determination**. Consider the journey of 'S's into 'M's here (it is fun to speak the last phrase through gritted teeth, all in the lips):

SUBTLE: I must use him
In some strange fashion now, to make him admire me.

Ben Jonson, *The Alchemist* (1610)

SIBILANT CONSONANCE

This often creates an effect of **Secrecy**, with the 'S's creating a sound like whispering. This is something the playwrights of the Renaissance were particularly adept at:

HUME: Seal up your lips and give no words but mum;
The business asketh silent secrecy.

William Shakespeare, *Henry VI Part Two* (1591)

This secretive effect often extends into things **Sexual**, as when the beguiling Mrs Allonby in Oscar Wilde's *A Woman of No Importance* (1893) asks Lord Illingworth to 'Define us as a sex'. He replies – splendidly sibilantly – 'Sphinxes without secrets'. This is hard to say – the lips must be very active, which creates a sensual, flirtatious effect.

A tight, hissed pronunciation can bring out the subtle **Sarcasm** of a line such as Bevan's in Alan Bennett's *People* (2012) when he suggests, if Dorothy does not open her stately home to the public, that 'At first sight not sharing might seem like selfishness'. Or consider this example, in which the traitor Scroop pleads for mercy with **Sycophantic** simpering. There are sixteen 'S' sounds in only twenty words:

> SCROOP: So service shall with steelèd sinews toil,
> And labour shall refresh itself with hope
> To do your grace incessant services.
> William Shakespeare, *Henry V* (c.1599)

PARIMION (pa-*rim*-ee-on) from the Greek meaning 'close resemblance'. Extreme ALLITERATION (see also CACEMPHATON 2).

Tongue twisters, of course, indulge in this device. Think of 'Peter Piper picked a peck of pickled pepper' or 'Around the rugged rocks the ragged rascal ran'. The muscularity required to shape the repeated sounds is both taxing and amusing. Because of this, there is often a playfulness in the use of PARIMION.

Emphasis In Julian Mitchell's *Another Country* (1982), the schoolboy Bennett exuberantly triumphs over his nemesis with 'The foul fiend Fowler felled at last!' – it is like a headline yelled by a newspaper vendor. Meanwhile, in Sarah Daniels' *Neaptide* (1986), another play set in a school, Roger greets his deputy head teacher, Claire, with glorious affectation: 'Good morning, deputy éclaire, our matriarch's mentor and minion'.

Comedy Unsurprisingly, such excessive ALLITERATION can have a ludicrously comic effect, as in:

> QUINCE: Whereat with blade – with bloody, blameful blade,
> He bravely broached his boiling bloody breast.
> William Shakespeare, *A Midsummer Night's Dream* (1595)

Comedy like this is often combined with extreme REPETITION too, as in this example:

> MRS SWABB: Now a scene setting scene to set the scene and see the set,
> set the scene up and see the set up.
> Alan Bennett, *Habeas Corpus* (1973)

Other effects achievable through PARIMION include:

Contempt Peter in Sean O'Casey's *The Plough and the Stars* (1926) lays into the Covey, who has been goading him, saying 'You lean, long, lanky lath of a lowsey bastard!'

Spite Elyot's ex-wife, Amanda, in Noël Coward's *Private Lives* (1930) derides his new wife, Sybil, with the acidly sibilant 'She seems so insipid, somehow'.

Melancholy Michael in *Someone Who'll Watch Over Me* (1992) by Frank McGuinness ruefully describes being made redundant from his university post with the comment 'One wave from the wicked witch's wand, and it's gone'.

THE ASSONANT FAMILY

If consonants carry the energy of our thoughts, then the vowel sounds are considered to bear the emotion. As you will see from the following family of devices, different vowel sounds and the internal sounds of words can have very particular effects – worth noting for actors, directors and writers alike.

ASSONANCE from the Latin meaning 'resounding'.
The repetition of identical vowel sounds in neighbouring words.

Again this is an idea familiar from school, but here, in the realm of drama, think how different vowel sounds relate to different emotions. For instance, hope is often represented by generous, open sounds, whereas criminality might be portrayed by tight, closed sounds.

Let's deal with each vowel in turn:

'A' sounds During a fatalistic tryst with Loveless in John Vanbrugh's comedy *The Relapse* (1696) Amanda states 'But we were clad in black mortality'. The short 'A's contribute to making her statement rather bald and even sinister – note that the short assonant 'A' in 'mortality' lands on the primary stress of the word. Conversely, the long 'A's in Steven Berkoff's *Greek* (1980) are steeped in derision, when Eddy vows to 'rid the world of half-assed bastards'. Consider also the keening 'AY' sounds in this example, in which Antony has just fallen on his sword:

> ANTONY: Death,
> Like a great man, takes state, and makes me wait
> For my admittance.
> John Dryden, *All for Love* (1677)

'E' sounds The short 'E' tends towards a more stark, dry effect, as when the Messenger in Marlowe's *Tamburlaine the Great: Part One* (1587) heralds that warrior's attack, saying that his 'jetty feathers menace death and hell'. The long 'E' sound is often employed when a yearning, begging effect is sought, as in Queen Margaret's 'O, let me entreat thee cease' in Shakespeare's *Henry VI Part Two* (1591). Alternatively, long 'E's can create an effect of ease and freedom, as in this example where the sound echoes the sense; pronouncing the long 'EE's causes the mouth to smile:

> PRINCESS: I'm breathing freely and deeply as if the panic was over.
> Tennessee Williams, *Sweet Bird of Youth* (1959)

'I' sounds In Oliver Goldsmith's comedy *She Stoops to Conquer* (1771) Marlow, besotted with Miss Hardcastle when she is dressed as a maid, utters the stupefied 'This simplicity bewitches me'. In English Received Pronunciation (RP) short 'E's are pronounced as short 'I's, thus rendering every vowel sound in this phrase the same. Conversely, in Congreve's *The Way of the World* (1700) Sir Wilfull, locked into a room with Mrs Millament, asks 'What a vixen trick is this?' – the sharp 'I's are brim-full of accusatory embarrassment. Meanwhile, here's the future Richard III creating the very smile of which he boasts by pronouncing the long 'I's:

> RICHARD: Why, I can smile, and murder whiles I smile.
> William Shakespeare, *Henry VI Part Three* (1591)

'O' sounds The Spaniard Biskey in Aphra Behn's *The Rover* (1677) mocks the English when he says 'These be the oaken rogues; all rogues and rovers'; the long 'O's emulate his perception of the English accent, adding to the mockery. Short 'O's tend to have an almost pert effect, as when Katherine in David Hare's *The Secret Rapture* (1988) says 'got to keep Max's cock hot in my pocket'. The long 'OO' sound often creates a sense of petulance, forcing the lips into a sulky pout:

> HELENA: Good troth, you do me wrong, good sooth, you do,
>   In such disdainful manner me to woo.
> William Shakespeare, *A Midsummer Night's Dream* (1595)

Also common are extensions of the 'O' sounds, which include 'OW' and 'OR'. Consider the phonetically pedantic Professor Higgins in Shaw's *Pygmalion* (1912) when he promises Eliza Doolittle that she will 'go up and down and round the town in a taxi every day'. The repeated 'OW' sound seems to reflect the circuitous route of the vehicle. And observe how this example creates the gaping yawn it speaks of by echoing the 'OR/AW' sound:

> THOMAS: Sucked into judgement by a cosmic yawn
>   Of boredom.
> Christopher Fry, *The Lady's Not For Burning* (1948)

'U' sounds The short 'U' sound can be very curt, as when Sylv refers to washing Mike's stained underwear in Steven Berkoff's *East* (1975, revised 1976), saying she has 'the emblem of his scummy lust to Persil out with hectic scrub'; wonderfully tough, terse assonant words. Conversely, the terminally cynical Jimmy in John Osborne's *Look Back In Anger* (1956) longs for 'a little ordinary human enthusiasm'; there is sense of yearning in the long 'YOO' sounds, tinged perhaps with a slight sarcastic edge, so typical of this character. And see how the repeated sound here echoes the 'UGH' sound of being punched:

> NED: I'm accused of being self-serving, as if it's fun getting slugged in the subway.
>
> Larry Kramer, *The Normal Heart* (1985)

ASSONANT 'KNITTING'

This is what we call ASSONANCE used to link crucial words for stress and sense.

Kinchela in Dion Boucicault's *The Shaughraun* (1874) says 'Every penny I possess is invested in this estate'. Here, all the words which share the same vowel sound hold the sense: every-penny-possess-invested-estate. And consider the long 'I's in this example:

> TAMBURLAINE: Wherein are rocks of pearl that shine as bright
> As all the lamps that beautify the sky!
>
> Christopher Marlowe, *Tamburlaine the Great: Part Two* (1588)

ASSONANT SYMPHONY

This is our term for when there is either a profusion of one vowel in its several forms, a progression of vowel sounds, or an antithesis of vowel sounds.

Profusion of One Vowel Felix, the socially awkward astro-physicist in Charlotte Jones' *Humble Boy* (2001), quietly despairs with 'I don't know how the world works'; the several different 'O' sounds create a hollow, sorrowful effect. And there are various 'A' sounds in this example, surging from the long to the short:

> LUCETTA: Faith, thy sweet face and shape have made me your absolute captive.
>
> Aphra Behn, *The Rover* (1677)

Progression of Vowel Sounds This can, for instance, be from closed to open, or from sharp to broad. Many actors will know the classic vocal warm-up exercise 'Who would know aught of art must learn and then take his ease', which moves through all the vowel sounds in order. It is these shifts of sound that are of interest here.

Cleopatra in Shakespeare's *Antony and Cleopatra* (1606) demands 'Give me some music – music, moody food / For us that trade in love'; the sounds move from a sharp 'I'

Dramatic Adventures in Rhetoric

through the lengthening 'O's to the soft sound of 'love'. Try pronouncing only the vowel sounds to hear the progression. And here various broad, open vowel sounds lead to the sharp 'I's of the final phrase:

> JOSEPH SURFACE: To smile at a jest which plants a thorn in another's breast is to become a principal in the mischief.
>> Richard Brinsley Sheridan, *The School for Scandal* (1777)

Antithesis of Vowel Sounds Elyot in Noël Coward's *Private Lives* (1930) comments on his and his ex-wife's convoluted honeymoon situation, saying to Victor, her new husband 'Primitive feminine instincts – warring males – very enjoyable'; the feminine has the tight, short 'I' sounds, whereas the male has the expansive open 'A' sounds: eminently playable. In Steven Berkoff's *Greek* (1980), Eddy refers to 'the seething heaving heap of world in which I was just a little dot'; pitting the long 'E's describing the 'world' against the short, sharp vowels representing his solitary presence in it. And note the distinct change of sound from bright, energized short 'I's into broad, darker long 'A's here:

> MORTON: His forward spirit
> Would lift him where most trade of danger ranged.
>> William Shakespeare, *Henry IV Part Two* (c.1598)

ASSONANT PAIR

This is what we call two assonant words deployed together to 'ping out' an image or idea (more subtle than ALLITERATIVE PAIRS above). Think of such common examples as 'high time', 'foul mouthed' and 'fiscal cliff'.

Consider Hamlet's reference to his father's Ghost as 'old mole' in Shakespeare's *Hamlet* (c.1601), creating a hollow, haunting effect. And in J.B. Priestley's *Dangerous Corner* (1932) Olwen's complaint of being thought a 'priggish spinster'; the tight neatness of those short 'I's is perhaps reflective of her spinsterhood. Terence Rattigan in *The Deep Blue Sea* (1952) has the ex-RAF pilot Freddie describe whisky as 'delicious oblivion'; a rhythmically pleasing phrase, with the primary stress of each word landing on the assonant 'I's, almost as if he is vocally savouring the alcohol as he swirls it in his glass. And then there's this extraordinary image, in which a grimace is caused by pronouncing the ASSONANT PAIR:

> LEANTIO: There's no harm in your devil, he's a suckling,
> But he will breed teeth shortly, will he not?
>> Thomas Middleton, *Women Beware Women* (1621)

Try out the inherent comic potential of such combinations as when Betty – again in J.B. Priestley's *Dangerous Corner* (1932) – asks whether the husband in a radio programme they have been listening to was 'the one with the adenoidy voice'; or when Ewan informs Harry 'You have to dance to their stupid tune' in David Hare's *Racing Demon* (1990) – his mockery implicit in the slightly silly sound of the repeated 'YU' sound.

Conversely, ASSONANT PAIRS can be delightfully pithy and curt. Tim in Alan Ayckbourn's *Ten Times Table* (1978) dismisses festival revellers as 'drunken scum'; and Hurst abruptly silences Sparky in John Arden's *Serjeant Musgrave's Dance* (1959) with 'Hold your noise, you dirty turd!'

Sound and Sense go together Consider the broad, smiling generosity of the long 'A's of the 'radiant lady' Pegeen hopes her cousin Shawn will find in J.M. Synge's *The Playboy of the Western World* (1907); or the tense pair of short 'E's when Dr Rance states 'The vexed question of motive is now clear' in Joe Orton's *What the Butler Saw* (1967). Or this wonderfully derisive description of Cleopatra's effect on Antony:

> VENTIDIUS: Oh, she has decked his ruin with her love,
> Led him in golden bands to gaudy slaughter.
> John Dryden, *All for Love* (1677)

COMBINED SOUNDS

The next few devices take repeated sounds a step further, away from the simple repetition of a single consonant or vowel sound into subtle combinations of sound and on towards out-and-out rhyme.

PARACHESIS (pa-ruh-*kee*-sis) from the Greek meaning 'heaping up beside'.
A general term for the repetition of any letter sounds in key or neighbouring words.

ALLITERATION and ASSONANCE are in fact forms of this device, but are far better known. For our purposes we have invested in PARACHESIS as the repetition of *combined* sounds, especially the combination of more than one consonant, or the marriage of ALLITERATION and ASSONANCE together. These can occur in various positions:

The Beginnings of Words This is an extended ALLITERATION. Think of such well-worn phrases as 'to add insult to injury', 'to forgive and forget', or – as in T.S. Eliot's *The Cocktail Party* (1949) – when Reilly quotes the ADAGE 'Honesty before honour'. It most commonly occurs with prefixes, either positive or – as in this example – negative:

> BRUCE: If I let him out he will have a breakdown and succumb to
> all the most horrifying symptoms of schizophrenia undiagnosed,
> unchecked, unsupervised and unmedicated.
> Joe Penhall, *Blue/Orange* (2000)

The Middle of Words Ayesha in Tanika Gupta's *Sanctuary* (2002) complains of her mother's boyfriend, saying 'Wish she'd chuck the fucker out'. And here Prince Edward praises his mother, Queen Margaret, to his father, Henry VI, saying she could make a coward valiant and:

> PRINCE: Infuse his breast with magnanimity,
>   And make him, naked, foil a man at arms.
>
> William Shakespeare, *Henry VI Part Three* (1591)

The Ends of Words PARACHESIS at the ends of words is called HOMOIOTELEUTON in rhetoric (see below).

The Beginnings and Ends of Words Such as the phrase 'forewarned is forearmed' (both words begin with the prefix 'fore' and end in an 'ed'). Most commonly, words might simply share the same first letters and last letters – as in the phrase 'born in a barn', or this example:

> BEATIE: It's like twenty other songs, it don't mean anything and it's sloshy and sickly.
>
> Arnold Wesker, *Roots* (1959)

It can also be the same first letters and same last syllables, such as when Michael in Tanika Gupta's *Sanctuary* (2002) claims 'There is an art to capturing and cornering your enemy'. Mari, meanwhile, in Jim Cartwright's *The Rise and Fall of Little Voice* (1992), who is getting ready to go out – with a drink in one hand and her hairspray in the other – declares 'Lacquer! Liquor! Lacquer! Liquor!' (also a fine example of ECPHONESIS). Conversely, it can be the same first syllables and same last letters, as when Richard Rich in Robert Bolt's *A Man for All Seasons* (1960) says that he 'would never repeat or report a thing like that'. Or, more cleverly, the same first syllables and last syllables, as when Boyle in Sean O'Casey's *Juno and the Paycock* (1924) declares that his friend Joxer is 'a prognosticator an' a procrastinator!' Perhaps cleverest of all is when only one letter is changed, as when Schuppanzigh in Peter Shaffer's *Black Comedy* (1965) proclaims a sculpture to be 'Ingenious, but not ingenuous!'

Consonants Only Such as the repeated 'PR' in the phrase 'to practise what you preach'. In Patrick Marber's play *Closer* (1997) Dan mocks Alice with 'You're the belle of the bullshit'; the repeated 'B' and 'L' sounds create a particularly derisive effect. The psychiatrist Robert in Joe Penhall's *Blue/Orange* (2000), meanwhile, berates his colleague with 'I'm not going to quibble over this twaddle'; the repeated near-rhyme is splendidly belittling.

PARACHESIC PAIR

This is what we call two parachesic words deployed together to 'ping out' an image or idea. This seems to be the most popular deployment of PARACHESIS in all periods of playwriting. A pair will always be more acoustically effective if the repeated sound is on the stressed syllable of each word.

Oscar Wilde had a particular skill at deploying these: Lady Hunstanton in *A Woman of No Importance* (1893) declares that the American class system is a 'strange arrangement'; the strangeness easy to relish in the repeated sound. In *The Importance of Being Earnest* (1895) Jack proclaims that Gwendolen has a 'capital appetite' – rhythmic and playful in its positivity. And Lady Bracknell urges the foundling Jack to make 'a definite effort' to find at least one parent; once again rhythmic, but rather less playful.

While always emphatic, PARACHESIC PAIRS are often used with an element of **Derision**. Willie in Eugene O'Neill's *The Iceman Cometh* (1939) refers to Don Parritt as 'this useless youth'; the repeated sound accentuating his attitude. Similarly, David Hare in *Amy's View* (1997) has Esme dismiss the village fête with 'All those ridiculous pickles'. Or how about this defence of medical trials:

> TOBY: Don't hide behind this fashionable trashing of it all.
> Lucy Prebble, *The Effect* (2012)

Sound Echoes Sense In Marlowe's *Edward II* (c.1592) the King refers to his rival for the throne as 'this haughty Mortimer' as he sends him to prison in the Tower of London; there is real mockery in the repeated sound. Ben Jonson has the eponymous character in *Volpone* (1605-6) congratulate his servant Mosca for his 'quick fiction' when he has made up a story to get them out of trouble; this time the sound is sharp and bright, echoing Mosca's wit. And consider this:

> ROXANNA: I'm regressing fast, turning into a jittery little girl...
> Stephen Poliakoff, *Playing With Trains* (1989)

HOMOIOTELEUTON (hom-*oy*-oh-tel-*you*-ton) from the Greek meaning 'same ending'. When adjacent or parallel words have the same or similar sounding endings.

This is a specific form of PARACHESIS which usually results in rhyme, as in the MAXIM 'cleanliness is next to godliness'. In fact this device is commonly employed in popular sayings, such as 'you snooze, you lose', 'from hero to zero', 'by hook or by crook' and 'doom and gloom'; or Phebe's 'Omittance is no quittance' in Shakespeare's *As You Like It* (c.1600). Other common endings to look out for include: -ic, -tion, -ing, -able, -ible, -ly and -ed.

Joe, the photographer in Lucy Kirkwood's *Chimerica* (2013), says he captured his iconic shot of Tank Man in Tiananmen Square by 'just spraying and praying'; with only one letter difference between the two words, this phrase is instantly catchy and memorable. Meanwhile, when exposed as a fraudster by his wife, the conniving Mr Fainall in William Congreve's *The Way of the World* (1700) declares 'My wife has played the jade with me' – the repeated sound laced with his bitterness and derision. And Don Juan, in Patrick Marber's modern reworking of the story of the infamous lothario, succinctly describes his sidekick Stan and himself:

> DJ: We can't be parted, we're joined at the groin! A runt and a cunt!
>
> Patrick Marber, *Don Juan in Soho* (2006)

This device often lends itself to consciously witty characters, such as the character of Bevan in Alan Bennett's play *People* (2012) who responds to the idea of celebrity eucharists with 'The host on toast!' And Pam in Edward Bond's *Saved* (1965) who surveys her surroundings and utters 'This dump gives me the 'ump.' Or:

> THOMAS: Where in this small-talking world can I find
> A longitude with no platitude?
>
> Christopher Fry, *The Lady's Not For Burning* (1948)

Most commonly appearing in twos – as in the examples above – this device often comes in the form of a TRICOLON (see Chapter 7: The Rule of Three), as in Ralph's praise of the convicts' production of *The Recruiting Officer* in Timberlake Wertenbaker's *Our Country's Good* (1988) as 'A pleasurable, intelligible and memorable evening'.

This device is also common with repeated verb endings – especially participles – as when Garry in Noël Coward's *Present Laughter* (1943) says 'I see myself all the time eating, drinking, loving, suffering'; the repetition accentuates his wallowing self-obsession. And look at this extreme example:

> ROBERT: ...the worst, most incompetent, drivelling snivelling jibbering jabbering idiot...
>
> George Bernard Shaw, *Saint Joan* (1923)

Multiple adverbs appear frequently too, such as when Cheviot in W.S. Gilbert's *Engaged* (1877) gushes 'I love you, madam, humbly, truly, trustfully, patiently'. Or this glorious cascade:

> PLAYER: They can die heroically, comically, ironically, slowly, suddenly, disgustingly, charmingly, or from a great height.
>
> Tom Stoppard, *Rosencrantz and Guildenstern Are Dead* (1967)

Finally, consider this packed example:

> SUBTLE: You shall be soaked, and stroked, and tubbed, and rubbed,
> And scrubbed, and fubbed, dear Don, before you go.
> You shall in faith, my scurvy baboon Don,

> Be curried, clawed, and flawed, and tawed, indeed.
>
> Ben Jonson, *The Alchemist* (1610)

HOMOIOTELEUTONIC PAIR

This is what we call two homoioteleutonic or rhyming words deployed together to 'ping out' an image or idea. It is surprisingly common due to the memorability of the pairings – think of 'big wig', 'hot shot', 'trolley dolly', 'hanky panky', 'hocus pocus', 'culture vulture', 'take a chill pill' and 'you need your head read'.

This is just the sort of acoustic wordplay that Noël Coward excelled at, being – as he was – a superlative lyricist. His famous 'Don't quibble, Sybil!' from *Private Lives* (1930) is a fine example, and one admirably echoed by Philip King in his farce *See How They Run* (1945) with 'Don't bicker, Vicar!' and, more recently, by Nancy Harris in *Our New Girl* (2012), in which Hazel, a middle-class housewife declares, 'I don't need a nanny, Annie'.

It need not always be witty, however; consider Sarah Kane's grim pronouncement in the autobiographical *4.48 Psychosis* (2000): 'still ill' – chilling in its monosyllabic simplicity. And here's a fine example from Shakespeare:

> BUCKINGHAM: ...his eye reviled
> Me as his object abject.
>
> William Shakespeare with John Fletcher, *Henry VIII* (1613)

PAROMOIOSIS (*pa*-ruh-moy-*oh*-sis) from the Greek meaning 'nearly alike'.

Neighbouring phrases or sentences of corresponding length whose words sound similar or identical.

This was a popular device used by Vaudevillian and Music Hall comics to get away with crude or 'blue' humour, as in the famous:

> COMIC: I'll *ti*ckle your *arse* with a *fe*ather!
> LADY: I beg your pardon!
> COMIC: Par*ti*cularly *na*sty *we*ather?
> LADY: Oh...yes, it is, isn't it?

If you assess the sounds of the stressed syllables of the Comic's lines (in italics), they are the same – a kind of extended PARACHESIS. The two lines are rhythmically almost identical too.

In *The Lady's Not For Burning* (1948) by Christopher Fry, the drunken character of Skipps calls for 'Peace on earth and good tall women', with the second phrase a slurred version of the more traditional Christmas benediction 'good will towards men'. In Steven Berkoff's *Greek* (1980), Eddy talks of 'robbery with violets and glorious bodily charm' in a deeply ironic take on 'robbery with violence and grievous bodily harm'.

Tom Stoppard, the master of such devices, takes this device to an extraordinary extreme here:

> CARR: Never in the whole history of human conflict was there anything to match the carnage – God's blood!, the shot and shell! – graveyard stench! – Christ Jesu! – deserted by simpletons, they damn us to hell – ora pro nobis – quick! no, *get me out*! I think to match the carnation, oxblood shot-silk cravat, starched, creased just so, asserted by a simple pin, the damask lapels – or a brown, no, biscuit – no – get me out the straight cut trouser with the blue satin stripe and the silk cutaway.
>
> Tom Stoppard, *Travesties* (1993 edition)

While it is possible simply to celebrate the language and achieve an acceptable rendition, the speech is unlocked by identifying the PARAMOIOSIS. The character literally replaces his words of war – almost syllable by syllable – with the description of his clothes, in his attempt to suppress his shell-shock in favour of sartorial perfection. Consider it laid out like this:

[an]ything to match the carnage – God's blood!, the shot and shell! – graveyard stench! –
I think to match the carnation,   oxblood   shot-silk   cravat, starched,

Christ Jesu!   –   deserted by simpletons, they damn us to hell –
creased just so, asserted by a simple pin, the damask lapels –

ora pro nobis – quick!   no,   *get me out*!
or a brown, no, biscuit – no – get me out [the straight cut trouser...]

It is debatable whether an audience would pick up on this, but for the actor and director it is a tremendous effect to conjure with in rehearsal and in performance.

SOUND EFFECTS

The following devices tend to be more prolonged and subtle, even musical. They can create effects – subconscious in an audience – that sway them in a particular emotional direction, much like background music in a film. The writers of the Renaissance – and to a lesser extent the Restoration – used these to great effect.

EUPHONY (*yoof*-uh-nee) from the Greek meaning 'sounding good'.
When there is a beauty of sound in the words, reflective of what they describe.

This device comes more easily to the playwrights of the Renaissance since they are writing predominantly in verse, which lends itself more readily to such heightened, poetic language. Think of Oberon's 'I know a bank where the wild thyme grows' speech in *A Midsummer Night's Dream* (1595) or Portia's 'The quality of mercy' in *The Merchant of Venice* (1596-7). Marlowe relished it too:

> MEPHISTOPHELES: As are the elements, such are the heavens,
> Even from the moon unto the empyrial orb,
> Mutually folded in each other's spheres,
> And jointly move upon one axle-tree,
> Whose termine is termed the world's wide pole.
> Christopher Marlowe, *Doctor Faustus* (c.1589)

EUPHONY usually involves the acoustic effects covered in this chapter. Consider Berowne's description of Love in *Love's Labour's Lost* (1594): 'His lines would ravish savage ears'; the repeated 'AV' sound and rhythm of 'ravish savage' has a splendidly sensual effect. Or the pleasing ALLITERATION and PARACHESIS in Ferdinand's description of the masque in *The Tempest* (1611): 'This is a most majestic vision, and / Harmonious charmingly'; the two polysyllabic words held together by the repeated 'arm' sound, adding to the ALLITERATION of the 'M's that goes before.

EUPHONY need not always be purely beautiful; it can also be playful or evocative. Consider Carr's description of Zurich in Tom Stoppard's *Travesties* (1993 edition) as 'the banking bouncing metropolis of trampolines'; a gloriously complex combination of ALLITERATION, HOMOIOTELEUTON, PARACHESIS and CONSONANCE. And look at the effect the polysyllabic words have in this example:

> HARRIET: I have not learned those softnesses and languishings which now in faces are so much in fashion.
> George Etherege, *The Man of Mode* (1676)

CACOPHONY (kak-*off*-uh-nee) from the Greek meaning 'sounding bad'.
When there are ugly, discordant or 'angular' sounds in the words, reflective of what they describe or the mood in which they are spoken.

Here is Tom Stoppard's *Travesties* (1993 edition) again: consider the harsh sounds and spitting SIBILANCE of Bennett, the communist butler, when he says anyone in support of the war is stigmatized as a 'lickspittle capitalist lackey'. Or Sheena in David Greig's *The Architect* (1996) who describes living in a condemned block of flats as being 'Stuck in boxes on the dockside waiting to be picked up'; her bitterness apparent in the harsh consonants she uses. Such phrases are angular and difficult to say, as is this description of British soldiers (the spelling is Synge's):

> PEGEEN: I wouldn't be fearing the looséd kharki cut-throats.
> J.M. Synge, *The Playboy of the Western World* (1907)

In Shakespeare's *Much Ado About Nothing* (c.1598), Benedick claims that any man who avoids marrying Beatrice will 'scape a predestinate scratched face'; the sharp combination of consonants and SIBILANCE help to create the vicious image of the scratching. Or consider this wonderful description of African pirates in which the sharp, angular, awkward sounds parallel the subject matter, ending with the violent 'K' and hard 'C' sounds:

> TAMBURLAINE: These are the cruel pirates of Argier,
> That damnèd train, the scum of Africa,
> Inhabited with straggling runagates,
> That make quick havoc of the Christian blood.
>
> Christopher Marlowe, *Tamburlaine the Great: Part One* (1587)

ONOMATOPOEIA (*on*-uh-*mat*-uh-*pee*-yuh) from the Greek meaning 'making of words'.

When words or phrases imitate the sounds of the objects or actions they describe.

We all recall from school such onomatopoeic words as 'pop', 'snap', 'splash', 'bark', 'creak', 'crunch', 'mumble' and 'murmur'. This playful, muscular device often appears in drama.

Professor Higgins in Shaw's *Pygmalion* (1912) chastises the crying Eliza Doolittle with 'cease this detestable boohooing instantly'. Elyot in Noël Coward's *Private Lives* (1930) goes even further by describing a hotel fountain as going 'plopplopplopplopplopplopplopplopplop'. And here is an extraordinarily evocative ONOMATOPOEIC description:

> FIRST VOICE: There's the clip clop of horses on the sunhoneyed cobbles of the humming streets, hammering of horse-shoes, gobble quack and cackle, tomtit twitter from the bird-ounced boughs, braying on Donkey Down.
>
> Dylan Thomas, *Under Milk Wood* (1954)

Two Word Effects In Nicholas Wright's *Cressida* (2000) the character of Shank talks of 'cannikins clinking'; a wonderfully evocative pairing of words to create the sound of the metal cups (cannikins) being raised in a toast. Salieri in Peter Shaffer's *Amadeus* (1979) claims that trumpets greeted music-blessed men 'when they entered the world, and trombones groaned when they left it!'

Sustained Effects In a dramatic context, subtler, more sustained effects are also possible. The playwrights of the Renaissance and Restoration often create ONOMATOPOEIC phrases. Shakespeare, of course, excels at these. On taking leave of his family, Launce the clown in *The Two Gentlemen of Verona* (c.1591) says of his sister 'Mark the moan she makes'; the ALLITERATION of the 'M's creates her groaning. In *The Comedy of Errors* (1594) Egeon describes the fateful shipwreck that separated his family with 'Our helpful ship was splitted in the midst'; the splintering of wood is echoed in the harsh consonants, splashy SIBILANCE and short, sharp 'I's.

SIBILANCE is often used to create such acoustic effects, as when Mary in T.S. Eliot's *The Family Reunion* (1939) describes a 'fish / Thrashing itself upstream'; the splashes of the creature's efforts replicated in the sound of the words. Here's Shakespeare again, creating nervous whisperings the night before the Battle of Agincourt:

> CHORUS: The hum of either army stilly sounds,
>   That the fixed sentinels almost receive
>   The secret whispers of each other's watch.
>
>   William Shakespeare, *Henry V* (c.1599)

Rhythm This can also be drawn upon for ONOMATOPOEIA. Staying with *Henry V*, the Chorus describes dawn on the day of the battle, and includes the sentence 'The country cocks do crow, the clocks do toll'; adding to the strong ALLITERATION and ASSONANT SYMPHONY of the 'O's the distinct rhythm of 'cock-a-doodle-do'. In Stephen Jeffreys' *The Libertine* (1994) the Earl of Rochester gloriously describes sex as 'the thump and slop of congress'; the monosyllabic ONOMATOPOEIA is particularly evocative of the less romantic rhythms of lovemaking.

Finally, words can conjure very particular images with their sounds, such as when the fop Witwoud in Congreve's *The Way of the World* (1700) cruelly mocks the enthusiastic greeting of his half-brother up from the country 'where great lubberly brothers slobber and kiss one another'; creating a wonderfully messy image! And consider the sly sarcasm of this example, addressed – as it is – to his mistrusted wife Celia:

> CORVINO: You smile
>   Most graciously, and fan your favours forth,
>   To give your hot spectators satisfaction!
>
>   Ben Jonson, *Volpone* (1605-6)

Chapter 3 Imagery

CHASUBLE: Were I fortunate enough to be Miss Prism's pupil, I would hang upon her lips. I spoke metaphorically. My metaphor was drawn from bees.

Oscar Wilde, *The Importance of Being Earnest* (1895)

The word 'imagery' has the same Latin root (*imago*, image or representation) as the word 'imagine', of course, and imagination is perhaps the foremost quality of those of us that work in the theatre. Our role – whether as actor, playwright or director – is to appeal to the collective imagination of the audience in order to tell our stories. When language is used skillfully to describe mental or sensuous images, it enriches the experience immeasurably. Consider Lord Darlington's famous assertion in Oscar Wilde's *Lady Windermere's Fan* (1892) that 'We are all in the gutter, but some of us are looking at the stars'; it is a glorious, witty and thought-provoking image that instantly ignites our imaginative fires.

Imagery must appeal to one or more of our senses. Look at the following example, in which John – the son of the play's title – dreams of a future away from his loathed upbringing in a brutal industrialist family:

JOHN: When I make a few thousands out of this little idea of mine I'm going to have everything I want, and forget all about the dirt and the ugliness, the clatter and bang of the machinery, the sickening hot smell of the furnaces – all the things I've hated from my soul.

Githa Sowerby, *Rutherford and Son* (1912)

By describing the world he wants to leave behind, he directly appeals to our senses of sight, hearing and smell. We are asked to invest in the filth, noise and stink of his surroundings, and are therefore drawn in to the character and the world he inhabits. This is a huge step on the journey to achieving 'a willing suspension of disbelief', to use Coleridge's celebrated phrase.

The language we use is the greatest tool we have in constructing our stories; with it we create characters and plot and every conceivable journey they can embark on. The language of theatre began centuries ago, but it was perhaps the playwrights of the Renaissance – justly renowned for their imagistic language – who pioneered what we know as theatre today, led of course by the image *meister* himself: William Shakespeare.

English was very plastic in this period, and Shakespeare coined many images that are now commonplace, such as to 'vanish into thin air' (*The Tempest*), 'I will wear my heart upon my sleeve' (*Othello*), 'as dead as a doornail' (*Henry VI Part Two*) and 'in the twinkling of an eye' (*The Merchant Of Venice*). If you consider these literally, they have an extraordinarily beautiful and inventive effect.

The images we use most commonly, which almost become clichés, are often taken for granted; we cease to make the imaginative leap they beg of us. But when writing or tackling a play, it is as well to re-invest in such images, even if a character uses them in an off-hand way.

For instance, Walter in Lorraine Hansberry's play *A Raisin in the Sun* (1959) proclaims 'I got some plans that could turn this city upside down'; it's a common enough turn of phrase, but consider the *actual* image: the potential of Walter's plans actually to turn the city on its head. It's terrific! We are suddenly in a cataclysmic world where buildings are turned upside-down and shaken like dolls houses, altering everyone's perspective.

Images can be comic too, of course. In George Etherege's *The Man of Mode* (1676) Mrs Loveit curses the philandering Dorimant with 'Lightning blast him!' We understand her feelings instantly, but the literal image has a wonderfully extreme, cartoon quality.

In this chapter, we introduce you to some old friends – such as SIMILE, METAPHOR and ALLUSION – and to some new acquaintances – such as CATACHRESIS, SYNAESTHESIA and EFFICTIO. Examine the imaginative possibilities each of them engender and really *see* the images they conjure up.

THROUGH COMPARISON

SIMILE from the Latin meaning 'alike'.
The comparison of different things to imply a resemblance between them – perhaps the most common way to cast an image. A SIMILE is usually heralded by 'like' or 'as' – or the often forgotten 'than'.

With 'Like' Typical examples include 'like water off a duck's back', 'to have a head like a sieve', 'to look like death warmed up', 'to stick out like a sore thumb'. So commonly used are they that we know exactly what they mean without investing in the actual image. Consider them again – they're amazing!

Oscar Wilde in *The Importance of Being Earnest* (1895) has Algernon utter 'You are like a pink rose, Cecily'; it is almost a cliché, but set – as it is – in a garden, he draws from his surroundings to allude to Cecily's unspoiled beauty and even her blushes by his choice of colour. Conversely, Alan Bennett in *Forty Years On* (1968) reaches for a brilliantly original SIMILE when Leithen says that Hannay's 'talk is like a fierce cordial'; a cordial should be refreshing, but to render it 'fierce' is especially energizing, even frightening. Alternatively, a SIMILE can be very funny, as when Lee in Jez Butterworth's *Jerusalem* (2009) claims 'That tortoise pisses like a shirehorse'. Picture that!

Often the wondrous poetry of an image can be overwhelmingly beautiful and effective. Here is the poet and playwright John Dryden's extraordinary description of Cleopatra's smile:

> DOLABELLA: Yet, now and then, a melancholy smile
> Breaks loose, like lightning in a winter's night,
> And shows a moment's day.
> John Dryden, *All for Love* (1677)

With 'As' This is often simply used in place of 'like', such as in this example:

> JUDITH: She's far too old for you, and she goes about using Sex as a sort of shrimping-net.
> Noël Coward, *Hay Fever* (1925)

However, more commonly 'As' SIMILES come in the form of Comparative Parallels (see also PARALLELISM). Although all SIMILES are comparisons, the following – which use the grammatical figure 'as *something* as *something*' – create a more overt comparison than the more poetic examples above. Commonly-used phrases include 'as bright as a button', 'as hard as nails', 'as dull as ditchwater', 'as fit as a fiddle', 'as hard as rock' or the mystifying 'as sick as a parrot'.

Stephen in Timberlake Wertenbaker's *Three Birds Alighting on a Field* (1991) condemns Jean, who writes about sensuality, with 'You look as sensual as a tube of toothpaste'. The farmer John Proctor in Arthur Miller's *The Crucible* (1953) speaks of the imminent Spring when he says 'It's warm as blood beneath the clods'; a rich, almost disturbing image that conjures up his suppressed sexual feelings as well as the issues of supposed witchcraft in his community. Here's a delightful double-whammy from an unfaithful doctor to his wife:

> JOHN: I've been as heartless as a crocodile and as unscrupulous as a typhoid bacillus.
> W. Somerset Maugham, *The Constant Wife* (1926)

It is very common for the first 'as' of each comparison to be omitted (as in the Miller example above) – see ELLIPSIS – though the SIMILES are equally strong. Consider this multiple example:

> BONIFACE: Sir, I have now in my cellar ten tun of the best ale in Staffordshire; 'tis smooth as oil, sweet as milk, clear as amber, and strong as brandy.
> George Farquhar, *The Beaux' Stratagem* (1707)

Dramatic Adventures in Rhetoric

With 'Than' It is often forgotten that the word 'than' heralds a SIMILE as often as 'like' and possibly more often than 'as'. Think of such examples as 'larger than life', 'whiter than snow' or 'faster than the speed of light'. These are all launched by a comparative adjective for the comparison to be achieved.

Jim in Peter Nichols' *Passion Play* (2000 edition) comments that being a lover is 'More thrilling than war and warmer than sunshine'. In Terry Johnson's *Hysteria* (1993) Freud uses a negative comparison: 'God is no more light in this darkness than a candle in a hurricane.' And here's a lovely one from Shakespeare:

> BASSANIO: The painter plays the spider and hath woven
> A golden mesh t' entrap the hearts of men
> Faster than gnats in cobwebs.
> William Shakespeare, *The Merchant of Venice* (c.1597)

It is possible to achieve a SIMILE *without* the use of 'like', 'as' or 'than' by using alternative phrases, such as 'in the style of' or – as in this example – 'after the manner of':

> LADY DUNDOWN: I am aware that you have been engaged, though, if I may say so, much after the manner of a public lavatory... often and for very short periods.
> Alan Bennett, *Forty Years On* (1968)

Similes Drawn from our own Experience It is very common in life, and therefore in drama, for characters to reach for the images from their own culture, background, surroundings, or – as here – education:

> JEREMY: The first compromise you make winds you like a rugger ball in the stomach. Stays with you like school porridge.
> Laura Wade, *Posh* (2012)

EXTENDED SIMILE
A SIMILE that moves beyond a simple comparison and expands upon it.

> SIR ANTHONY ABSOLUTE: Madam, a circulating library in a town is as an ever-green tree of diabolical knowledge. It blossoms through the year! And depend upon it, Mrs Malaprop, that they who are so fond of handling leaves, will long for the fruit at last.
> Richard Brinsley Sheridan, *The Rivals* (1775)

As in this example, most extensions seem naturally to expand into METAPHORS (see below). In the following example the word 'matrimonial' is used metaphorically within the SIMILE, and brings the image back to its original context:

AMANDA: That was the trouble with Elyot and me, we were like two violent acids bubbling about in a nasty little matrimonial bottle.

Noël Coward, *Private Lives* (1930)

This device seems particularly popular amongst the Renaissance playwrights. The heightened form of writing in verse allowed for such flights of fancy:

LEANTIO: O thou the ripe time of man's misery, Wedlock,
When all his thoughts, like over-laden trees,
Crack with the fruits they bear, in cares, in jealousies!
O that's a fruit that ripens hastily
After 'tis knit to marriage. It begins
As soon as the sun shines upon the bride
A little to show colour.

Thomas Middleton, *Women Beware Women* (1621)

This elevated realm of imagery continued into the prose plays of the late Renaissance and even beyond into the Restoration.

ANTAPODOSIS (*an*-ta-*pod*-uh-sis) from the Greek meaning 'repayment' or 'reward'. An extended SIMILE in which several aspects of the comparison correspond.

ARCHER: I can play with a girl as an angler does with his fish; he keeps it at the end of his line, runs it up the stream, and down the stream, till at last he brings it to hand, tickles his trout, and whips it into his basket.

George Farquhar, *The Beaux' Stratagem* (1707)

METAPHOR from the Greek meaning 'transference'.
When a descriptive word or phrase is applied directly and imaginatively to something with which it would not normally be associated, in order to create an evocative image. This differs from SIMILE in not having a signal word, such as 'like' or 'as'. It is more immediate and poetic.

We use many metaphorical words in everyday speech – 'dull' for stupid, 'sharp' for clever, 'monstrous' for awful – as well as metaphorical phrases such as 'in a nutshell', 'to know which side your bread is buttered' and 'to make your blood run cold'. It is interesting to consider when a commonly used METAPHOR might have appeared in terms of history. A phrase like 'to work at the coalface' cannot have come into common usage until the Industrial Revolution, and to call someone a 'live wire' must have arrived with the dawn of the electrical age.

Here are some more metaphors from everyday life: 'to knock the wind out of your sails', 'to have your head in the sand' or 'to get on like a house on fire'; 'to smell a rat', 'to take the bull by the horns', or 'to throw the cat among the pigeons'; to have 'a bee in your bonnet', 'fingers in many pies' or 'a skeleton in the closet'; or the marvellous images of 'a storm in a teacup' or 'when the shit hits the fan'. We take these common images for granted, but consider each of them in turn and visualize the actual image – they're brilliant! Is it any wonder that playwrights reach for METAPHORS with such alacrity? Not only are they vibrant, witty and imaginative, but it is clear that they play a huge part in how humanity communicate with each other.

Shakespeare is justly famous for his use of METAPHOR, as when Claudius in *Hamlet* (c.1601) observes 'When sorrows come, they come not single spies / But in battalions.' – painting his 'sorrows' as a cloak-and-dagger army. Leontes, eaten up by jealousy in *The Winter's Tale* (c.1610), talks of a man not knowing that his wife 'has been sluiced in's absence, / And his pond fished by his next neighbour'; an extraordinarily repellant image for adultery. And here is one of sad beauty:

> RICHARD: O that I were a mockery king of snow,
> Standing before the sun of Bolingbroke,
> To melt myself away in water drops.
>
> William Shakespeare, *Richard II* (1595)

This is by no means the preserve of Shakespeare alone – all the Renaissance playwrights were at it:

> EDWARD: But what are kings, when regiment is gone,
> But perfect shadows in a sunshine day?
>
> Christopher Marlowe, *Edward II* (c.1592)

> BOSOLA: A politician is the devil's quilted anvil:
> He fashions all sins on him, but the blows
> Are never heard.
>
> John Webster, *The Duchess of Malfi* (1624)

> SERAPION: How stands the queen affected?
> ALEXAS: Oh, she dotes,
> She dotes, Serapion, on this vanquished man,
> And winds herself about his mighty ruins.
>
> John Dryden, *All for Love* (1677)

METAPHORS can be deployed in a variety of ways:

The Direct Exchange This is when something actual is simply exchanged with something imagistic. Mrs Tilehouse in Edward Bond's *The Sea* (1973) warns the redoubtable Mrs Rafi not to challenge the draper, Mr Hatch, with 'What foolishness to bait an unchained lion'. She directly swaps Mr Hatch for the animal, thereby achieving a beautifully simple but effective image. Or this overwhelmingly romantic example:

> SIR ROBERT CHILTERN: I am a ship without a rudder in a night without a star.
>
> Oscar Wilde, *An Ideal Husband* (1895)

The Surprise Image This is when a sudden image comes out of nowhere, as when the suicidal Hester in Terence Rattigan's *The Deep Blue Sea* (1952) refers to her feelings for her younger lover as 'A great tidal wave of illogical emotions'. Or this poetic description of a lesion, the first sign of AIDS:

> PRIOR: The wine-dark kiss of the Angel of Death.
>
> Tony Kushner, *Angels in America* (1991)

The Image Explained This is when an image is launched, and then its aptness is made explicit, as when John Proctor in Arthur Miller's *The Crucible* (1953) claims 'I have made a bell of my honor! I have rung the doom of my good name....' Or this example:

> HARRY: Betty, you are a star in my sky. Without you I would have no sense of direction.
>
> Caryl Churchill, *Cloud Nine* (1979)

The Image as Qualification This is when a statement is made, and then clarified with an image, as when Maggie in Tennessee Williams' *Cat on a Hot Tin Roof* (1955) says to Brick 'I am not living with you. We occupy the same cage'. Or this example from another American great:

> LINDA: Be loving to him. Because he's only a little boat looking for a harbour.
>
> Arthur Miller, *Death of a Salesman* (1949)

The Direct Comparison This is when two things are set in direct comparison, as when Lydia in Sheridan's *The Rivals* (1775) claims 'the rude blast that overset your boat was a prosperous gale of love to him'. Or this charmingly simple example:

> RAFE: They talk about the beauty of this garden. Compared to you it's a desert!
>
> Peter Whelan, *The Herbal Bed* (1996)

Images of our Experience This is when a character reaches for a METAPHOR of their trade or surroundings. In the following example, Troy is a former baseball player. There is something touching and vulnerable about a character who can only express themselves by what they know.

> TROY: Maybe I come into the world backwards, I don't know. But... you born with two strikes on you before you come to the plate. You got to guard it closely... always looking for the curve-ball on the inside corner. You can't afford to let none get past you. You can't afford a call-strike. If you going down... you going down swinging.
> August Wilson, *Fences* (1985)

Metaphors Clarified by Similes Playwrights loved this particular form during the Restoration. In this example, the image is launched by the word 'adrift' and is then clarified by the SIMILE of the 'leaky hulk':

> FAINALL: Your darling daughter is turned adrift, like a leaky hulk, to sink or swim as best she may in the doubtful currents of this lewd town.
> William Congreve, *The Way of the World* (1700)

EXTENDED METAPHOR
This is when an image is prolonged and invested in further.

Slight Extension This example conjures a wonderfully precise image of Freud's character. The METAPHOR is created with the word 'snared', but is then extended into the psychoanalyst's painstaking and fastidious mounting of his fears as displayed insects:

> FREUD: I hunted down my fears, and snared them. Throughout the summer, mounted, pinned and labelled each of them.
> Terry Johnson, *Hysteria* (1993)

Greater Extension Here Tom describes Rose Trelawny's growth as an actress; he takes the image of the well surprisingly – even ludicrously – far, showing us the extent of his obsession with her:

> TOM: Yes, deep down in the well of that girl's nature there has been lying a little, bright, clear pool of genuine refinement, girlish simplicity. And now the bucket has been lowered by love; experience has turned the handle; and up comes the crystal to the top, pure and sparkling.
> Arthur Wing Pinero, *Trelawny of the 'Wells'* (1898)

Two Characters Here one character picks up on a METAPHOR launched by another:

> CHARLES COURTLY: My dear madam, how fares the plot? Does my governor nibble?
> LADY GAY SPANKER: Nibble! He is caught and in the basket. I have just left him with the hook in his gills, panting for very lack of element.
> Dion Boucicault, London Assurance (1841)

MIXED METAPHOR

This is when two or more metaphors are interwoven – either accidentally or deliberately – usually for comic effect. Playwrights always create a MIXED METAPHOR deliberately, of course, but their characters may not.

The most common MIXED METAPHORS tend to be muddled PROVERBS: Lady Rumpers in Alan Bennett's comedy *Habeas Corpus* (1973) mistakenly mixes up two proverbs for pregnancy – to be 'in the club' and to have 'a bun in the oven' – and arrives at 'I had a bun in the club'. Amanda in Noël Coward's *Private Lives* (1930) announces to Elyot that she does not 'believe in crying over my bridge before I've eaten it', thereby muddling the proverbs of 'crying over spilt milk', 'crossing a bridge before you come to it', and 'having your cake and eating it'. In this case it is no mistake; Amanda is fully aware of her own cleverness, as is Elyot, who wittily proclaims it 'Very sensible'! Try unpicking this brilliantly chaotic muddle of 'home and dry', 'high and dry', 'out of my depth', 'over my dead body' and 'coming to a head'. Good luck!

> GUILDENSTERN: We'll soon be home and high – dry and home – I'll –
> ROSENCRANTZ: It's all over my *depth* –
> GUILDENSTERN: I'll hie you home and –
> ROSENCRANTZ: – out of my head –
> GUILDENSTERN: – and dry you high –
> ROSENCRANTZ: *(cracking, high)* – over my step over my head body! – I tell you it's all stopping to a death, it's boding to a depth, stepping to a head, it's all heading to a dead stop –
> Tom Stoppard, Rosencrantz and Guildenstern Are Dead (1967)

PROGRESSIO (prog-*ress*-ee-oh) from the Latin meaning 'progress' or 'advancement'. To use a series of different comparisons to make a point.

Here is an overly-romantic example, from a suitably named character:

> VALENTINE: You're a woman, one to whom Heaven gave beauty, when it grafted roses on a briar. You are the reflection of Heaven in

a pond, and he that leaps at you is sunk. You are all white, a sheet of lovely spotless paper, when you are first born; but you are to be scrawled and blotted by every goose's quill.

William Congreve, *Love for Love* (1695)

SYNCRISIS (*sin*-criss-iss) from the Greek meaning 'comparison' or 'combination'.
1) A comparison achieved through several parallel clauses.

Here Evelyn states the literal situation first, then draws on images from Shakespeare's *The Merchant Of Venice* (c.1597), the myth of Pygmalion and Galatea, and even Adam and Eve:

EVELYN: But to marry one whom you could adore and whose heart is closed to you, to yearn for the treasure and only to claim the casket, to worship the statue that you never may warm to life, oh, such a marriage would be a hell the more terrible because paradise was in sight.

Edward Bulwer-Lytton, *Money* (1840)

2) When opposing things are compared; an antithetical SIMILE or METAPHOR.

Here, a wife appraises her late husband's prodigious mind in clearly penile terms:

BRADSHAW: Getting his ugly reasoning out, his great moral purpose, showing it in public, and his wisdom! Could not walk with him five minutes but he had his wisdom out, forever exhibiting his mind, was ever a mind hung out so much in public, dirty thing it was, great monster of a mind so flashed and brazenly dangled?

Howard Barker, *Victory* (1983)

CATACHRESIS (cat-uh-*kree*-sis) from the Greek meaning 'misuse'.
An unlikely METAPHOR using a word outside its normal sphere.

A servant in Shakespeare and Middleton's *Timon of Athens* (1605), once the eponymous character has ceased to be generous with his money, refers to it being 'Deepest winter in Lord Timon's purse', thereby conjuring an image of chilly emptiness by the inventive application of the word 'winter'. The Headmaster in Alan Bennett's *The History Boys* (2004) claims to be 'corseted by the curriculum' when asked to find more class time by a new teacher; it creates a hilarious image. And here's a stylish example:

JULIA: I want to be a gentleman too, detached, elegant, self-sufficient, with a cashmere mind.

Timberlake Wertenbaker, *Three Birds Alighting on a Field* (1991)

This device is often used to create an effect of **Affectation**. The Landlord in Goldsmith's *She Stoops to Conquer* (1771) claims Marlow and Hastings, newly arrived in the countryside from London, 'look woundily like Frenchman'; he is purposefully using such language to mock their urbanity and style. In Noël Coward's *Present Laughter* (1943) Liz describes her husband's exhausted secretary, Monica, as looking 'absolutely congealed'; an arch turn of phrase, typical of the playwright and the period. And here's a terrific term for an argument from Lady Teazle to her hapless husband:

> LADY TEAZLE: Now, Sir Peter, since we have finished our daily jangle,
> I presume I may go to my engagement with Lady Sneerwell.
>
> Richard Brinsley Sheridan, *The School for Scandal* (1777)

HYPERBOLE (hy-*pur*-buh-lee) from the Greek meaning 'overshooting'. Emphasis through exaggeration.

Most commonly this is **Numerical**, as when Ruth in Lorraine Hansberry's *A Raisin in the Sun* (1959) scolds her son Travis with the classic 'A thousand times I have told you not to go off like that'. In Peter Shaffer's *Amadeus* (1979) Mozart flatters the Emperor with 'Let me kiss your royal hand a hundred thousand times!' And here Cleopatra's deceitful eunuch gushes sycophantically to Antony:

> ALEXAS: A thousand wishes, and ten thousand prayers,
> Millions of blessings wait you to the wars;
> Millions of sighs and tears she sends you too,
> And would have sent
> As many dear embraces to your arms,
> As many parting kisses to your lips;
> But those, she fears, have wearied you already.
>
> John Dryden, *All for Love* (1677)

HYPERBOLE can equally be used to create **Overstatement** in terms of imagery. In Arthur Miller's *A View from the Bridge* (1956) Eddie says 'I seen spiders could stop a Buick' – picture it! And Mrs Tilehouse in Edward Bond's *The Sea* (1973) resorts to BIBLICAL ALLUSION to describe her reaction to an unfortunate incident involving cloth shears in the draper's shop in which her friend, Mrs Rafi, is cut: 'After this I shall regard Gomorrah as a spa resort'. And here's a typically high-blown piece of hyperbolic imagery from the Renaissance:

> ISABELLA: O gush out, tears, fountains and floods of tears,
> Blow, sighs, and raise an everlasting storm:
> For outrage fits our cursèd wretchedness.
>
> Thomas Kyd, *The Spanish Tragedy* (c.1592)

PERSONIFICATION from the Latin meaning 'making a character or mask'.
To give human characteristics to an inanimate object or an abstract concept.

Shakespeare personifies **Abstract Entities** as actual characters: Time appears in Act IV Scene i of *The Winter's Tale* (c.1610) to describe the passing of 16 years, and Rumour speaks the opening chorus of *Henry IV Part Two* (c.1598), describing the chaos of information – some true, some false – following the Battle of Shrewsbury that ends *Henry IV Part One* (c.1597).

Shakespeare often makes reference to other characters as being personified abstracts, such as when Benedick in one of his spats with Beatrice in *Much Ado About Nothing* (c.1598) calls her 'my dear Lady Disdain'. And here the Abbess in *The Comedy of Errors* (1594) describes what happens when a wife denies her husband sleep, good food and sex:

> ABBESS: Sweet recreation barred, what doth ensue
> But moody and dull Melancholy,
> Kinsman to grim and comfortless Despair,
> And at her heels a huge infectious troop
> Of pale distemperatures and foes to life.

More recent playwrights use PERSONIFICATION in similar ways. Kay in J.B. Priestley's *Time and the Conways* (1937) states 'There's a great devil in the universe, and we call it Time', thereby clarifying her view of the relationship between the passing years and her family – the very core of the most famous of Priestley's Time Plays. Sir Percy in Alan Bennett's *Habeas Corpus* (1973) gloriously claims 'King Sex is a wayward monarch'. And here laughter and tears are pictured as two children:

> MARGARET: I am sure the laugh just went off with the tear to comfort
> it, and they have been playing about that stream ever since.
> J.M. Barrie, *Dear Brutus* (1917)

ANTHROPOMORPHISM (*an*-throp-uh-*mor*-fiz-um) from the Greek meaning 'change into a human'.
To describe inanimate objects or animals in human terms.

In Noël Coward's *Blithe Spirit* (1941) Madame Arcati talks of the 'beckoning finger of adventure'; a classic image for temptation. Dylan Thomas in *Under Milk Wood* (1954) says 'the smell of fried liver sidles out with onions on its breath'; an extraordinary evocation of a smell as a human. And here the world is portrayed as an old drunk going to bed with the sun as his candle:

MR DAZZLE: When the world puts on its nightcap and extinguishes the sun, then comes the bottle.
> Dion Boucicault, *London Assurance* (1841)

CHREMAMORPHISM (*krem*-uh-*mor*-fiz-um) from the Greek meaning 'change into a thing'.
To assign the attributes of objects to humans.

We speak of film 'stars', or a sociable person as 'social glue', or someone dependable as 'a brick', which Arthur Miller takes a step further here:

FRANCIS: My wife is the very brick and mortar of the church...
> Arthur Miller, *The Crucible* (1953)

ZOOMORPHISM (*zoh*-uh-*mor*-fiz-um) from the Greek meaning 'change into something living'.
To view or imagine someone or something in terms of an animal.

Lady Sneerwell in Sheridan's *The School for Scandal* (1777) refers to 'the envenomed tongue of slander'; conjuring the image of a poisonous snake. Antonio in Middleton's *The Revenger's Tragedy* (1607), condemning the Duchess' son, speaks of 'the ravenous vulture of his lust'; brutally predatory. And here Jennet pictures herself as a caught fish:

JENNET: You've cast your fishing-net
    Of eccentricity,
    Caught me when I was already lost
    And landed me with despairing gills on your own
    Strange beach. That's too inhuman of you.
> Christopher Fry, *The Lady's Not For Burning* (1948)

SYNAESTHESIA (sin-ees-*theez*-yuh) from the Greek meaning 'with sensation'.
When one sensation is described in terms of another. Also spelled SYNESTHESIA.

This is surprisingly common. We often talk of the 'bitter cold' (touch as taste), a 'loud shirt' (visual as sound) or a 'blue note' (sound as colour).

The artist Galactia, in Howard Barker's *Scenes from an Execution* (1984), talks of her epic depiction of the Battle of Lepanto as a 'noisy painting'; sight as sound. Kali in Bryony Lavery's play *Stockholm* (2007) says 'the coffee smelled like a door opening'; an extraordinarily evocative image created by describing smell in visual terms. And here we get mood as smell (the spelling is O'Casey's):

> JERRY: Have you forgotten, Mary, all the happy evenin's that were as
> sweet as the scented hawthorn that sheltered the sides o' the road
> as we saunthered through the country?
>
> Sean O'Casey, Juno and the Paycock (1924)

ALLUSION from the Latin meaning 'playing with'.

A reference to another artistic or inspirational form, including quotations or even misquotations. These come in many forms, of course, some of which we touch on below.

RELIGIOUS ALLUSION

Any reference to religion or religious texts.

Reference Malcolm in Shakespeare's *Macbeth* (1606) refers to Lucifer (the bearer of light) in relation to Macbeth, saying 'Angels are bright still, though the brightest fell'. Jonathan in Joseph Kesselring's *Arsenic and Old Lace* (1941) enters his childhood home and says 'I hope there's a fatted calf awaiting the return of the prodigal' in reference to the parable of The Prodigal Son. Dearth in J.M. Barrie's *Dear Brutus* (1917) asks Purdie 'if you find the tree of knowledge in the wood bring me back an apple'; a teasing reference to Original Sin. And here's a flirtatious interchange:

> LORD ILLINGWORTH: Let us stay here. The Book of Life begins with a
> man and a woman in a garden.
> MRS ALLONBY: It ends with Revelations.
>
> Oscar Wilde, A Woman of No Importance (1893)

Quotation Direct quotations from any religious text, such as the Bible's 'an eye for an eye, a tooth for a tooth' or 'turn the other cheek' are obvious ALLUSIONS. Weatherill in James Graham's *This House* (2012) warns his political opponent with 'Pride cometh before the fall, Walter' referring to the fall of Adam. English-language plays were – up until about fifty years ago – largely in the Christian tradition and therefore tend to draw on the Bible, but other religions are alluded to in more recent writing, such as in this example:

> AMIRA: In Koran, it say: 'Whoever is removed from fire and admitted
> unto paradise, shall win great victory'.
>
> David Edgar, Pentecost (1994)

Misquotation is as much an ALLUSION as a direct quote. Guildenstern in Tom Stoppard's *Rosencrantz and Guildenstern Are Dead* (1967) remarks (with the stage direction 'low, dry rhetoric') 'Give us this day our daily mask'. And Dr Prentice in Joe Orton's *What the Butler Saw* (1967) declares that his 'marriage is like the peace of God – it passeth all understanding'; a witty misappropriation and slight misquotation of the famous verse from Philippians.

CLASSICAL ALLUSION

Any reference to Greek or Roman myths or writings. A famous example is referring to someone's weak spot as their 'Achilles' heel'.

Reference Because education during the Renaissance and Restoration relied heavily on Latin and Greek texts – especially Ovid's *Metamorphoses* – playwrights refer easily and often to the Greek myths. For instance, 15th- and 16th-century writers often allude to Promethean fire with regard to the light in lovers' eyes; or, when someone is overwhelmed by grief, to Niobe, who wept so much when her many children were killed by the gods that she turned into a rock, from which a spring poured forth. We still relate vain and self-obsessed people to Narcissus, the beautiful youth who fell in love with his own reflection.

The Trojan War provides many opportunities for ALLUSION too. Perhaps the best-known is in Marlowe's *Doctor Faustus* (c.1589), when the ill-fated doctor asks of the image of Helen 'Was this the face that launched a thousand ships / And burnt the topless towers of Ilium?' But there are also numerous references to the Trojan Horse, as here:

> FLAMINEO: Couple together with as deep a silence
>   As did the Grecians in their wooden horse.
> John Webster, *The White Devil* (1612)

Richardetto in John Ford's *'Tis Pity She's a Whore* (c.1629) plans his rival's death, saying 'If he had / As many heads as Hydra had, he dies'; referring to the many-headed serpent slain by Hercules. Judd in Julian Mitchell's *Another Country* (1982) asks 'Has an eagle descended on your Ganymede?' – a EUPHEMISM for homosexual activity, since Zeus fell in love with Ganymede and ravished him, in the guise of an eagle. And here's another:

> HELEN: ...then you'll be light, weightless and fast not tied like Ulysses
> to a mast / afraid to hear unchained the Sirens' blast...
> Steven Berkoff, *Decadence* (1981)

HISTORICAL ALLUSION

It is common in the realms of history and politics – including their depiction in the theatre – to reference other moments from history or other leaders that have gone before.

Reference The Labour Party whip Michael Cocks in James Graham's *This House* (2012) suggests 'Let's perform the old Trafalgar, split the fleet' in preparation for a meeting with the opposition whips. Lady Bracknell in Oscar Wilde's *The Importance of Being Earnest* (1895) compares Jack's having been discovered in a handbag with 'the worst excesses of the French Revolution'; something of an OVERSTATEMENT.

Quotation The reputed words of Julius Caesar in winning the Pontic Wars – 'veni, vidi, vici' (I came, I saw, I conquered) – reported by Roman historians Plutarch and Suetonius, are referenced here:

> FALSTAFF: He saw me; and yielded; that I may justly say, with the hook-nosed fellow of Rome, three words, 'I came, saw, and overcame'.
>
> William Shakespeare, *Henry IV Part Two* (c.1598)

Misquotation At the Riot Club dinner in Laura Wade's *Posh* (2012) Hugo alludes to the Roman gladiators' salutation to the Emperor 'We who are about to die salute you' when he proclaims 'We who are about to dine, salute you' – the simple addition of a single letter provides a witty WORDPLAY.

LITERARY ALLUSION
Reference to any other work of literature.

Reference Think of such common terms as Quixotic (Cervantes' *Don Quixote*), Room 101 (George Orwell's *1984*), 'grinning like a Cheshire cat' (Lewis Carroll's *Alice Through the Looking-Glass)* and 'O what a tangled web we weave' (Sir Walter Scott).

In Stewart Parker's *Pentecost* (1987), one character refers repeatedly to Northern Ireland – 'this teeny weeny province of ours and its little people' – as Lilliput, after the miniature kingdom in Jonathan Swift's *Gulliver's Travels*. And this reference is to Oscar Wilde's *The Portrait of Dorian Gray*:

> SYLVIA: You look like shit.
>
> OLIVER: Funny, I was convinced there was a portrait somewhere in the attic that was doing that for me.
>
> Alexi Kaye Campbell, *The Pride* (2008)

Quotation Getting nowhere in an argument with his wife Susan, Gerald in Alan Ayckbourn's *Woman in Mind* (1985) reaches for Kipling with 'East is East. Never the twain shall meet', thereby somewhat monumentalizing their row by comparing it to the cultural division between East and West. And here is a quotation from the 19th-century poet and novelist George Meredith (mis-assigned by the character in the play to William Blake):

> BILL: Wally, try not to let me have anything to drink at lunch-time. O.K.?
>
> HUDSON: I'll do my best.
>
> BILL: 'And if I drink oblivion of a day, so shorten I the stature of my soul.'
>
> John Osborne, *Inadmissible Evidence* (1964)

Misquotation Jeff, the eponymous journalist in Keith Waterhouse's *Jeffrey Bernard is Unwell* (1989), wryly describes Denis Shaw – an actor who used to play villains in British B movies of the 1950s and 1960s – as 'The face that closed a thousand cinemas', a mischievous reference to Marlowe's famous description of Helen of Troy in *Doctor Faustus* (c.1589). And here Tennyson's *The Charge of the Light Brigade* is wittily misquoted:

> CARR: Entente to the left, détente to right, into the valley of the invalided blundered and wandered myself when young.
>
> Tom Stoppard, *Travesties* (1993 edition)

ALLUSION to FABLES and FAIRY TALES
Reference to any story or character from fairy tale, fable, folk lore or nursery rhyme.

Fairy Tales Any remark starting with 'Once upon a time...' immediately puts you in mind of fairy tales, and thereby alludes to the form. The psychiatrist Robert in Joe Penhall's *Blue/Orange* (2000) defends himself by saying 'I'm not the big bad wolf'; we instantly know what he means through our collective cultural reference bank. And here's one that has playfully muddled *Cinderella* and *The Sleeping Beauty*:

> JOHNNY: Well I'll tell you something, Cinderella: Your Prince Charming has come. Wake up before another thousand years go by!
>
> Terrence McNally, *Frankie and Johnny in the Clair de Lune* (1987)

Nursery Rhyme We commonly make references to such classic nursery rhymes as *Jack and Jill*, *Jack Sprat,* and *Boys and Girls Come Out to Play*. Here's an example which equates the irreversibility of white families leaving an area as more black families buy into it with – of all things – Humpty Dumpty:

> KARL: ...once that process begins, once you break that egg, Bev, all the king's horses, etcetera –
>
> Bruce Norris, *Clybourne Park* (2010)

Aesop Interestingly, although fairy tales have existed in the oral tradition for many centuries, the phrase 'fairy tale' did not become established until the late 17th century, so earlier playwrights tended to reach for the ancient Greek storyteller, Aesop, whose myriad fables include *The Tortoise and the Hare*, *The Crow and the Pitcher* and *The Boy Who Cried Wolf*. Here is reference to another:

> FLAMINEO: Love a lady for painting or gay apparel? I'll unkennel one example more for thee. Aesop had a foolish dog that let go the flesh to catch the shadow.
>
> John Webster, *The White Devil* (1612)

SHAKESPEAREAN ALLUSION

Either to the man himself, one of his characters or his writings.

Reference So entrenched in our common psyche is William Shakespeare, it should be no surprise how often we make reference to him without realizing. Who has not referred to 'the long and the short of it', or to someone being 'a tower of strength' or something that 'set your teeth on edge'? Here the fop, Witwoud, describes Lady Wishfort with an very unflattering ALLUSION to *Macbeth*:

> WITWOUD: Your lady mother came in like Banquo's angry ghost and stopped the proceedings.
>
> William Congreve, *The Way of the World* (1700)

Quotation We quote Shakespeare – knowingly or unknowingly – daily. Here is a particularly witty example, in which the schoolteacher Mrs Merriman is fully aware of her cleverness in quoting the moment Bottom the weaver is turned into an ass; though here she uses Bottom in the literal sense, since Gwen has fallen asleep in the sun and suffered sunburn:

> MERVYN: Are you pink at the back, too?
> GWEN: Yes I am, if it amuses you to know.
> MRS MERRIMAN: Bottom, thou art translated.
>
> Rodney Ackland, *The Dark River* (1937)

Misquotation In Timberlake Wertenbaker's *Our Country's Good* (1988) Captain Collins accuses Captain Campbell of mocking the officers in the production of *The Recruiting Officer* he has directed, saying 'Et tu, Campbell?' By alluding – via Shakespeare – to the last words of Julius Caesar, 'et tu' has become synonymous with treachery and betrayal. And here a misquote of *Henry V* ironically congratulates Nora for finding a missing file in a newspaper's cuttings library:

> JOHN: Cry God for Nora, England and Saint Jude.
> *Geoffrey makes a cheering noise.*
> Saint Jude being the patron saint of lost causes.
>
> Michael Frayn, *Alphabetical Order* (1975)

MUSICAL ALLUSION

Any reference to a composer, a musical style, lyrics or annotation.

Reference Algernon in Wilde's *The Importance of Being Earnest* (1895) guesses that his aunt, Lady Bracknell, has arrived from the way she rings the doorbell, saying 'Only relatives or creditors ever ring in that Wagnerian manner'; he conjures up her character by relating her to the composer's epic orchestral music.

Quotation Thinking a deal has been struck from which he will benefit, Potts in Jez Butterworth's *Mojo* (1995) says 'All we know is 'Fish are jumping and the cotton is high'.' The Gershwin's song *Summertime* – from which this lyric comes – has become synonymous with good times.

Misquotation Carr in Tom Stoppard's *Travesties* (1993 edition) quips 'If you knew Iolanthe like I knew Iolanthe'; interweaving the 1920's song *If You Knew Susie* with the heroine of a Gilbert and Sullivan opera – a playful mismatch.

CINEMATIC ALLUSION

Any reference to a particular film or filmic style.

Bri in Peter Nichol's *A Day In The Death Of Joe Egg* (1967) comments on his teaching job by saying 'It's not exactly Goodbye Mr Chips', in reference to the film of that name about the retirement of a much-loved teacher. In Lucy Prebble's *Enron* (2009) Fastow has named his virtual money schemes Raptors, after the ferocious velociraptors of *Jurassic Park*. They appear in the play as *actual* dinosaurs and, on seeing them, Fastow utters the final words of game warden Robert Muldoon (played by Bob Peck) before he is devoured: 'Clever girls.' The irony being that these virtual dinosaurs will end up 'devouring' the whole company. And in this example two miners are in trouble with their boss, known as the Colonel. The reference is from Stanley Kubrick's 1960 film *Spartacus*, in which numerous rebels attempt to cover for their leader by standing up and declaring 'I am Spartacus'.

> JIMMY: He started it.
> COLONEL: I don't give a fuck. Both of you out.
> MALCOLM: He's right, it was me.
> COLONEL: Don't come all Spartacus on me now, sunshine.
> Beth Steel, Wonderland (2014)

SEXUAL ALLUSION

Any reference with either blatant or subtle sexual overtones. Also known as INNUENDO. Perhaps the wittiest form of this is DOUBLE ENTENDRE, which can be read innocently, but has a second, dirtier meaning. This was often used to get risqué humour past the Lord Chancellor in the days of censorship.

Here's a filthy example from Shakespeare. Cloten is trying to woo his step-sister Imogen and appears beneath her window with musicians, whom he instructs:

> CLOTEN: I would this music would come: I am advised to give her music a mornings, they say it will penetrate. *(Enter musicians)* Come on, tune: if you can penetrate her with your fingering, so; if not, we'll try with tongue too.
> William Shakespeare, Cymbeline (1610)

'Fingering' refers to playing a woodwind instrument, and 'tongue' refers to singing; however, their *alternative* meanings are fairly obvious, we think. And here's a more recent example, in which Doalty is allegedly talking about his theodolite, but the stage direction – *He now grabs BRIDGET around the waist* – suggests his true subject:

> DOALTY: What d'you make of that for an implement, Bridget? Wouldn't that make a great aul shaft for your churn?
>
> Brian Friel, *Translations* (1981)

THROUGH EXAMPLE

ANALOGY from the Greek meaning 'in proportion'.
The use of a similar or parallel example to clarify a point. This is quite close to ALLUSION – but ANALOGY is expressly to make a point, as opposed to a passing reference.

Here, for instance, a novelist dismisses the untrained efforts of a young writer:

> HENRY: This thing here, which looks like a wooden club, is actually several pieces of particular wood cunningly put together in a certain way so that the whole thing is sprung, like a dance floor. It's for hitting cricket balls with. If you get it right, the cricket ball will travel two hundred yards in four seconds, and all you've done is give it a knock like knocking the top off a bottle of stout, and it makes a noise like a trout taking a fly... (*He clucks his tongue to make the noise.*) What we're trying to do is to write cricket bats, so that when we throw up an idea and give it a little knock, it might... travel...
>
> Tom Stoppard, *The Real Thing* (1982)

ALLEGORY from the Greek meaning 'speaking otherwise'.
A story with two meanings – one literal and one symbolic or figurative – used to make a point.

In this example, the eponymous Duchess tries to impress upon Bosola, who has said her husband is too lowly for her, that her husband is in fact better than her.

> DUCHESS: Sad tales befit my woe: I'll tell you one.
>   A salmon, as she swam unto the sea,
>   Met with a dogfish, who encounters her
>   With this rough language: 'Why art thou so bold
>   To mix thyself with our high state of floods,

Being no eminent courtier, but one
That for the calmest and fresh time o' th' year
Dost live in shallow rivers, rank'st thyself
With silly smelts and shrimps? And darest thou
Pass by our dog-ship without reverence?'
'O', quoth the salmon, 'sister, be at peace;
Thank Jupiter we both have passed the net.
Our value never can be truly known
Till in the fisher's basket we be shown;
I' th' market then my price may be the higher,
Even when I am nearest to the cook and fire.'
So to great men the moral may be stretchèd:
Men oft are valued high when th' are most wretchèd.

John Webster, The Duchess of Malfi (1624)

PARABLE from the Greek meaning 'placing beside'.
A parallel story or extended METAPHOR used particularly to teach a moral lesson.

Here, Rodolpho tries to advise Catherine how to proceed in the situation with her over-protective uncle:

> RODOLPHO: Catherine. If I take in my hands a little bird. And she grows and wishes to fly. But I will not let her out of my hands because I love her so much, is that right for me to do?
>
> Arthur Miller, A View from the Bridge (1956)

EXEMPLUM from the Latin meaning 'model' or 'pattern'.
A true or fictitious story cited as an illustrative example, usually with a moral angle. Mediaeval preachers used 'exempla' in their sermons, usually in the form of fables or folklore.

Here, Graves tries to prove that men are capable of not being covetous:

> GRAVES. I know one man, at least, who, rejected in his poverty by one as poor as himself, no sooner came into a sudden fortune than he made his lawyer invent a codicil which the testator never dreamt of, bequeathing independence to the woman who had scorned him.
>
> Edward Bulwer-Lytton, Money (1840)

PARADIGM from the Greek meaning 'pattern' or 'model'.
A very clear example – true or fictitious – illustrating a pattern of typical human behaviour.

In this example, Sherbert, who works in a beauty salon, argues why she wants to grow old gracefully:

> SHERBERT: There's this one woman who comes in – I feel sorry for her in a way – and she's got this photograph of what she looked like when she was nineteen. She must be fifty if she's a day now. Anyway, she comes in and she shows me this photograph and – fucking hell! – was she beautiful! 'This was me', she says. It's as if that photograph captured her at the happiest moment of her life. Perhaps it's like that. Perhaps we reach our peak when we're nineteen and – for one glorious summer – we're in control of our lives and we look wonderful and everything is perfect. And then it's never the same again.
>
> Philip Ridley, *The Fastest Clock in the Universe* (1992)

APOMNEMONYSIS (ap-*om*-nem-on-*ee*-sis) from the Greek meaning 'recalling from memory'.
To quote a higher authority, often religious.

Religious When Miss Prism in Oscar Wilde's *The Importance of Being Earnest* (1895) says 'As a man sows, so shall he reap', she is issuing a warning by way of an appeal to the collective moral code provided by the Bible. And in the following example, a prisoner, who of course is power*less*, says 'Fetch me the Koran that I may read of power':

> ADAM: *(He reads from the Koran)* In the name of God, the Merciful,
> the Compassionate.
> Behold, we sent it down on the Night of Power:
> And what shall teach thee what is the Night of Power?
> The Night of Power is better than a thousand months;
> In it the angels and the Spirit descend,
> By the leave of The Lord, upon every command.
> Peace it is, till the rising of dawn.
>
> Frank McGuinness, *Someone Who'll Watch Over Me* (1992)

Non-religious This can be as simple as saying such things as 'my instincts tell me...' or 'my gut feeling is...' Or it can allude to people in authority, such as a parent – as when Stan in Neil Simon's *Brighton Beach Memoirs* (1983) quotes his father, saying 'you always have to do what you think is right in this world and stand up for your principles'. Alternatively it can be a figure in power, as when Arthur, in Terence Rattigan's *The Winslow Boy* (1946), staves off his daughter's differing opinion of Sir Robert Morton by saying 'in the words of the Prime Minister let us wait and see!' (alluding to Anthony Asquith, who famously used to bluff his adversaries by saying 'We had better wait and see').

Philosophy To quote an established philosopher also, of course, carries great authority, as here:

> BOHR: ...no sooner has man become, as Protagoras proclaimed him, the measure of all things, than we're pushed aside again by the products of our own reasoning!
>
> Michael Frayn, *Copenhagen* (1998)

Shakespeare In this example the ex-actor Tyrone, who is an inveterate quoter of Shakespeare, drives his sons to distraction:

> TYRONE: There's nothing wrong with life. It's we who – (*He quotes.*) 'The fault, dear Brutus, is not in our stars, but in ourselves that we are underlings.'
>
> Eugene O'Neill, *Long Day's Journey Into Night* (c.1940)

MIMESIS (mim-*ee*-sis) from the Greek meaning 'imitation' – itself from *mimos*, 'imitator' or 'actor'.
The direct imitation of someone either vocally or physically.

There is a certain overlap with ETHOPOEIA below – the distinction we have drawn is that MIMESIS tends towards a mockery, whereas ETHOPOEIA is an attempt to put oneself into another's emotional situation.

In this example Public Gar mocks his undemonstrative father, for whom he works:

> PUBLIC: Instead of saying to me: (*grandly*) 'Gar, my son, since you are leaving me for ever, you may have the entire day free,' what does he do? Lines up five packs of flour and says: (*in flat dreary tones*) 'Make them up into two-pound pokes.'
>
> Brian Friel, *Philadelphia, Here I Come!* (1964)

Playwrights who write in a vernacular are creating a whole mimetic world. Consider the Cockney of the grocer Ablett in Arthur Wing Pinero's *Trelawny of the 'Wells'* (1898): 'Jest as I was preparin' to clean myself, the 'ole universe seemed to cry aloud for pertaters'. Or the Newcastle dialect of the miners in Lee Hall's *The Pitmen Painters* (2008): 'Ye de de art, divvint ye?' Or the Scottish of the Doctor in Harold Brighouse's *Hobson's Choice* (1915): 'Aye, it's a gay, high-sounding sentiment, ma mannie, but ye'll nae do it'. This is not mockery, of course, but merely how the characters should sound according to the writer.

Moving further afield, how about the broad New York tones of Rocky in Eugene O'Neill's *The Iceman Cometh* (1939): 'dat louse Hickey's coitinly made a prize coupla suckers outa youse'. Or this example of a West Indian patois:

> BAYGEE: Well, he sister tell me that the wife tell she, that he just look at her, and then he look at this young stallion dat making Thelma shout ting he doe hear in he life and he heart just give up so, gang, he drop and dead.
>
> Kwame Kwei-Armah, *Elmina's Kitchen* (2003)

ETHOPOEIA (eeth-oh-*pee*-yuh) from the Greek meaning 'enacting a character'.
To imagine oneself in another person's position in order to understand or convey their feelings or actions better. This device tends to be descriptive, and a deliberately empathetic action, sometimes involving MIMESIS (see above).

For instance, here Quentin recalls his friend Lou who, faced with the anti-communist investigations, has committed suicide:

> QUENTIN: "Please be my friend, Quentin" is what he was saying to me, "I am drowning, throw me a rope!"
>
> Arthur Miller, *After The Fall* (1964)

MARTYRIA (mar-*ti*-ree-uh) from the Greek meaning 'proof'.
To confirm something through previous experience.

In this example, Mary berates her husband:

> MARY: You were swindled again as you always are, because you insist on secondhand bargains in everything.
>
> Eugene O'Neill, *Long Day's Journey Into Night* (c.1940)

FORESHADOWING
The mention of something that subsequently occurs. In dramatic terms, this is important structurally – but from a *character's* point of view, they imagine a future action or situation. Hence the link to DRAMATIC IRONY.

It can be comic, as in this example from Oscar Wilde's *The Importance of Being Earnest* (1895), describing his fiancée Gwendolen's meeting with his ward, Cecily:

> JACK: I'll bet you anything you like that half an hour after they've met, they will be calling each other sister.

Which indeed they do in Act III, after they have 'called each other a lot of other things first':

GWENDOLEN: My poor wounded Cecily!
CECILY: My sweet wronged Gwendolen!
GWENDOLEN: You will call me sister, will you not?

Alternatively it can be emotive, as in this example from Githa Sowerby's *Rutherford and Son* (1912). Janet – spinster daughter of the tyrannical industrialist of the title – recounts a dream she has had to her sister-in-law Mary:

JANET: I had a dream – a dream that I was in a place wi' flowers, in the summer time, white and thick like they never grow on the moor – but it was the moor – a place near Martin's cottage. And I dreamt that he came to me with the look he had when I was a little lass, with his head up and the lie gone out of his eyes.

Then, towards the end of the play, she revisits her dream in a poignant moment when she tries to persuade her lover, Martin, to choose her over returning to work for his boss, her father:

JANET: We'll begin again. We'll be happy – happy. You and me, free in the world! All the time that's been'll be just like a dream that's past, a waiting time afore we found each other – the long winter afore the flowers come out white and thick on the moors –

He, of course, had not been privy to the description of the dream before, so he hears only the wild poetry of her hopes for them. Such use of FORESHADOWING can be very moving for an audience.

TAXIS (*tak*-sis) from the Greek meaning 'arrangement' or 'order'.
To assign everything its proper place in life.

Morris in Noël Coward's *Present Laughter* (1943) uses a simple form of this when he utters 'God's in his heaven and all's right with the world'. But here is a darker and more fulsome example:

PIZARRO: There's the world. The eagle rips the condor; the condor rips the crow. And the crow would blind all the eagles in the sky if once it had the beak to do it. The clothed hunt the naked; the legitimates hunt the bastards, and put down the word Gentleman to blot up the blood.
Peter Shaffer, *The Royal Hunt of the Sun* (1964)

THROUGH DESCRIPTION

PATHOS from the Greek meaning 'suffering'.
When language and imagery are used to elicit a strong emotional response from another character or the audience or, most probably, both.

Think of Macbeth's famous 'Tomorrow and tomorrow and tomorrow' speech, in response to the news of his wife's death in Act V Scene v of *Macbeth* (1606). And here's a rather sickening example in which Michael describes the part he played in the Rwandan genocide:

> MICHAEL: Hobble the children first. Slash their Achilles tendons so that they could not move far. Then the parents would come running to protect them... those were my orders. It took four days and nights. When the dogs heard the cries of the people. They too began to howl.

> Tanika Gupta, *Sanctuary* (2002)

ENARGIA (en-*ar*-jee-uh) from the Greek meaning 'visible' or 'distinct'.
A general term for any form of vivid description, including Chronographia (description of a past or recurring event), Chorographia (description of a particular nation), Oneirographia (description of a dream), Hodographia (description of a journey), Hydrographia (description of water) and Dendrographia (description of a tree – we kid you not).

The suffix '-graphia' comes from the Greek *graphein*, to draw or paint, which gives us the word graphic, of course. This form of active description is rather out of fashion. Nowadays, playwrights are encouraged to 'show, not tell', and off-stage action is deemed *un*dramatic. However, examples can still be identified, and the following are the more common types to be found in drama.

PRAGMATOGRAPHIA (*prag*-mat-uh-*graf*-ee-uh) from the Greek meaning 'depicting a deed'.
The detailed description of an event or action.

It is often used in plays to describe what has happened offstage, much in the style of the messengers in Greek Tragedy. The Bloody Sergeant in *Macbeth* (1606) is very much in this tradition.

Here is a more simple and comic example, the description of a duel:

> CRABTREE: Charles's shot took effect, as I tell you, and Sir Peter's missed; but, what is very extraordinary, the ball struck against a little bronze Shakespeare that stood over the fireplace, grazed out of the

window at a right angle, and wounded the postman, who was just coming to the door with a double letter from Northamptonshire.

Richard Brinsley Sheridan, *The School for Scandal* (1777)

TOPOGRAPHIA (*top-oh-graf-ee-uh*) from the Greek meaning 'depicting a place'. The detailed description of a place.

Here is a rather wonderful example:

OLD MARTIN: You call them the Andes. Picture a curtain of stone hung by some giant across your path. Mountains set on mountains: cliffs on cliffs. Hands of rock a hundred yards high, with flashing nails – where the snow never moved, scratching the gashed face of the sun. For miles around the jungle lay black in its shadow.

Peter Shaffer, *The Royal Hunt of the Sun* (1964)

TOPOTHESIA (*top-oh-theez-yuh*) form the Greek meaning 'arranging a place'. The description of an imaginary or imagined place, often heaven or hell.

Here is Edgar's description of an imagined cliff edge for his suicidal blind father to jump off:

EDGAR: Come on, sir; here's the place. Stand still! How fearful
And dizzy 'tis to cast one's eyes so low!
The crows and choughs that wing the midway air
Show scarce so gross as beetles. Halfway down
Hangs one that gathers samphire – dreadful trade!
Methinks he seems no bigger than his head.
The fishermen that walk upon the beach
Appear like mice, and yon tall anchoring bark
Diminished to her cock; her cock, a buoy
Almost too small for sight. The murmuring surge
On th' unnumbered idle pebble chafes
Cannot be heard so high. I'll look no more,
Lest my brain turn, and the deficient sight
Topple down headlong.

William Shakespeare, *King Lear* (c.1606)

THANATOGRAPHIA (*tha-nat-uh-graf-ee-uh*) from the Greek meaning 'depicting a death'.
The description of a death.

Shakespeare's history plays are full of them, of course – such as Talbot in *Henry VI Part One* (1592) – but here's a more modern one: the description of the redoubtable Giles Corey's demise:

> ELIZABETH: Great stones they lay upon his chest until he plead aye or
> nay. (*With a tender smile for the old man*) They say he give them but
> two words. "More weight," he says. And died.
> Arthur Miller, *The Crucible* (1953)

PROSOPOGRAPHIA (*pross*-op-uh-*graf*-ee-uh) from the Greek meaning 'depicting a face'. The description of a person's face.

Here's a particularly emotive example:

> HIERONIMO: Within thy face, my sorrows I may see.
> Thy eyes are gummed with tears, thy cheeks are wan,
> Thy forehead troubled, and thy mutt'ring lips
> Murmur sad words abruptly broken off.
> Thomas Kyd, *The Spanish Tragedy* (c.1592)

EFFICTIO (ef-*ik*-tee-oh) from the Latin meaning 'creation' or 'portrayal'. The detailed description of someone's body, usually from top to bottom.

For a much extended version, see Dromio of Syracuse's description of Nell the kitchen wench in Act III Scene ii of Shakespeare's *The Comedy of Errors* (1594). Here, however, is one from Ben Jonson, in which Mistress Littlewit is described in equine terms:

> KNOCKEM: Is't not pity my delicate dark chestnut here – with the fine
> lean head, large forehead, round eyes, even mouth, sharp ears, long
> neck, thin crest, close withers, plain back, deep sides, short fillets,
> and full flanks; with a round belly, a plump buttock, large thighs, knit
> knees, straight legs, short pasterns, smooth hoofs, and short heels
> – should lead a dull honest woman's life, that might live the life of
> a lady?
> Ben Jonson, *Bartholomew Fair* (1614)

THROUGH QUALIFICATION

APPOSITION from the Latin meaning 'placing nearby'.
A qualifying word or phrase placed next to the noun it qualifies. This most often occurs

when we describe people in relation to their jobs (my neighbour, the lawyer) or their relationships (Emily, Stuart's wife).

Here's a strong, metaphorical example from Oscar Wilde:

> HESTER: Till you count what is a shame in a woman to be an infamy in a man, you will always be unjust, and Right, that pillar of fire, and Wrong, that pillar of cloud, will be made dim to your eyes...
> Oscar Wilde, *A Woman of No Importance* (1893)

EPITHET from the Greek meaning 'adding on'.
A word or phrase used as a qualifying description or substitute for someone or something.

Simple Description Iago, the villain of Shakespeare's *Othello* (c.1604), is referred to and addressed as 'honest Iago' by the very characters whose downfall he is engineering: a grim IRONY. And here is Marlowe helpfully referencing the term itself:

> TAMBURLAINE: Ah, fair Zenocrate! Divine Zenocrate!
> Fair is too foul an epithet for thee.
> Christopher Marlowe, *Tamburlaine the Great: Part One* (1587)

Substitution In Oscar Wilde's *The Importance of Being Earnest* (1895) Jack's imaginary brother, Ernest – whom he uses as an excuse to go up to London – is referred to by several characters as 'That unfortunate young man, his brother'. And here is Jimmy's cruelly witty description of his brother-in-law:

> JIMMY: The Platitude from Outer Space – that's brother Nigel.
> John Osborne, *Look Back in Anger* (1956)

HYPALLAGE (hy-*pal*-uh-jee) from the Greek meaning 'exchange'.
A transferred epithet; the agreement of a word with one it does not logically qualify (see also CATACHRESIS above).

Shakespeare loves this device when he is at his most economically poetic. Othello talks of Desdemona lapping up his exotic stories with a 'greedy ear'; it is not her ear that is ravenous, of course, but her appetite for his tales. Amid the farcical confusions of *The Comedy of Errors* (1594) Antipholus of Ephesus is locked out of his own house, and says later 'upon me the guilty doors were shut'; it is not the doors that were in the wrong, but the people that locked them.

Here are some examples by other playwrights: roused from sleep in Thomas Kyd's *The Spanish Tragedy* (c.1592) Hieronimo asks 'What outcries pluck me from my naked bed?' – it is not the bed, but Hieronimo himself that is naked. In Terry Johnson's *Hysteria* (1993) Yahuda asserts to Freud that there are 'No scantily-clad secrets in your closet'; a clue to what he had hoped those secrets might be. And here is one from the Restoration, in which the blood rises in her cheeks, not the confession itself:

> FAINALL: I see the warm confession reddening on your cheeks, and sparkling from your eyes.
>
> William Congreve, *The Way of the World* (1700)

THROUGH ECONOMY

COMPOUNDS

An inventive and economic combination of words to conjure up a single image, usually hyphenated (see also NEOLOGISM). Shakespeare, of course, coined many of these that have gone into common parlance: 'blood-stained', 'high-pitched', 'ill-tempered', 'low-spirited', 'well-behaved', a 'bold-faced lie' or 'star-crossed lovers'.

Nominal Think of such classics as 'heart-strings' or 'marriage-knot'. And here is a provocative one:

> TZARA: ... it was the artist who became the priest-guardian of the magic that conjured the intelligence out of the appetite.
>
> Tom Stoppard, *Travesties* (1993 edition)

David Rudkin takes the traditionally hyphenated compounds a step further with truly Germanic compound words such as 'dwellingplace' and the gloriously poetic 'golden soldierspine' in *The Sons of Light* (1977), which is set on a remote Scottish island and written in a specific dialect. Jez Butterworth does similarly in *Jerusalem* (2009), in which Davey asks Lee about his imminent trip to Australia: 'You ready for your dreamquest then?'

Adjectival Think of such combinations as 'smooth-tongued', 'high-handed' or 'wrong-headed'. And here is a pleasing one:

> SYLV: I wrap my goodies up for special heroes crashing thigh-clutched Harleys...
>
> Steven Berkoff, *East* (1975, revised 1976)

Verbal Most usually with a prefix such as in the terms to 'out-do', 'out-run' or this description of the garrulous servant, Tranio:

> GREMIO: What, this gentleman will out-talk us all!
>
> William Shakespeare, *The Taming of the Shrew* (c.1591)

Insults Compounds seem particularly favoured for insults and general INVECTIVE, as when Captain Ross in Timberlake Wertenbaker's *Our Country's Good* (1988) condemns Australia as 'this scrub-ridden, dust-driven, thunder-bolted, savage-run, cretinous colony'. Or in Ben Jonson's *Volpone* (1605-6) when Volpone himself dismisses a rabble of charlatans as 'These turdy-facy-nasty-paty-fartical rogues!' Or this riotous rant at the Mayor:

> THOMAS: You bubble-mouthing, fog-blathering,
> Chin-chuntering, chap-flapping, liturgical,
> Turgidical, base old man!
> Christopher Fry, *The Lady's Not For Burning* (1948)

ALLITERATIVE COMPOUNDS

It seems to be especially popular and memorable to combine COMPOUNDS with ALLITERATION, such as in the well-worn (there's one) examples 'hard-hearted', 'tongue-tied', 'high-heels', 'mealy-mouthed', 'high-handed', 'pill-popping', 'penny-pinching', 'tempest-tossed', 'far-fetched', 'fat-face', 'fart-face', 'fuck-face'... we could go on!

Shakespeare was a prodigious exponent of this form of the device: Juliet's 'fiery-footed steeds', Hamlet's 'muddy-mettled rascal' and Hubert's 'fair-faced league' in *King John* (1596) to name but three. The Renaissance was a period of enormous linguistic invention, and all the playwrights were at it. Ben Jonson talks of the 'furrow-faced sea' in *Volpone* (1605-6); and John Ford has Soranzo – husband to Annabella, who is pregnant by her own brother in *'Tis Pity She's a Whore* (c.1629) – refer to her 'corrupted, bastard-bearing womb'.

SIBILANT COMPOUNDS

Again, Shakespeare seems fond of these, with Juliet's 'sober-suited matron', Prospero's 'spell-stopped' enemies, and Henry V's threat to the hapless citizens of Harfleur that his army will 'Defile the locks of your shrill-shrieking daughters'. Here's a 20th-century one – the spelling is O'Casey's own Irish vernacular:

> MRS BOYLE: There'll never be any good got out o' him so long as he goes with that shouldher-shruggin' Joxer.
> Sean O'Casey, *Juno and the Paycock* (1924)

ASSONANT COMPOUNDS

The combination of the COMPOUND with the repeated vowel sounds of ASSONANCE, such as 'slim-hipped', 'hard-arsed', 'loud-mouthed' or 'foul-mouthed'.

In this marvellously terse example, two teachers are discussing their sexually ambiguous pupil, Dakin:

> MRS LINTOTT: You always think they're sad, Hector, every, every time. Actually I wouldn't have said he was sad. I would have said he was cunt-struck.
>
> Alan Bennett, *The History Boys* (2004)

PARACHESIC COMPOUNDS

This is where a combination of sounds is repeated either at the beginning of linked words, such as in Bryony Lavery's play *Stockholm* (2007) in which Kali describes her mother as 'phone-phobic'. Or in the middle, such as the repeated 'un' sound in 'punch-drunk', or the 'horse-courser' mentioned by the Book-Holder in Ben Jonson's *Bartholomew Fair* (1614).

It is surprisingly common for both the beginnings and ends of each word to share the same sounds, as in 'topsy-turvy' or this example from Steven Berkoff's *East* (1975, revised 1976), in which he refers to the yobs of the East End as 'jesting-jousting lads'. Such combinations are eminently memorable; think of 'zig-zag', 'flim-flam', 'shilly-shally', 'dilly-dally', 'pitter-patter' and 'wishy-washy'. Interestingly all these share the same change of vowel sound – from 'I' to 'A' – as does this example:

> EYRE: Peace, my fine Firk! Stand by with your pishery-pashery, away!
>
> Thomas Dekker, *The Shoemaker's Holiday* (1599)

HOMOIOTELEUTONIC COMPOUNDS

This is the particular form of PARACHESIS when the ends of each word in a COMPOUND are the same, as in 'chick-flick', 'hanky-panky', 'hoity-toity', 'razzle-dazzle', 'pell-mell' and 'helter-skelter'.

Returning to Bryony Lavery's *Stockholm* (2007), Kali's boyfriend Todd refers to their 'pleassic-jurassic sofa'. And now, as an eccentric finale, in Thomas Tomkis' little-known Jacobean play *Albumazar* (1615) the eponymous fraudulent astronomer uses compounds to befuddle his audiences, inventing such terms as:

> ALBUMAZAR: Necro-puro-geo-hydro-cheiro-coscinomancy

THROUGH SUBSTITUTION

METONYMY (met-*on*-im-ee) from the Greek meaning 'change of name'.
When one word or phrase stands for another with which it is associated; a part for the whole.

For instance, Hollywood stands for the American film industry, the White House for US government, or the Crown for British royalty. T.S. Eliot coined the phrase 'object correlative' to describe an image that encapsulates the idea, such as an apple for the fall of man, which is a form of METONYMY.

In *Richelieu* (1839), Edward Bulwer-Lytton coined the most famous example of METONYMY with 'The pen is mightier than the sword'; with the 'pen' representing written diplomacy and the 'sword' active combat. Equally famously, Christopher Marlowe refers to Helen of Troy in *Doctor Faustus* (c.1589) as 'the face that launched a thousand ships'; her face represents her matchless beauty and, more importantly, her status as a political trophy. Here's another, representing a happy disposition and a smart appearance:

> CHARLEY: He's a man way out there in the blue, riding on a smile and a shoeshine.
>
> Arthur Miller, *Death of a Salesman* (1949)

METONYMIC HENDIADYS (see also HENDIADYS)
The more poetic conjuring of an image through two entities associated with it joined together with a conjunction.

Commonly used examples include 'hearts and minds' (emotion and intellect), 'hand and heart' (practical and emotional), 'heart and soul' (emotional and spiritual), 'body and soul' (physical and spiritual), 'flesh and blood' (actual body and genetic line) and 'shock and awe' (action and effect).

Tom Stoppard in *Travesties* (1993 edition) succinctly encapsulates the horrors of First World War trenches with the 'mud and wire'; the 'mud' represents the natural obstacles and 'wire' the man-made. And here's an extraordinary one, describing the South of England from a northerner's point of view:

> ANN: They tell me there's a deal of sunshine and wickedness in them parts.
> Githa Sowerby, *Rutherford and Son* (1912)

This device often combines with ALLITERATION as well, such as in the phrase 'bed and board' (comfort and sustenance) and 'brain and brawn' (intellect and physical strength). The Earl of Rochester in Stephen Jeffreys' *The Libertine* (1994) claims that he and his cronies are 'the froth and fizz of the reign'. While Timon in Shakespeare and Middleton's *Timon of Athens* (1605) decries the morals of the time with 'Lust and liberty / Creep in the minds and marrows of our youth' a double whammy!

SYNECDOCHE (sin-*ek*-duh-kee) from the Greek meaning 'with interpretation'.
A kind of METONYMY in which a part is substituted for the whole or the whole for a part.

Part for a Whole As in 'the boards' representing the stage. It was common among Renaissance playwrights to use a phrase such as 'Take thy face hence', meaning 'go away'; the 'face' represents the whole body, but it gives the added sense of 'I'm sick of the sight of you'! In this example the tongue represents all that it pronounces:

HARRIET: Your tongue is so famed for falsehood 'twill do the truth an injury.

George Etherege, *The Man of Mode* (1676)

Whole for a Part As in 'the law' representing the police. In *Absolute Hell* (1988) Rodney Ackland has the talent-spotting film producer, Maurice, approach an American GI at the bar with 'Turn around, America, let's see your profile' – the whole country represents one soldier serving it. Or consider this:

SANDRA: I'm talking about having enough handbag to get a decent pair o' shoes...

Jonathan Harvey, *Beautiful Thing* (1993)

METALEPSIS (met-uh-*lep*-sis) from the Greek meaning 'substitution'.
Another form of METONYMY in which one thing is referred to by something else more *remotely* associated with it.

Larry in Patrick Marber's *Closer* (1997) claims 'I'm a refugee escaping from the glittering babble'. He gives both a visual and aural sense of the *beau monde* he's trying to avoid. And here a fop alludes to his own levity and fashion (and perhaps, unwittingly, his own stupidity) by his use of the word 'feather':

FOPPINGTON: Through all record, no prince was ever slain
By one who had a feather in his brain.
John Vanbrugh, *The Relapse* (1696)

DIAPHORA (dy-*af*-or-ruh) from the Greek meaning 'distinction' or 'difference'.
To use a simple word instead of a person's name as representative of that person.

In the Renaissance, an old man would often be referred to as a 'beard', as representative of his age and gravity. Mortimer in Joseph Kesselring's comedy *Arsenic and Old Lace* (1941) refers to his copy-setter, Joe, as 'the third machine from the left'. And Frank in Arnold Wesker's *Roots* (1959) asks about Beattie's boyfriend, who is late, saying 'where is this article we come to see?' In the following example – from another play by John Vanbrugh – an adjective is applied without its noun as representative of whom it describes (see also ANTIMERIA):

LADY FANCIFUL: 'Tis more than natural such a rude fellow as he and such a little impertinent as she should be capable of making a woman of my sphere uneasy.

John Vanbrugh, *The Provok'd Wife* (1697)

ANTONOMASIA (*an*-tuh-noh-*maz*-ee-yuh) from the Greek meaning 'instead of a name'. When a word or phrase is used instead of a person's name, usually suggesting a quality related to them. Think of women waiting for Mr Right to come along or Frank Sinatra being known as Ol' Blue Eyes.

Word Here one of the Jurors berates another, who is a sportsman:

> 6TH JUROR: Listen, baseball, why don't you stop making smart remarks all the time?
>
> Reginald Rose, *Twelve Angry Men* (1956)

Phrase Whereas here the guy who has just installed the telephone refers to Connie by her new telephone number:

> DELIVERY MAN: Well, Eldorado five-eight-one-nine-one – have a nice marriage.
>
> Neil Simon, *Barefoot In The Park* (1965)

Another form of this device, popular in the Renaissance and the Restoration, is when characters create a name using an appropriate attribute, as when Leontes in Shakespeare's *The Winter's Tale* (c.1610) talks acidly of 'Sir Smile, his neighbour' as being a possible adulterer; and Lady Teazle in Sheridan's *The School for Scandal* (1777) addresses Joseph Surface as 'Good Mr Hypocrite'.

EPONYM (*ep*-on-im) from the Greek meaning 'named after'.
To substitute for a particular attribute the name of a famous person or thing recognized for that attribute: a succinct form of ALLUSION (see above).

Greek Myths These provide us with a few popular ones. Someone self-engrossed is a Narcissus, a horrifying or vicious woman is a Gorgon, a peddler of doom and gloom is a Cassandra.

History Someone clever is an Einstein; a philanderer is a Casanova; a Napoleon of Industry is a what we would now term a Corporate Fat Cat. And here is a good one for a somewhat dictatorial teacher:

> GILBERT: The headmaster said you ruled them with a rod of iron. He called you the Himmler of the lower fifth.
>
> Terence Rattigan, *The Browning Version* (1948)

Literature Someone miserly is a Scrooge (the central character in Dickens' *A Christmas Carol*), and young men in love are Romeos. Fairy Tales give us Prince Charming or the Big Bad Wolf. In the following example, Jimmy passes comment on the overbearing nature of one of his wife's friends by alluding to Oscar Wilde, mocking her class on the way:

> JIMMY: Pass Lady Bracknell the cucumber sandwiches, will you?
> John Osborne, *Look Back In Anger* (1956)

Bible A Herod is someone despotic, a Job is wise, a Jezebel is a fallen women, and a Judas is treacherous, of course. Here is a nice example, leveled at the Reverend Hale, who is allowing Proctor's wife to be arrested and is likened to the man who presided over the trial of Jesus Christ:

> PROCTOR: Pontius Pilate! God will not let you wash your hands of this!
> Arthur Miller, *The Crucible* (1953)

Things We commonly refer to 'an ocean of tears' or 'a mountain of paper work'. Both are fine examples of imagistic HYPERBOLE. Here is a more precise version of the last one:

> HESTHER: I've got an Everest of papers to get through before bed.
> Peter Shaffer, *Equus* (1973)

Chapter 4 Wit

MARGARET: Oh, Father, don't be witty!
MORE: Why not? Wit's what's in question.
ROPER: *(quietly)* While we are witty, the Devil may enter
us unawares.

Robert Bolt, *A Man for All Seasons* (1960)

In this chapter, we are dealing with the notion of *conscious* wit. Playwrights who create witticisms and WORDPLAY invariably *mean* to do so, and usually – though not always – their characters are aware of their own wit and cleverness too. A character's facility with words tells us a great deal about them – their background and education, and the way they think and communicate. Witty characters are profoundly useful; they draw an audience in through their humour – although they often wear their wit as a veneer, to cover their intentions or insecurities.

However, there is wit and there is wit: funny wit and clever wit. In the early Renaissance this distinction was epitomized in the difference between Clowns and Fools. A Clown was usually a low-status character who did not know that he was funny, whereas a Fool was *paid* to be funny: it was his job. The Clown was often deployed at moments of high drama to provide light relief, but also, paradoxically, this served to intensify the dramatic tension – think of the Clown who delivers the asp to Cleopatra in *Antony and Cleopatra* (1606). The task of the Fool, on the other hand, was to expose the follies of mankind, which often necessitated sailing very close to the wind; he was therefore extremely clever and knew exactly how to play his audience to best advantage. The Fool in *King Lear* (c.1606) is a prime example. By Shakespeare's time the two terms had become interchangeable, though there are still clearly two types of 'funny man':

FESTE: Better a witty fool, than a foolish wit.

William Shakespeare, *Twelfth Night* (c.1602)

In the theatre there is a terrific *energy* to wit, linked to the speed of thought of the witty characters. This energy is very often supported by the sprung rhythms of our language and bolstered by rhetorical devices such as those in this chapter, and in those that follow on STRUCTURE, REPETITION and the RULE OF THREE. Consider the inverted repetition of Feste's line above (a form of CHIASMUS called ANTIMETABOLE). It is stunningly neat, exact and economical. So much so, in fact, that it takes a moment to comprehend it fully. An audience enjoys running to keep up with such characters and the wit they dispense.

The devices in this chapter mostly belong to these clever, witty, knowing characters. With this in mind, plunge into this chapter with alacrity. There is much to enjoy.

PLAY ON WORDS

This first section covers the devices which literally play with words. Some of the devices will be very familiar, such as IRONY and PARONOMASIA, better known as the PUN. Others will be utterly new – we hope you relish meeting them.

Writers in all media have always enjoyed playing with words. Hilaire Belloc (of *Cautionary Tales* fame) famously hoped that people would say of him that 'His sins were scarlet, but his books were read'. He uses the word 'scarlet' to mean 'scandalous', but balances its more usual meaning of the colour against the PUN on 'read', which sounds like the colour 'red'. It is terrifically clever and deeply pleasing.

Another dizzying example – attributed to the painter Francis Bacon – is 'Champagne for my real friends, real pain for my sham friends'; a brilliant play on the two syllables of 'champagne' and the words they sound like (homonyms, in case you were wondering).

In everyday life we probably come across such WORDPLAY most often in advertising. A witty slogan is more appealing and, crucially, more memorable. Think of the Adidas campaign 'Impossible Is Nothing'; a clever inversion of the usual phrase. Or the Nintendo slogan 'Get N or Get Out'; playing on the sound of the letter 'N' and the word 'in'. Or the Conservative Party's advert in the run-up to the 1979 election, at a time of high unemployment, 'Labour Isn't Working'; a simple double meaning.

WORDPLAY
When words are used playfully and inventively, usually for clever or comic effect.

True Wordplay The former RAF pilot Freddie in Terence Rattigan's *The Deep Blue Sea* (1952) complains that he wants to fly planes rather than sit behind a desk, saying 'I want something airborne – not chairborne'; the rhyme (or HOMOIOTELEUTON) is integral to his embittered wit. One of the schoolboys in Alan Bennett's *The History Boys* (2004) reports their teacher Mrs Lintott as saying 'This is history not histrionics'; this time the repeated first syllable or PARACHESIS points up the cleverness. And how about this one:

> AGNES: I'll see her in the poorhouse. Though perhaps the whorehouse would suit her better.
>
> Peter Nichols, *Passion Play* (2000 edition)

Literal and Metaphoric Wordplay In *Volpone* (1605-6), Ben Jonson's titular character exclaims that health is 'The blessing of the rich! The riches of the poor!' – the rich are literally well-off, but health for the poor is their metaphorical 'riches'. Similarly, Terence

Rattigan in *The Winslow Boy* (1946) has Sir Robert describe the House of Commons as having 'Too little ventilation and far too much hot air'; the 'hot air' is both literal, due to the poor ventilation, and metaphorical due to the blustering talk of the politicians. We can surmise a lot about a character who can produce such playful language. Consider this wonderfully mischievous play on words:

> ROGER: I can't stand here all day discussing the ins and outs
> of hermaphrodites.
>   Sarah Daniels, *Neaptide* (1986)

Playing with Proverbs (see also PUN 2 below) WORDPLAY often relies on the listeners – both other characters and the audience – having a common knowledge of established phrases or PROVERBS. Here's another example from Sarah Daniels' *Neaptide* (1986), in which Jean says of a case of lesbianism in her school 'better latent than never'; a witty twist on 'better late than never'. Similarly Dr Wicksteed in Alan Bennett's *Habeas Corpus* (1973) riffs on the saying 'he who laughs last, laughs longest' when he says 'He whose lust lasts, lasts longest'. And here is an established proverbial phrase taken literally to playful effect:

> MORTIMER: You see, insanity runs in my family. It practically gallops.
>   Joseph Kesselring, *Arsenic and Old Lace* (1941)

Just Plain Silly This example proved too much to resist, playing on the quaint word 'tantamount' – say it out loud:

> BISHOP: Such callousness is astounding! It's tantamount
> to slaughter.
> CLIVE: *(miserably)* Oh, it can't amount to tantamount to slaughter.
>   Philip King, *See How They Run* (1945)

PUN thought to be from the Old English 'pundrigion', meaning a 'fanciful formation'. Also known as **PARONOMASIA** (*pa*-ruh-noh-*maz*-ee-yuh) from the Greek meaning 'beside the name'. This device comes in two common forms:
1) The use of the same or similar sounding words for comic, clever or ironic effect.

Same Word, Different Meanings Mercutio in Shakespeare's *Romeo and Juliet* (1595) says, when he has been mortally stabbed, 'You shall find me a grave man', with 'grave' meaning both serious and a place of burial. Staying with Shakespeare, Benedick in *Much Ado About Nothing* (c.1598) claims 'Till all graces be in one woman, one woman shall not come in my grace', with 'grace' first meaning 'virtue' and then 'favour'. And here is a fun example from a more recent play:

PRIOR: Oh my queen; you know you've hit rock bottom when even drag is a drag.

Tony Kushner, *Angels in America* (1991)

Same Sounding Words, Different Meanings Once again Shakespeare excels at this. The King in *Henry V* (c.1599) talks of the three traitors having been paid by 'the gilt of France – O guilt indeed!' Sam Shepard, in *Buried Child* (1997 version), has his character Dodge state with great simplicity that 'the past is passed'. And here is a pleasing example that has become colloquial due to its wit and memorability:

ROCKY: We're goin' to beat it down to Coney Island and shoot the chutes...

Eugene O'Neill, *The Iceman Cometh* (1939)

Similar Sounding Words, Different Meanings The Schoolmaster in Alan Bennett's *Forty Years On* (1968) claims that he has been 'cosseted and corseted from a very early age'. Benny in Kevin Elyot's *My Night With Reg* (1994), meanwhile, describes a noisy ex-lover as enjoying 'the sound of his own vice'; a witty take on the more usual 'voice'. And in Athol Fugard's *Hello and Goodbye* (1965) Johnnie, in the midst of a nervous breakdown, advises himself to 'Arrive in peace not in pieces'.

2) The witty juxtaposition of words or phrases for comic or ironic effect.

The Lord Chief Justice in Shakespeare's *Henry IV Part Two* (c.1598) says to the fat, poor and heavy-drinking knight Sir John Falstaff 'Your means are slender, but your waste is great'; a wonderful play on 'waste' and 'waist'. Geoffrey in Michael Frayn's *Alphabetical Order* (1975) states 'silence reigned and we all got wet'; a delightful play on 'reigned' and 'rained', which creates a rather extraordinary image. And here Alan Bennett mischievously tweaks an established metaphorical phrase:

RUSSELL: I had no contact with my own body until the spring of 1887, when I suddenly found my feet.

Alan Bennett, *Forty Years On* (1968)

Playing with Proverbs It is common to play with established proverbial phrases, as when the convict Duckling in Timberlake Wertenbaker's *Our Country's Good* (1988) refuses to appear in a performance of *The Recruiting Officer* with a hangman, claiming 'The words would stick in my throat'; or when Lady Broughton in James Graham's *This House* (2012) describes the great clock of Big Ben stopping as 'causing a bit of a ding-dong'. And here one character creates a mischievous play on words from what another character has said, a classic piece of REPARTEE (see below):

FOWLER: I've half a mind to ask Barclay for permission to beat you.
JUDD: Well – you've half a mind. We can all agree on that.

Julian Mitchell, Another Country (1982)

ADIANOETA (*ad*-ee-an-*ee*-tuh) from the Greek meaning 'incomprehensible'.
When something is said that seems to mean one thing, but on closer inspection has a hidden, usually negative, meaning; it is consciously ambiguous.

Corvino in Ben Jonson's *Volpone* (1605-6) pronounces the conniving Mosca 'honest'; Mosca replies 'You do lie, sir'. Corvino reads this as false modesty, but we – the audience – know it to be true. Lady Brocklehurst in J.M. Barrie's *The Admirable Crichton* (1902) comments on Mr Woolley's memoirs (of his time shipwrecked on a deserted island), which she suspects are not a truthful representation, saying 'It is as engrossing, Mr Woolley, as if it were a work of fiction'; an ambiguity enjoyed by the audience who know her suspicions are well-founded. And here, in the final lines of another play, two murderous old ladies offer their guest a glass of poisoned homemade alcohol:

WITHERSPOON: You don't see much elderberry wine nowadays –
I thought I'd had my last glass of it.
ABBY: Oh, no –
MARTHA: *(handing him glass of wine)*. No, here it is.

Joseph Kesselring, Arsenic and Old Lace (1941)

ZEUGMA (*zyoog*-muh) from the Greek meaning a 'bond' or 'yoke'.
This is an inventive form of ELLIPSIS, where one word or phrase is 'yoked' to two or more other words or phrases in a variety of ways.

PROZEUGMA (proh-*zyoog*-muh) from the Greek meaning 'yoked in front'.
When the 'yoking' word or phrase *precedes* those 'yoked'.

Here the verbal phrase 'She wore' governs the two following phrases:

LORD GORING: She wore far too much rouge last night, and not quite enough clothes.

Oscar Wilde, An Ideal Husband (1895)

MESOZEUGMA (mess-oh-*zyoog*-muh) from the Greek meaning 'yoked in the middle'.
When the 'yoking' word or phrase is *in between* those 'yoked'.

Here, a wife imagines her husband's reaction to finding her with a lover – the 'yoking' phrase is 'would go to pot':

> CHARLOTTE: His sentence structure would go to pot, closely followed by his sphincter.
>
> Tom Stoppard, *The Real Thing* (1982)

HYPOZEUGMA (hy-poh-*zyoog*-muh) from the Greek meaning 'yoked under'. This appears to have two meanings, the first of which is perhaps the simplest and therefore most common form of ZEUGMA.

1) When the 'yoking' word or phrase *follows* those 'yoked'.

> FAY: Formaldehyde and three morticians have increased my wife's allure.
>
> Joe Orton, *Loot* (1966)

2) When two or more subjects are governed by one verb, usually placed at the end.

> LOU: No – your eleven-room apartment, your automobile, your money are not worth this.
>
> Arthur Miller, *After The Fall* (1964)

DIAZEUGMA (dy-uh-*zyoog*-muh) from the Greek meaning 'yoked apart'. When a single subject has two or more verbs.

In this rather delightful example, Hellena is talking of her sister's proposed husband; 'the giant' governs all six subsequent clauses:

> HELLENA: The giant stretches itself, sighs a belch or two, stales in your pot, farts loud as a musket, throws himself into bed and expects you in his foul sheets.
>
> Aphra Behn, *The Rover* (1677)

HYPERZEUGMA (hy-pur-*zyoog*-muh) from the Greek meaning 'yoked across'. When each clause in a sentence has its own verb, usually – though not necessarily – governed by the same subject (almost identical to DIAZEUGMA above; see also HYPOZEUXIS).

Here, Mrs Frail rebuffs the advances of the uncouth Benjamin Legend, who was raised at sea:

> MRS FRAIL: Oh, see me no more, for thou wert born amongst rocks, suckled by whales, cradled in a tempest, and whistled to by winds.
>
> William Congreve, *Love for Love* (1695)

SYLLEPSIS (sil-*lep*-sis) from the Greek meaning 'taking together'.
A form of ZEUGMA in which a word is understood differently with each of two or more others; often understood with one word literally and the other metaphorically.

Celia in Shakespeare's *As You Like It* (c.1600) informs Rosalind that Orlando (with whom Rosalind fell in love when he won a wrestling match) has arrived in the forest. She says to her friend that Orlando 'tripped up the wrestler's heels and your heart both in an instant'; he *literally* tripped up the wrestler and *metaphorically* tripped up Rosalind's heart. In *The Pillowman* (2003) Martin McDonagh uses this device when Michal, who has been beaten up by his brother, says 'You've hurt my feelings. And my head'. And here's a mischievous one:

> CRABTREE: Did you ever hear how Miss Piper came to lose her lover
> and her character last summer at Tunbridge?
>
> Richard Brinsley Sheridan, *The School for Scandal* (1777)

SPARRING

The devices in this section tend to be the preserve of High Comedy across the ages, although elements of them appear in many other plays.

REPARTEE from the French meaning 'set off again'.
An exchange of witty retorts, each one 'capping' or 'besting' the last – derived from a fencing term meaning a smart return blow.

The famous sparring couples of the High Comic tradition – such as Shakespeare's Benedick and Beatrice (*Much Ado About Nothing*, c.1598), Congreve's Mirabel and Millamant (*The Way of the World*, 1700), Wilde's Lord Illingworth and Mrs Allonby (*A Woman of No Importance*, 1893) and Coward's Amanda and Elyot (*Private Lives*, 1930) – are all adepts at REPARTEE.

Here is a rather vicious example, with Mr and Mrs Sullen constantly 'capping' each other:

> SULLEN: You're impertinent.
> MRS SULLEN: I was ever so, since I became one flesh with you.
> SULLEN: One flesh! Rather two carcasses joined unnaturally together.
> MRS SULLEN: Or rather a living soul coupled to a dead body.
> DORINDA: So, this is fine encouragement for me!
> SULLEN: Yes, my wife shows you what you must do.
> MRS SULLEN: And my husband shows you what you must suffer.
> SULLEN: 'Sdeath, why can't you be silent?

> MRS SULLEN: 'Sdeath, why can't you talk?
> SULLEN: Do you talk to any purpose?
> MRS SULLEN: Do you think to any purpose?
>
> George Farquhar, *The Beaux' Stratagem* (1707)

BADINAGE (*bad*-in-*arj*) from the French meaning 'jokery'.
Also known as **PERSIFLAGE** (*pur*-sif-*larj*) from the French meaning 'banter'.
A form of REPARTEE that includes playful, humorous banter or ridicule. It is generally accepted to be frivolous, not serious.

This is very common between masters and servants in the Renaissance, and between male friends in Restoration Comedies and in the later High Comedies, as here:

> ALGERNON: My dear fellow, the way you flirt with Gwendolen is perfectly disgraceful. It is almost as bad as the way Gwendolen flirts with you.
> JACK: I am in love with Gwendolen. I have come up to town expressly to propose to her.
> ALGERNON: I thought you had come up for pleasure? I call that business.
> JACK: How utterly unromantic you are!
> ALGERNON: I really don't see anything romantic in proposing. It is very romantic to be in love. But there is nothing romantic about a definite proposal. Why, one may be accepted. One usually is, I believe. Then the excitement is all over. The very essence of romance is uncertainty. If ever I get married, I'll certainly try to forget the fact.
> JACK: I have no doubt about that, dear Algy. The Divorce Court was specially invented for people whose memories are so curiously constituted.
>
> Oscar Wilde, *The Importance of Being Earnest* (1895)

RAILLERY (*ray*-luh-ree) from the French meaning 'jest'.
This is generally accepted to be synonymous with BADINAGE above, but we have found it to have a harder edge. It is indeed playful banter, but is often laced with anger or bitterness, and therefore has an ambiguous feel.

Here's a typically witty spat between a playwright and actress couple about a production of *'Tis Pity She's a Whore* she might perform in:

HENRY: Anyway, I thought you were committing incest in Glasgow.
ANNIE: I haven't said I'll do it.
HENRY: I think you should. It's classy stuff, Webster. I love all that Jacobean sex and violence.
ANNIE: It's Ford, not Webster. It's Elizabethan, not Jacobean. *And* it's Glasgow.
HENRY: Don't you work north of Cambridge Circus, then?
ANNIE: I was thinking you might miss me – pardon my mistake.
HENRY: I was thinking you might like me to come with you – pardon mine.

> Tom Stoppard, *The Real Thing* (1982)

ASTEISMUS (ass-tay-*iz*-mus) from the Greek meaning 'of the city' or 'urbane', and therefore 'witty'.
A witty response to a person, usually by deliberately misunderstanding their meaning. It can be foolish or – as in this example – snide:

ROWLEY: What can have happened to trouble you since yesterday?
SIR PETER TEAZLE: A good question to a married man!
ROWLEY: Nay, I'm sure, Sir Peter, your lady can't be the cause of your uneasiness.
SIR PETER TEAZLE: Why, has anybody told you she was dead?

> Richard Brinsley Sheridan, *The School for Scandal* (1777)

CACEMPHATON (kak-*em*-fuh-ton) from the Greek meaning 'seeming bad'.
1) A rude joke or double entendre (see also SEXUAL ALLUSION in Chapter 3).

Here's a camp bit of rudery between gay friends:

DANIEL: And you should see him drive his bus! I had the misfortune to be on it once. Never again! I was sitting on the top, screaming.
JOHN: Wouldn't be the first time.

> Kevin Elyot, *My Night with Reg* (1994)

2) It can also mean ugly, jarring sounds in words, especially through over-repetition or excessive alliteration – see also CACOPHONY and PARIMION.

Tony Lumpkin in Oliver Goldsmith's *She Stoops to Conquer* (1771) dismisses his step-sister Miss Hardcastle as a 'tall, trapseing, trolloping, talkative maypole'; his pejorative terms gaining syllables as the sentence progresses. On a Monday morning – in Sarah Daniels' play *Neaptide* (1986) – Physics teacher Cyril berates the English teacher for 'cracking on like a crazed cockatoo, Cunningham'; the extreme ALLITERATION might encourage an actor to invest in the character's derision more. And here the pedant Holofernes improvises a ridiculous rhyme by way of showing off his cleverness:

> HOLOFERNES: The preyful Princess pierced and pricked a pretty pleasing pricket.
>
> William Shakespeare, *Love's Labour's Lost* (c.1595)

SAYINGS

The application of apt SAYINGS plays a huge part in people's communication with each other. These SAYINGS often come from such authoritative sources as the Bible or Aesop, but just as many have been established from practical experience; what we might call folklore or old wives' tales.

Playwrights have also provided us with many sayings, led of course by Shakespeare, such as 'neither a borrower or a lender be' from *Hamlet* (c.1601). Felicity in Tom Stoppard's *The Real Inspector Hound* (1968) observes 'Hell hath no fury like a woman scorned, Simon.' Although this saying is proverbial, it is actually paraphrased from William Congreve's lesser-known play *The Mourning Bride* (1697) – the original is 'Heav'n has no rage like love to hatred turned, / Nor Hell a fury like a woman scorned'. A lovely antithetical couplet.

The various types of SAYING in this section have huge areas of cross-over; the Venn diagram would look like a dahlia! Through our research we have tried to make fine distinctions between them to help differentiate them.

PROVERB from the Latin meaning literally 'before the word' and so an 'old saying'. A concise and memorable statement of a well-established truth. There is a sense that PROVERBS – useful as a source of practical wisdom – have been handed down from generation to generation, attaining an almost folkloric status. It is, after all, a book in the Bible.

PROVERBS often involve a metaphorical image – think of 'people in glass houses shouldn't throw stones', 'a bird in the hand is worth two in the bush' or 'the straw that broke the camel's back' – and it is quite common for lovers to wish themselves a proverbial PARADIGM for their successes or failures.

In Shakespeare's *Troilus and Cressida* (1602) the go-between, Pandarus, says 'Let all constant men be Troiluses, all false women Cressids, and all brokers-between Pandars!' And here's another:

> JULIA: If ever, without such cause from you as I will not suppose possible, you find my affections veering but a point, may I become a

proverbial scoff for levity and base ingratitude.
                    Richard Brinsley Sheridan, *The Rivals* (1775)

Due to the fact that PROVERBS are so commonly used in everyday speech, they have naturally made it into the realm of drama throughout the ages. For instance, Laurence in Mike Leigh's *Abigail's Party* (1977) says 'I'm at your service, Mrs Cushing: he who pays the piper calls the tune!' Or when Mrs Bryant in Arnold Wesker's *Roots* (1959) compares her husband to her daughter, claiming 'The apple don't fall far from the tree – that it don't'.

Many proverbial sayings are so well-known they can be only partially quoted and the point is still made; think of 'too many cooks... [spoil the broth]', 'when in Rome... [do as the Romans do]', 'if it ain't broke... [don't fix it]' and so on. Such an ELLIPSIS creates a pleasing colloquialism.

Dr James in Lucy Prebble's *The Effect* (2012) describes disagreeing with the idea that depression is a curable disease of the brain as 'bolting the door after the horse has, you know'; conveying a slight embarrassment at stating the obvious. Alternatively, the end of the PROVERB can be replaced with the word 'proverbial', as when George in Charlotte Jones' *Humble Boy* (2001) says 'Water under the proverbial', or this example:

MICHAEL: I wasn't very complimentary, but a mention is better than
a kick up the proverbial.
                    Kwame Kwei-Armah, *Statement Of Regret* (2007)

Once established, PROVERBS lay themselves open to reinterpretation, subversion or ridicule, as when Kit in Shelagh Delaney's *The Lion in Love* (1960) takes her shoes off with a grunt, complaining that 'Hell hath no fury like a woman's corns'; a lovely subversion of the Congreve quote at the top of this section, who is at it himself in his play *Love for Love* (1695), in which Valentine warns 'He that follows his nose always will be very often led into a stink'. Or this double example, in which Hobson, disapproving of his daughter Maggie's marriage, is offered a piece of wedding cake:

HOBSON: The milk's spilt and I'll not cry.
MAGGIE: *(holding plate)* Then there's your cake, and you can eat it.
                    Harold Brighouse, *Hobson's Choice* (1915)

Alternatively they can be *mis*quoted to witty or ironic ends, such as when James in Peter Nichols' *Passion Play* (2000 edition) says 'There's no place like bed'; a step further than the traditional 'There's no place like home'. In the same playwright's *A Day In The Death Of Joe Egg* (1967) Bri grimly pronounces 'Every cloud has a jet-black lining' instead of the familiar 'silver lining'. And Kali in Bryony Lavery's *Stockholm* (2007) comments on her boyfriend's supposed unfaithfulness with 'A leopard does not change his... acne'.

MAXIM from the Latin meaning 'greatest', as in the greatest idea or proposition.
A form of PROVERB which states concisely what does or should happen in life; a fundamental principle of conduct, such as 'to err is human: to forgive divine', 'when the cat's away, the mice will play' or 'in all things moderation'. It's a form echoed in advertising slogans such as Häagen-Dazs' 'Pleasure is the path to joy' – isn't it just!

Polonius' oft-quoted advice to his parting son, Laertes, in *Hamlet* (c.1601) includes 'to thine own self be true'; admirably concise. Captain Plume in Farquhar's *The Recruiting Officer* (1706) declares 'those who know the least obey the best'; a perfect EPIGRAM. And here is a rather fulsome example:

> GRACE: The man that misses sunrise loses the sweetest part of his existence.
>
> Dion Boucicault, *London Assurance* (1841)

SENTENTIA (sen-*ten*-tee-uh) from the Latin meaning 'opinion' or 'judgement'.
To apply a general truth to a situation by quoting a MAXIM (see above), as in this example:

> JEREMY: You think the country's gone to the dogs and we're going with it, but you're wrong. You can't turn a ship on a sixpence, you know?
>
> Laura Wade, *Posh* (2012)

This is often accompanied with the phrase 'as they say' or its equivalent. Here Arthur apologizes for the small dowry he offers his daughter's prospective husband:

> ARTHUR: Not as generous as I would have liked, I'm afraid. However – as my wife would say – beggars can't be choosers.
>
> Terence Rattigan, *The Winslow Boy* (1946)

AXIOM from the Greek meaning 'of worth'.
A form of MAXIM that states a widely accepted principle for life or a self-evident truth, such as 'a stitch in time saves nine', 'let sleeping dogs lie' or 'riches are a snare'.

Here is one we would do well to observe in this era of text and email and social networking:

> EDDIE: Just remember, kid, you can quicker get back a million dollars that was stole than a word that you gave away.
>
> Arthur Miller, *A View from the Bridge* (1956)

APHORISM (*af*-uh-riz-um) from the Greek meaning 'definition' or 'distinction'.
A pithy form of MAXIM embodying an original thought or an astute observation. A true APHORISM should be conjured in the moment, and its economy will often be in the form of an EPIGRAM.

Estragon in Samuel Beckett's *Waiting for Godot* (1955) pronounces with the accompanying stage direction *'aphoristic for once'*: 'We all are born mad. Some remain so.' Professor Higgins in George Bernard Shaw's *Pygmalion* (1912) offers 'What is life but a series of inspired follies?' And here is an old man who loves life:

> CLIFTON: It is only possible to live as long as life intoxicates us.
> Kwame Kwei-Armah, *Elmina's Kitchen* (2003)

DICTUM from the Latin meaning 'saying'.
A kind of MAXIM that has a formality to it.

The eponymous soldier of John Arden's *Serjeant Musgrave's Dance* (1959) proclaims that 'A soldier's duty is a soldier's life'; the ANAPHORA of each phrase leads us deftly to the key words 'duty' and 'life'. Grandma, the fount of all knowledge in Neil Simon's *Lost In Yonkers* (1990), warns her daughter Bella with 'Look for trouble, you'll find trouble'; this time the ANTISTROPHE of the two phrases accentuates the ANTITHESIS of the verbs. And here HOMOIOTELEUTON aids the formality and memorability (the spelling is O'Casey's):

> JOXER: Ah, him that goes a borrowin' goes a sorrowin'!
> Sean O'Casey, *Juno and the Paycock* (1924)

ADAGE (*ad*-idge) from the Latin meaning 'nearly a saying', and so an 'assertion'.
A short, memorable saying which often displays a philosophical or ethical element.

Mrs Erlynne in Oscar Wilde's *Lady Windermere's Fan* (1892) rebuffs her host, who has rebuked her for gate-crashing a party, with 'manners before morals, Lord Windermere'; the saying made all the more pithy by its ALLITERATION. The mysterious Unidentified Guest in T.S. Eliot's *The Cocktail Party* (1949) pronounces gnomically 'To try to forgive is to try to conceal'. And here's a well known one from Shakespeare:

> JOHN OF GAUNT: Teach thy necessity to reason thus:
> There is no virtue like necessity.
> William Shakespeare, *Richard II* (1595)

TRUISM (*troo*-iz-um) thought to be from the Old English 'treowe', meaning 'truce'.
An obviously true and often hackneyed statement.

Dr Rance in Joe Orton's *What the Butler Saw* (1967) claims 'Just when one least expects it, the unexpected always happens'. And here is a classic, uttered as the characters have to leave their church garden which has been sold to property developers:

> JENNY: But all good things must come to an end and we must leave our lovely Garden of Eden, I'm afraid.
> > Tanika Gupta, *Sanctuary* (2002)

CLICHÉ from the French meaning 'stereotype'.
One step on from a TRUISM, this is when a saying has become overused, such as 'the cat's out of the bag', 'keep it under your hat' or any number of ghastly corporate phrases like 'run it up the flagpole and see who salutes'!

Here is another classic in action:

> CHARLES: Don't you think, Madame Arcati, that perhaps we've had enough séances? After all they haven't achieved much, have they?
> MADAME ARCATI: Rome wasn't built in a day, you know.
> > Noël Coward, *Blithe Spirit* (1941)

IRONY

IRONY from the Greek meaning 'evasion' or 'mockery'.
A deliberate ambivalence of expression, where the intended meaning is different from, and even opposite to, the literal sense – a very common device, usually used for humour or emphasis.

It can be the simple irony of Winnie's 'What is that unforgettable line?' in Samuel Beckett's *Happy Days* (1961); or a more conscious joke by an author:

> PHILIP: My trouble is, I'm a man of no convictions. *(A longish pause)* At least, I think I am.
> > Christopher Hampton, *The Philanthropist* (1970)

Or the glorious bluntness of:

> TRUSCOTT: If I ever hear you accuse the police of using violence on a prisoner in custody again, I'll take you down to the station and beat the eyes out of your head.
> > Joe Orton, *Loot* (1966)

Or the sly wit of:

> BRANDT: ...under capitalism man is oppressed by man – under socialism
> it's the other way round...
>
> Michael Frayn, *Democracy* (2003)

DRAMATIC IRONY

A form of IRONY in which the audience know things that the characters do not. It can take various forms:

Situation When a character misreads a moment, but the audience is fully aware of what is happening, as in the following example, where Jane finds the suicidal Eva trying to gas herself in the oven. Jane is blithely unaware of the dark PUNS she makes, but for the audience the black humour is highly relishable:

> JANE: Don't you worry about that oven now. That oven can wait. You
> clean it later. No point in damaging your health for an oven, is there?
> Mind you, I know just what you feel like, though. You suddenly get
> an urge, don't you? You say, I must clean that oven if it kills me.
>
> Alan Ayckbourn, *Absurd Person Singular* (1972)

Foreshadowing In J.B. Priestley's *Time and the Conways* (1937) Carol, the youngest daughter, is determined to make the most of her life, saying 'Never mind about money and positions and husbands with titles and rubbish – I'm *going to live*'. However, we learn in Act II (set in 1937) that she dies tragically young in 1920, only a year after the action of Act I. The audience is armed with this knowledge and that of all the characters' futures when they return to 1919 in Act III. Dramatic ironies abound, and very movingly – typical of Priestley's time plays.

Here is a more immediate example in which the IRONY is in the fact that the audience know that Vindice is planning to kill Lussurioso.

> LUSSURIOSO: 'Tis a good name that.
> VINDICE: Ay, a revenger.
> LUSSURIOSO: It does betoken courage; thou shouldst be valiant
>   And kill thine enemies.
> VINDICE: That's my hope, my lord.
>
> Thomas Middleton, *The Revenger's Tragedy* (1607)

UNDERSTATEMENT

A form of IRONY in which something is represented as less than it is, in order to draw attention to it (see also LITOTES below).

Loomis in Simon Gray's *Quartermaine's Terms* (1981) describes his language school's threatened closure as 'a slight crisis'; typical English UNDERSTATEMENT. In Joseph Kesselring's *Arsenic and Old Lace* (1941) Mortimer rebukes his aunts, declaring that their actions have 'developed into a very bad habit', when what they have been doing is murdering lonely old men! And here George undersells the vicious, embittered interchanges between him and his wife, Martha, to their hapless guests:

> GEORGE: It gets pretty bouncy around here sometimes.
> Edward Albee, *Who's Afraid of Virginia Woolf?* (1962)

OVERSTATEMENT

A form of IRONY in which something is represented as more than it is, to draw attention to it (see also HYPERBOLE).

Mama in Lorraine Hansberry's *A Raisin in the Sun* (1959) berates her children for not packing up the house for a move, claiming they have 'got all the energy of the dead'. Celia in Christopher Hampton's *The Philanthropist* (1970) humiliates her fiancé, Philip (who has attempted unwillingly to be unfaithful to her, and failed), accusing him of 'a triumph of emotional incompetence'; a glorious PARADOX (see below). Or there's the simple HYPERBOLE of Meenah in Ayub Khan-Din's *East Is East* (1996) who, when asked what the matter with her younger brother Sajit is, says 'Nothing decapitation couldn't fix'. And in this example the parents observe their sleeping young son, who is undergoing the ordeal of a court case:

> GRACE: I expect he's over-excited.
> *(ARTHUR and GRACE both look at the tranquilly oblivious form.)*
> ARTHUR: A picture of over-excitement.
> Terence Rattigan, *The Winslow Boy* (1946)

AMPHIBOLOGY (*am*-fib-*ol*-uh-jee) from the Greek meaning 'ambiguity'.

An ambiguous structure in a sentence, that means that it can be interpreted in more than one way. Sometimes playwrights use this grammatical ambiguity for ironic effect.

In this example, Young Mortimer has ordered the death of King Edward by way of a note written in Latin. He uses the ambiguous possibilities of translation as his defence:

> MORTIMER: This letter, written by a friend of ours,
> Contains his death, yet bids them save his life:
> *(Reads) Edwardum occidere nolite timere bonum est,*
> *Fear not to kill the king, 'tis good he die.*
> But read it thus, and that's another sense:

Edwardum occidere nolite timere bonum est,
Kill not the king, 'tis good to fear the worst.
Unpointed as it is, thus shall it go.
> Christopher Marlowe, *Edward II* (c.1592)

SARCASM from the Greek meaning literally the 'tearing of flesh', and so 'bitter speech'. Harsh or witty derision, often overtly ironic. SARCASM is, of course, very commonly used in everyday life. It is often referred to as 'the lowest form of wit, but the highest form of intelligence', a line attributed to Oscar Wilde.

In this example, the SARCASM passes between two characters – both are MPs: Harrison is a bullish, northern Labour member and Atkins a privately educated Conservative:

> HARRISON: Do your private school kids break up the same time as our state school kids or is that different too?
> ATKINS: Well done, Walter, three minutes in and you've already played the class card. I think that's a record. I take it the swearing is due to start shortly as well?
> HARRISON: Bollocks, bugger, piss.
> ATKINS: How lovely, you know walking into here is like walking into a Noël Coward play, isn't it, Jack?
> > James Graham, *This House* (2012)

DEFLATION

ANTICLIMAX from the Greek meaning 'down the ladder'.
An insignificant or disappointing conclusion, especially when a CLIMAX was expected. A CLIMAX is achieved through any number of structural devices (see Chapters 6, 7 and 8), so to break such a *crescendo* will create an ANTICLIMAX. It does not seem a natural ally to drama, but an intentional ANTICLIMAX can elicit humour or even sympathy (see BATHOS below).

Here Miss Hardcastle, whose expectations are so high, shows her disappointment in having met her nervous beau, Marlowe. Goldsmith creates for her a rhythmic list of positive traits, before puncturing the mood with his sudden departure:

> MISS HARDCASTLE: He treated me with diffidence and respect; censured the manners of the age; admired the prudence of girls that never laughed; tired me with apologies for being tiresome; then left the room with a bow, and 'Madam, I would not for the world detain you'.
> > Oliver Goldsmith, *She Stoops to Conquer* (1771)

BATHOS from the Greek meaning 'depth'.
A form of ANTICLIMAX in which there is a sudden change in style from the sublime to the ridiculous. It is usually thought of as unintentional, though invariably it is used deliberately by the playwright, to produce a humorous effect.

Accidental Mrs Rafi, rehearsing her version of the Orpheus myth, indulges in a wonderfully Gothic description of Orpheus' arrival at the River Styx, and concludes with:

> MRS RAFI: Wearily I sit down on a rock and survey the dismal scene.
> I take out my lute and sing 'There's no place like home'.
> Edward Bond, *The Sea* (1973)

Deliberate A character is usually unaware of the bathetic effect, as in the example above, though not always. In the following example, it is fun to build up the hefty description of the Mediterranean and then plunge into the silliness beyond:

> DYSART: All my wife has ever taken from the Mediterranean – from that
> whole vast intuitive culture – are four bottles of Chianti to make into
> lamps, and two china condiment donkeys labelled Sally and Peppy.
> Peter Shaffer, *Equus* (1973)

Tom Stoppard is a huge fan of this device: Henry in *The Real Thing* (1982) dismisses opera as 'a sort of foreign musical with no dancing which people were donating kidneys to get tickets for'; so much for the elitist pretensions of high art! Thomasina in *Arcadia* (1993), meanwhile, deflates the political effects of Cleopatra's love life, saying 'away goes the empire like a christening mug into a pawn shop'. And in *The Real Inspector Hound* (1968), Simon comments on the play-within-the-play in which he has been replaced by one of the critics:

> SIMON: To say that it is without pace, point, focus, interest, drama,
> wit or originality is to say simply that it does not happen to be my
> cup of tea.

BELITTLEMENT

MEIOSIS (my-*oh*-sis) from the Greek meaning 'diminishing'.
To belittle something as less than it is; a form of SARCASM (see above). A prime example is referring to America as being 'across the pond' – the pond being the Atlantic Ocean.

Examples of this include the schoolboy Rudge's definition of history in Alan Bennett's *The History Boys* (2004) as 'just one fucking thing after another'. Or Bruce's description of rugby in Joe Penhall's *Blue/Orange* (2000) as a 'Bunch of hairy twats running around biting each other's ears off'.

Alternatively, it can be to describe a person as less than they are, as in this example:

EMMA: What am I arguing with you for? You don't know enough medicine to treat a mouse. You don't know enough science to study boiled water.

Larry Kramer, *The Normal Heart* (1985)

TAPINOSIS (tap-in-*oh*-sis) from the Greek meaning 'humiliation'.
To belittle someone by lessening their status, as when a shop assistant calls a man 'mate' instead of 'sir', or a woman 'love' instead of 'madam'.

Nurse Guinness in Shaw's *Heartbreak House* (1919) calls everyone 'ducky', reducing them to the status of the children she is used to dealing with. Similarly, Hickey in Eugene O'Neill's *The Iceman Cometh* (1939) addresses the drunks and whores of Harry Hope's saloon as 'boys and girls' in an attempt to maintain his status as their father figure. In this example Jerome addresses the ridiculous social worker, Mervyn Bickerdyke:

JEROME: If we're having to rely on decisions from people like you, matey, what's it matter anyway?

Alan Ayckbourn, *Henceforward* (1987)

ANTIPHRASIS (an-*ti*-fruh-sis) from the Greek meaning 'expressing by the opposite'.
The ironic use of a word or short phrase, as when lawyers call their legal opposition 'my learnèd friend' or when politicians call their opponents 'honourable members', when they would far rather be calling them something else!

This device is often used in nicknames, as when someone a bit dim is known as 'Sparky', or someone very fat or very tall is known as 'Tiny'. Pets' names reach for this device too; in Tom Stoppard's *Arcadia* (1993) the tortoise is gloriously called Lightning. Here Falstaff addresses the young Boy, his servant:

FALSTAFF: Sirrah, you giant, what says the doctor to my water?

William Shakespeare, *Henry IV, Part Two* (c.1598)

PARADOX

PARADOX from the Greek meaning 'unexpected'.
A seemingly true statement which creates a contradiction or defies logic, such as the phrase 'an accident waiting to happen' – by its very nature an accident cannot wait to happen; it is of the moment.

Quentin in Arthur Miller's *After The Fall* (1964), for instance, compliments Maggie with the overwhelming 'You're so beautiful it's hard to look at you'. Hamm in Samuel Beckett's *Endgame* (1957), meanwhile, asks Clov 'What time is it?' to which comes the typically Beckettian reply 'The same as usual'. It is sometimes the play between a literal statement and a metaphorical one, as in Jamie's description of his mother's addiction to morphine in Eugene O'Neill's *Long Day's Journey Into Night* (c.1940) as 'She'll be here but she won't be here'.

Shakespeare was a fine purveyor of PARADOX, and many of his phrases have moved into common parlance. Think of the prince's 'I must be cruel only to be kind' or Polonius saying 'By indirections find directions out' in *Hamlet* (c.1601). Or Petruchio's 'This is a way to kill a wife with kindness' in *The Taming of the Shrew* (c.1591). Or this conniving observation:

> IAGO: When devils do the blackest sins put on,
>   They do suggest at first with heavenly shows.
>   William Shakespeare, *Othello* (c.1604)

Oscar Wilde was (if you'll excuse the PUN) wild about this. Algernon cynically declares 'Divorces are made in heaven' in *The Importance of Being Earnest* (1895), and there is Lord Darlington's wonderful 'I can resist everything except temptation' in *Lady Windermere's Fan* (1892). Here's another from the same play:

> MR DUMBY: In this world there are only two tragedies. One is not getting what one wants, and the other is getting it.

OXYMORON (ox-ee-*mor*-ron) from the Greek meaning literally 'sharp-dull', and therefore 'keenly stupid'.
A succinctly expressed PARADOX.

Sir Cautious Fulbank in Aphra Behn's *The Lucky Chance* (1686) is kept awake at night by 'a kind of a silent noise'; on examination this makes no sense, but we know exactly what he means. The psychiatrist Dysart in Peter Shaffer's *Equus* (1973) refers to his clientele as 'The usual unusual'. And here's a glorious indictment of the world of high finance:

> SKILLING: Every dip, every crash, every bubble that's burst, a testament to our brilliant stupidity.
>   Lucy Prebble, *Enron* (2009)

Once again Shakespeare excels: Berowne in *Love's Labour's Lost* (c.1595) refers to Cupid as a 'giant-dwarf'. Theseus in *A Midsummer Night's Dream* (1595) pronounces the Mechanicals' proposed play – advertised as 'merry and tragical' and 'tedious and brief' – as 'wondrous hot ice'. And here's a glorious run of OXYMORONS from Juliet, in response to the news that Romeo has murdered her cousin, Tybalt. These highlight how emotionally torn she is:

> JULIET: Beautiful tyrant! Fiend angelical!
> Dove-feathered raven! Wolvish-ravening lamb!
> Despisèd substance of divinest show!
> Just opposite to what thou justly seem'st:
> A damnèd saint, an honourable villain!
>
> William Shakespeare, *Romeo and Juliet* (1595)

PARAPROSDOKIAN (*pa*-ruh-pross-*dok*-ee-un) from the Greek meaning 'against expectation'.

An unexpected ending to a sentence or idea, usually put in the mouth of clever and witty characters.

Oscar Wilde relished using this device; it plays into the hands of his admirable mischief and sense of social satire.

> LORD ILLINGWORTH: Women represent the triumph of matter over mind – just as men represent the triumph of mind over morals.
>
> Oscar Wilde, *A Woman of No Importance* (1893)

We think we are heading for the well-established phrase 'mind over matter', but instead we land with a bump in the land of morals.

Here are some more Wildean surprises: Cecil Graham in *Lady Windermere's Fan* (1892) warns his friend Tuppy not to be 'led astray into the paths of virtue'; we expect the well-established ANTITHESIS 'vice'. Lady Bracknell in *The Importance of Being Earnest* (1895) remarks upon the appearance of her friend, Lady Harbury, following her husband's death, with 'I never saw a woman so altered; she looks quite twenty years younger'; not 'older' as we expect.

PARAPROSDOKIAN most often plays with established phrases, such as when Archie Rice in John Osborne's *The Entertainer* (1957) subverts the usual 'I can't hear myself think' with 'I wish you'd stop yelling, I can't hear myself shout'. Mr M in Athol Fugard's *My Children! My Africa!* (1989) dreams of 'a comfortable bed for a good night's insomnia'; we, of course, expect him to say a good night's *sleep*. And Sir in Ronald Harwood's *The Dresser* (1980) says of a rival actor-knight 'I saw his Lear. I was pleasantly disappointed'; not the expected *surprised*.

Well-worn PROVERBS are an equally rich vein: Steve in Steven Berkoff's *Decadence* (1981) cynically subverts the PROVERB 'absence makes the heart grow fonder' with 'absence makes the heart grow colder'. And in this example the playwright plays mischievously with the famous TRICOLON 'See no evil, speak no evil, hear no evil':

> BRIAN: I see no evil, hear no evil, speak utter filth, me.
>
> Terry Johnson, *Dead Funny* (1994)

PROLEPSIS (proh-*lep*-sis) from the Greek meaning 'taking in advance' or 'anticipation'. When a future event is presumed to have happened – a flash forward.

The classic example is 'dead man walking'. This seems to be a popular concept in drama: Thomas More in Robert Bolt's *A Man for All Seasons* (1960) declares 'I am a dead man', as does Keller in Arthur Miller's *All My Sons* (1947) who says 'I'm a dead man, I'm an old dead man, nothing's mine'. And here Harry, returning home after eight years, is wisely commented on by his aunt:

> AGATHA: The man who returns will have to meet
>   The boy who left.
>
> T.S. Eliot, *The Family Reunion* (1939)

CLEVERNESS

PARODY from the Greek meaning literally 'against the ode', and so a 'burlesque poem'. A humorous and often exaggerated imitation of an author or literary style, usually witty and often a deliberate and extended misquotation (see also ALLUSION).

Literary Parody When one writer consciously puts the style of another in the mouth of a character, as in this superb example:

> HUGO: Once more unto the drink, dear friends, once more.
>   And give a roar for all our English drunk.
>   In peace there's nothing so becomes a man
>   As Milo's sweetness and sobriety;
>   But when the call to drink rings in his ears,
>   He'll imitate the action of the Tubester;
>   Stiffen the member, summon up the sword,
>   Disguise understanding with hard-drinking rage;
>   Then look like Guy with terrible aspect;
>   Burning eyes 'neath the wiggage of the head
>   Like the George Balfour; let the brow o'erwhelm it
>   As fearfully as does the Grecian frown

O'erhang and jutty poor Dimitri's face,
Steeped in the wild and wanton Ouzo.
Now be like Ryle and stretch the gullet wide,
Be Harry brave, and hold up every sabre
To its full height. On, on you noblest Riot,
Whose blood is fet from vodka 80 proof!
Drinkers that, like so many Old Etonians,
Have in these parts from morn to even drank,
Then drank some more for love of Leighton.
Dishonour not dead members; now attest
That Knights like our Lord Riot did beget you.
Be envy now to clubs of weaker blood,
And teach them how to drink. The game's afoot!
Pour out the spirits, and with glasses charged
Cry, 'God for Harry, Dimitri and Alistair, James, Toby,
Edward, Milo, Hugo, Guy and George!'
> Laura Wade, *Posh* (2012)

This is a witty PARODY of the great rallying speech of King Henry outside the walls of Harfleur in Shakespeare's *Henry V* (c.1599). Both the audience and the other characters in the play will respond to such a PARODY similarly. By way of comparison, seek out the original.

WELLERISM named after the character Sam Weller, Pickwick's witty servant in *The Pickwick Papers* by Charles Dickens.
A witticism often with the form 'as somebody said when...', like the famous 'as the actress said to the bishop' riposte. As a definition, this term seems to have expanded to include a well-known quotation followed by a facetious response – which seems common in drama.

TRIGG: You could say in a way it's almost flattering to be cast as Helen of Troy. Didn't she have the face that launched a thousand ships?
ALEX: That was when the war *began*. This is seven years later.
She probably couldn't launch a leaky life-boat.
> Nicholas Wright, *Cressida* (2000)

Equally, it can be the subversion of a well-known saying:

SANDRA: The leopard never changes its spots, and the slapper never changes her knickers!
> Jonathan Harvey, *Beautiful Thing* (1993)

EPIGRAM from the Greek meaning 'inscription'.

A brief, clever, usually memorable statement. An EPIGRAM is usually recognized as having a perfect form and balance, often involving ANTITHESIS, CHIASMUS, ZEUGMA or various forms of REPETITION (see also SAYINGS above).

Oscar Wilde is justly famed for his skill with EPIGRAMS. Consider these: Lord Darlington in *Lady Windermere's Fan* (1892) defines a cynic as 'A man who knows the price of everything and the value of nothing'; a lovely employment of ANTITHESIS. Mrs Allonby in *A Woman of No Importance* (1893) says that the Ideal Man 'should always say much more than he means, and always mean much more than he says'; this time using a pleasing CHIASMUS. And lastly, one of his great social observations:

> ALGERNON: All women become like their mothers. That is their tragedy.
> No man does. That is his.
>
> Oscar Wilde, *The Importance of Being Earnest* (1895)

Here are some other examples of EPIGRAMS through the ages. The aptly named rake Mr Dazzle in Dion Boucicault's *London Assurance* (1841) claims that 'Love ends in matrimony, wine in soda water'; a simple PARALLELISM, and a witty comparison. The politician Blackborough in Harley Granville Barker's *Waste* (1907) says that 'what one's friends lose one's enemies gain'; a clean double ANTITHESIS. And Lady Croom in Tom Stoppard's *Arcadia* (1993) wisely pronounces that 'A lesson in folly is worth two in wisdom'; so beautifully balanced that it has the ring of a well-established MAXIM about it.

NEOLOGISM (nee-*ol*-uh-*jiz*-um) from the Greek meaning 'new word'.

A newly coined word or phrase (see also ANTIMERIA below).

Standard Invention Made-up words such as 'thingummyjig' and 'thingummybob' have become accepted replacements for ones you have forgotten, along with 'gobbledegook' to describe something incomprehensible. Fabritio in Thomas Middleton's *Women Beware Women* (1621) uses a forerunner of these when he speaks of 'tricks and jiggambobs'.

Shakespeare famously coined an astounding number of words, many of which survive to this day – 'butchered', 'domineering' and 'assassination' among them. Here are a few that did not survive: 'exsufflicate' (puff up), 'chirurgeonly' (like a doctor), 'empiricutic' (experimental) or this term for a cannibal, here in reference to Falstaff:

> HOST: Go, knock and call. He'll speak like an anthropophaginian unto thee.
>
> William Shakespeare, *The Merry Wives of Windsor* (c.1598)

In more recent times, new words are often an **Extension of an Existing Word**, such as when Miss Prism in Oscar Wilde's *The Importance of Being Earnest* (1895) rather artlessly coins the word 'womanthrope' as an opposite to 'misanthrope'. And here the Private Gar inventively bad-mouths his ex, Kathy Doogan, to his Public self:

> PRIVATE: Just like her stinking rotten father and mother – a bugger and a buggeress – a buggeroo and a buggerette!!
> Brian Friel, *Philadelphia, Here I Come!* (1964)

Another way of creating a NEOLOGISM is by the **Combination of Words**. Carr in Tom Stoppard's *Travesties* (1993 edition) talks of the 'comraderaderie' in Red Square, wittily combining the words 'comrade' and 'camaraderie'. Kwaku in Kwame Kwei-Armah's *Statement Of Regret* (2007) uses 'politricks', combining 'politics' and 'tricks' in reference to black politics in the UK. These are WORDPLAY at its most cleverly economical.

ANTIMERIA (*an*-tim-*air*-ree-uh) from the Greek meaning 'one part for another'. Also spelled ANTHIMERIA.
A form of NEOLOGISM in which a word is used in a different part of speech than intended, most often appearing as:

Nouns Used as Verbs such as in this example:

> LEAR: The thunder would not peace at my bidding.
> William Shakespeare, *King Lear* (c.1606)

Shakespeare excelled at this in an age when language was burgeoning through invention. He particularly enjoyed using nouns in verbal forms and making them negative: Aufidius says in *Coriolanus* (1608) that the titular warrior 'hath widowed and unchilded many'. Hermione in *The Winter's Tale* (c.1610) playfully berates Polixenes with 'You would seek t' unsphere the stars with oaths'. Meanwhile, here's *Richard II* (1595) at the point of his deposition:

> RICHARD: 'God save King Henry', unkinged Richard says.

Examples of nouns used as verbs from elsewhere include Captain Hook in J.M. Barrie's *Peter Pan* (1904), who says of the lost boy, Nibs, 'He is only one, and I want to mischief all the seven'. Old Martin in Peter Shaffer's *The Royal Hunt of the Sun* (1964) says of the captured Inca king, Atahuallpa, 'He was allowed to audience his nobles'. And here's another good one:

> SIR PETER TEAZLE: I am sneered at by all my acquaintance, and paragraphed in the newspapers.
> Richard Brinsley Sheridan, *The School for Scandal* (1777)

Adjectives Used as Nouns This was a particular fad in the 1920s and '30s, such as when Mr Manningham in Patrick Hamilton's *Gaslight* (1938) says to his wife 'I wish you weren't such a perfect little silly'. It occurs elsewhere, though: Mrs Warren in George Bernard Shaw's *Mrs Warren's Profession* (1893) says 'I should go melancholy mad'; a beautifully poetic combining of two adjectives. And here Mrs Rafi condemns the hapless draper, Mr Hatch:

> MRS RAFI: Your catalogue is full of interesting items but none of them are in your shop. You offer only shoddy.
> Edward Bond, *The Sea* (1973)

Nouns Used as Adjectives This is less common, and much more poetic. Consider this example:

> STEPHEN: Why don't you write about pots and pans and stop smearing art with your lipstick mind?
> Timberlake Wertenbaker, *Three Birds Alighting on a Field* (1991)

Prepositions Used as Nouns As in the popular phrases 'ups and downs' or 'ins and outs'. In Shakespeare's *Cymbeline* (1610) Imogen describes her longing for her banished husband as 'beyond beyond'; a form that Sean O'Casey borrows in *The Plough and the Stars* (1926) when Fluther says that likening their home to penal servitude is 'goin' beyond th' beyonds in a tenement house'.

Prepositions Used as Verbs are rare, but two commonly used examples are the phrase 'he's upped and gone' and the term to 'out' someone.

LITOTES (ly-*toh*-teez) from the Greek meaning 'plainness' or 'simplicity'
1) To state a positive by negating a negative – the correct term for a double negative.

This device is very common and can be used in a variety of ways, usually emphatic, as in the lawyer Alfieri's pronouncement 'To promise not to kill is not dishonourable' in Arthur Miller's *A View from the Bridge* (1956). It can be begrudging too, as when Lady Bracknell – averse to the engagement between Jack and her only daughter, Gwendolen, in Wilde's *The Importance of Being Earnest* (1895) – allows that his answer to one of her questions is acceptable with 'That sounds not unsatisfactory'; her particular grammar shows her reluctance. Consider this example, in which Flora is talking about her facial surgery:

> FLORA: Your father wanted me to – (*carefully*) he didn't not want me to – he knew what it meant to me.
> Charlotte Jones, *Humble Boy* (2001)

'FALSE' LITOTES is when the *double* negative stands for a *single* negative, either due to idiom or dialect (see also IGNORANCE below). One of the best-known examples of this, outside the world of drama, is Mick Jagger's declaration 'I can't get no satisfaction'.

In terms of theatre writing such a colloquialism is very useful for placing characters in their social class. Lee in Sam Shepard's *True West* (1980) says 'I don't even hardly recognize it'; meaning 'I hardly recognize it'. Ruth in Lorraine Hansberry's *A Raisin in the Sun* (1959) says wearily to her husband 'Honey, you never say nothing new'; meaning 'you never say *anything* new'. Or how about this fine piece of advertising (a vizard is a prostitute):

> VIZARD: You won't never find a tighter one than mine.
> Stephen Jeffreys, *The Libertine* (1994)

2) An UNDERSTATEMENT (see above) achieved by denying the contrary.

Mrs Prentice in Joe Orton's *What the Butler Saw* (1967) claims 'I was angry and not a little frightened'; meaning, of course, that she was *very* frightened. The Member for Peebles in James Graham's *This House* (2012), when asked whether he would support a vote of No Confidence in the government, carefully states 'We don't currently *not* have confidence in you.' 'Spoken like a true politician' comes the wry reply. And here's a classic example between two characters (the 'she' referred to has just tried to commit suicide):

> FREDDIE: I'm just a bloke who's having a couple of drinks because
> he's feeling ruddy miserable –
> JACKIE: I don't expect she can be feeling exactly happy herself –
> Terence Rattigan, *The Deep Blue Sea* (1952)

ENALLAGE (en-*al*-uh-jee) from the Greek meaning 'exchange' or 'alternative'.
The intentional misuse of grammatical form, usually for comic or familiar effect. Think of such common phrases as 'no can do' or 'what can I do you for?'

Dimitri, a highly-educated Oxford student in Laura Wade's *Posh* (2012), rebuts the casual racism of his fellow Riot Club members with 'Is it cos I is Greek?' – echoing the catchphrase of the comedian Sacha Baron Cohen's character Ali G: 'Is it cos I is black?' And this example shows a common form of ANTIMERIA (see above), using an adjective as a noun:

> SKILLING: I like guys with spikes. I didn't know you had any till I heard
> you took on a pack of traders. That takes a special kind of stupid.
> Lucy Prebble, *Enron* (2009)

MISNOMER (miss-*noh*-muh) from the Old French meaning 'name wrongly'.
Deliberate misuse of similar sounding words for comic effect (see also PUN and WORDPLAY above).

Martha, in a dysfunctional marriage to George in Edward Albee's *Who's Afraid of Virginia Woolf?* (1962), details the contents of her wedding bouquet as 'Pansies! Rosemary! Violence!' – instead of *violets*. And how about:

> TZARA: For your masterpiece
> I have great expectorations
> For you I would evacuate a monument.
> Art for art's sake – I am likewise defecated.
>
> Tom Stoppard, *Travesties* (1993 edition)

Stoppard lets the Dadaist wilfully mix 'expectorations' for 'expectations', 'evacuate' for 'excavate', 'defecated' for 'dedicated' in his purposeful mockery of James Joyce.

It is common for a second character deliberately to play on a word that the other character has used, creating REPARTEE. In this example they are talking of Felicity's father, Doctor Wicksteed:

> FELICITY: Perhaps he could heal you.
> DENNIS: Him? He couldn't heel a shoe.
>
> Alan Bennett, *Habeas Corpus* (1973)

IGNORANCE

MALAPROPISM from the Latin meaning 'badly put', and named after the character Mrs Malaprop in Sheridan's play *The Rivals* (1775).
The habitual and unintentional misuse of similar sounding words to comic effect. This is entirely conscious by the playwright, as is MISNOMER above. The difference between the two devices is that MISNOMER is a *deliberate* misuse of words by the character, whereas with a MALAPROPISM the character remains oblivious to their mistake.

Overwhelmed by the well-bred attentions of Captain Absolute, Mrs Malaprop pronounces him 'the very pineapple of politeness!' – intending to say *pinnacle*. She denounces Lydia as being 'as headstrong as an allegory on the banks of the Nile' – meaning, of course, an *alligator*; and she asks her to forget Ensign Beverley, 'to illiterate him, I say, quite from your memory'; instead of *obliterate*. And enjoy this riot of inaccuracy:

> MRS MALAPROP: I am sure I have done everything in my power since I exploded the affair! Long ago I laid my positive conjunctions on her, never to think on the fellow again – I have since laid Sir Anthony's preposition before her – but I'm sorry to say she seems resolved to decline every particle that I enjoin her.
>
> Richard Brinsley Sheridan, *The Rivals* (1775)

Need some help? She uses 'exploded' for exposed, 'conjunctions' for injunctions, 'preposition' for proposition and 'particle' for article. Glorious!

This device is also known as **DOGBERRYISM**, after Constable Dogberry in Shakespeare's *Much Ado About Nothing* (c.1598). Preceding Mrs Malaprop by almost two hundred years, he makes such statements as 'comparisons are odorous' (meaning *odious*), and 'Is our whole dissembly appeared?' (meaning *assembly*), along with the declaration that:

> DOGBERRY: Our watch, sir, have indeed comprehended two auspicious persons.

He means, of course, 'apprehended' and 'suspicious'.

Dogberry is not the only Shakespearean character who indulges in this device. Abraham Slender, nervous suitor to Anne Page in *The Merry Wives of Windsor* (c.1598), says 'I will marry her – that I am freely dissolved, and that dissolutely'; meaning *resolved* and *resolutely*. Mistress Quickly in the same play has all manner of linguistic quirks, but often says 'speciously' when she means *specially*. Launce in *The Two Gentlemen of Verona* (c.1591) says 'I have received my proportion, like the prodigious son', meaning that he has received his *portion* like the *prodigal* son.

Coming into the modern age, Mari, the mother in Jim Cartwright's *The Rise and Fall of Little Voice* (1992), drunkenly complains, 'I'm trying to make an impression and she can't even be swivel to a friend' (she means *civil*) – and later assures her lover, '...you can depend on me. One hundred pesetas.' (instead of *per cent*). And here's a lovely reported example which you can work out for yourself:

> AKASH: He said it again – 'If Pradip is *heavily* seduced, he may get some sleep.'
>
> Tanika Gupta, *The Waiting Room* (2000)

SPOONERISM Named after the Rev William Spooner, Warden of New College, Oxford, who was apparently prone to this.
An accidental error in speech in which letters or syllables are switched between words.

The flustered Birdboot in Tom Stoppard's *The Real Inspector Hound* (1968), for instance, complains 'I find it simply intolerable to be pillified and villoried'; meaning to say 'vilified and pilloried'.

SOLECISM (*sol*-iss-iz-um) from the Greek meaning 'speaking incorrectly'.
The ignorant misuse of grammar. The playwright is aware of the misuse, though the characters are not. Most playwrights will consciously write SOLECISMS as part of characterization.

Class Musgrave in John Arden's *Serjeant Musgrave's Dance* (1959) states that 'agitators is agitators, in or out the Army'; using the singular 'is' for *are* and missing out the *of* in the second phrase. The maid Edith in Noël Coward's *Blithe Spirit* (1941) wails 'I haven't done nothing nor seen nobody'; a splendid double LITOTES, a classic form of SOLECISM. Here's another maid:

> DENMAN: It's Sergeant Winchell is here, my Lord,
> And wants to see your Lordship very urgent...
> T.S. Eliot, *The Family Reunion* (1939)

Vernacular Teach in David Mamet's *American Buffalo* (1975) says 'he might of been a different hospital'; a classic SOLECISM in replacing *have* with 'of', and missing out the preposition *in*. Keller in Arthur Miller's *All My Sons* (1947) urges his son to action with 'That's the only way you lick 'em is guts!' And here Johnny, indulging in one of his evasive flights of fancy, relates what occurs when he responds to a knock at the door of his caravan:

> JOHNNY: I get up and I answers, and standing outside are all five
> birds off of Girls Aloud.
> Jez Butterworth, *Jerusalem* (2009)

He uses the wrong verbal form – 'I answers' – and commits the classic SOLECISM: 'off of'. Both common colloquialisms belonging to certain accents or dialects.

A word here on the SPLIT INFINITIVE. An educated character before the 1960s would never split an infinitive. Nowadays, it seems entirely acceptable, possibly even preferred. We blame *Star Trek* and the Starship Enterprise's claim 'to boldly go where no man has gone before' for this.

Nowadays, it is commonly used to emphasize a negative or an adverb, as when the psychiatrist Dysart in Peter Shaffer's *Equus* (1973) wants to help Alan Strang find a way 'to finally tell me what happened in that stable'; or when Mary in Eugene O'Neill's *Long Day's Journey Into Night* (c.1940) scolds her younger son Edmund, saying 'You don't have to always take Jamie's part'.

SYNESIS (*sin*-iss-iss) from the Greek meaning a 'meeting together' or 'understanding'. The agreement of words according to logic, not grammatical form.

Quentin in Arthur Miller's *After The Fall* (1964) sees a room full of bouquets and asks 'What's all the flowers?' – the flowers are plural and therefore require 'are', but the colloquial singular is used here. Similarly, Charles in Mike Bartlett's verse play *King Charles III* (2014) asks 'But where's / The children' about his grandchildren. By his use of the singular (when the plural is required) Charles indicates how he lumps the children together as a single entity in his mind. Here is David Mamet's *American Buffalo* (1975) again:

> TEACH: They treat me like an asshole, they are an asshole.

The point is more punchily made by repeating the singular noun, rather than changing it to the correct plural. The audience, and indeed the other character, may find the effect and Teach's indignation more pathetic.

EVASION

EUPHEMISM from the Greek meaning the 'use of auspicious words'.
An inoffensive or circumlocutory term for something unpleasant, indecent or socially unacceptable; what Alan Bennett refers to as 'a verbal fig-leaf' in *The History Boys* (2004). We are all used to hearing or using EUPHEMISMS, whether through politeness, coyness or embarrassment.

Death is perhaps the most commonly euphemized topic. The phrases 'passed away', 'gone before' or 'at peace' are often used, as are the more religious 'passed over', 'gone to meet his maker' or 'gone to Abraham's bosom'. The more coy ones include 'in the next room' or 'gone upstairs'; and the more playful ones 'cash in your chips', 'kick the bucket' or 'pop your clogs'.

Sex supplies a rich vein, of course, led by traditional English prurience. The sexual act itself is often referred to simply as 'it', as in the phrases 'at it', 'doing it' and 'having it off'. Laertes in Shakespeare's *Hamlet* (c.1601) tentatively refers to his sister's virginity as her 'chaste treasure'. Laurie in Neil Simon's *Brighton Beach Memoirs* (1983) wonders whether her stomach cramps might be the onset of her first period, saying 'Maybe I'm getting my "ladies"'. And here's a wonderful example from the valet Waitwell, who has just married the maid, Foible:

> WAITWELL: My wife here and I have indeed been solacing in lawful delights.
>
> William Congreve, *The Way of the World* (1700)

Prostitution is referred to as 'the oldest profession' or being 'on the game', and prostitutes themselves as 'street walkers' or 'ladies of the night'. **Homosexuality**, meanwhile, has always produced a dizzying array of euphemistic alternatives, such as 'light on his loafers', 'bats for the other team', 'dances at the other end of the ballroom' and, of course, 'friends of Dorothy'. Barclay in Julian Mitchell's *Another Country* (1982) reports the sexually dubious Vaughan Cunningham is 'the ripest of fruit, apparently'. And in the following example, Patrick Marber has fun with the convolutions of the obituarist:

> DAN: "He was a convivial fellow," meaning he was an alcoholic.
> "He valued his privacy" – gay.
> "He *enjoyed* his privacy" ... raging queen.
> Patrick Marber, *Closer* (1997)

Going to the **Lavatory** provides a riot of terms, of course, such as 'powdering your nose', 'paying a little visit' and 'visiting the smallest room'. Having a pee is 'spending a penny', 'straining the greens' or 'number ones', as opposed to doing a poo, which is 'number twos', 'releasing the otters' or 'dropping the kids at the pool'.

> HONEY: I want to...put some powder on my nose.
> GEORGE: *(as MARTHA is not getting up)* Martha, won't you show her where we keep the... euphemism?
> Edward Albee, *Who's Afraid of Virginia Woolf?* (1962)

Poverty is often referred to delicately as 'reduced circumstances', and to be without money at all is to be 'stony broke', 'on your uppers' or 'financially embarrassed'.

Stupidity Someone who is not very bright is 'not the sharpest knife in the drawer' or 'the lights are on, but no-one's home', while people who are mentally challenged might be 'a sandwich short of a picnic', 'a couple of coupons short of a pop-up toaster' or any number of other un-PC phrases, including this example:

> JAY: Aunt Bella...She's a little – *(Points to his head)* – you know – closed for repairs.
> Neil Simon, *Lost In Yonkers* (1990)

CHARIENTISMUS (*cah*-ree-en-*tiz*-mus) from the Greek meaning 'elegant wit'.
1) To couch something unpleasant in more positive terms.

In this example, Raleigh, a young officer newly arrived in the trenches of the First World War, is guided by the protective 'Uncle' Osborne:

> OSBORNE: There's something rather romantic about it all.
> RALEIGH: *(eagerly)* Yes. I thought that, too.

OSBORNE: Think of it all as – as romantic. It helps.

R.C. Sherriff, *Journey's End* (1929)

2) To brush off a cruel or aggressive remark with a joke, usually laced with SARCASM:

CLAIRE: If you dropped dead, I'd kiss everything in this school, including the dog shit in the playground.
ROGER: You'd do that for me. I'm so honoured.

Sarah Daniels, *Neaptide* (1986)

PERIPHRASIS (pe-*ri*-fruh-sis) from the Greek meaning 'talk around'.
Also known as **CIRCUMLOCUTION**, from the Latin also meaning 'talk around'.
1) To talk round a subject to avoid raising it.

In this example, Amanda and Elyot, once married to each other and now wed to other people, try to avoid talking about their ongoing love for each other, and have agreed to talk about 'outside things', starting with Elyot's trip to Asia:

AMANDA: Did you eat sharks' fins, and take your shoes off, and use chopsticks and everything?
ELYOT: Practically everything.
AMANDA: And India, the burning Ghars, or Ghats, or whatever they are, and the Taj Mahal. How was the Taj Mahal?
ELYOT: *(looking at her)* Unbelievable, a sort of dream.
AMANDA: That was the moonlight, I expect; you must have seen it in the moonlight.
ELYOT: *(never taking his eyes off her face)* Yes, moonlight is cruelly deceptive.
AMANDA: And it didn't look like a biscuit box did it? I've always felt that it might.
ELYOT: *(quietly)* Darling, darling, I love you so.
AMANDA: And I do hope you met a sacred elephant. They're lint white, I believe, and very, very sweet.
FIYOT: I've never loved anyone else for an instant.
AMANDA: *(raising her hand feebly in protest)* No, no, you mustn't – Elyot – stop.

Noël Coward, *Private Lives* (1930)

2) To substitute several words where one would do, to avoid saying that word.

For instance, Mrs Manningham tries here not to say the word 'murderer':

MRS MANNINGHAM: How can you imagine my husband is – what you imagine he may be?

Patrick Hamilton, *Gaslight* (1938)

SCHEMATISMUS (skee-mat-*iz*-mus) from the Greek meaning 'configuration' or 'form'. To hide meaning though evasive speech, motivated by anxiety, good manners or a sense of humour; a more deliberate PERIPHRASIS.

In this example, Marge is trying to get Evelyn to admit to having an affair with Paul:

MARGE: It's been brought to my notice that you and Paul – have – well...
EVELYN: What?
MARGE: I think you know what I'm talking about.
EVELYN: No.
MARGE: That you and her husband have been – is this true? Yes or no?
EVELYN: Is what true?

Alan Ayckbourn, *Absent Friends* (1974)

LEPTOLOGIA (*lep*-toh-*lodj*-ee-uh) from the Greek meaning 'subtle speech'. A sly or deliberately evasive form of CIRCUMLOCUTION.

Here, Valentine tries to avoid talking about the money he owes the lawyer, Mr Trapland, while also attempting to get him drunk:

TRAPLAND: There is a debt, Mr Valentine, of £1,500, of pretty long standing –
VALENTINE: I cannot talk about business with a thirsty palate.
(To JEREMY) Sirrah, some sack.
TRAPLAND: And I desire to know what course you have taken for the payment.
VALENTINE: Faith and troth, I am heartily glad to see you.
My service to you. Fill, fill, to honest Mr Trapland, fuller.
TRAPLAND: Hold, sweetheart. This is not to our business. My service to you, Mr Scandal *(Drinks)* – I have forborne as long –
VALENTINE: T'other glass, and then we'll talk. Fill, Jeremy.
TRAPLAND: No more, in truth. I have forborne, I say –
VALENTINE: Sirrah, fill when I bid you. And how does your handsome daughter? Come, a good husband to her. *(Drinks)*
TRAPLAND: Thank you; I have been out of this money –
VALENTINE: Drink first.

William Congreve, *Love for Love* (1695)

APOPLANESIS (*ap*-oh-plan-*ee*-sis) from the Greek meaning 'leading astray'. To avoid a tricky subject by going off on a tangent or generally digressing.

In this example, Falstaff expertly evades the Lord Chief Justice's accusations:

> LORD CHIEF JUSTICE: Sir John, I sent for you – before your expedition to Shrewsbury.
> FALSTAFF: An't please your worship, I hear his majesty is returned with some discomfort from Wales.
> LORD CHIEF JUSTICE: I talk not of his majesty. You would not come when I sent for you.
> FALSTAFF: And I hear, moreover, his highness is fallen into this same whoreson apoplexy.
> LORD CHIEF JUSTICE: Well, God mend him! I pray you let me speak with you.
> FALSTAFF: This apoplexy, as I take it, is a kind of lethargy, an't please your worship, a kind of sleeping in the blood, a whoreson tingling.
> LORD CHIEF JUSTICE: What tell you me of it? Be it as it is.
> FALSTAFF: It hath its original from much grief, from study, and perturbation of the brain. I have read the cause of his effects in Galen; it is a kind of deafness.
> LORD CHIEF JUSTICE: I think you are fallen into the disease, for you hear not what I say to you.
>
> William Shakespeare, *Henry IV, Part Two* (c.1598)

APOSIOPESIS (a-*poss*-ee-oh-*pee*-sis) from the Greek meaning 'falling silent'. An abrupt halt conveying unwillingness or inability to complete a thought (see also ANAPODOTON), either through evasiveness, embarrassment, confusion, forgetfulness or emotion.

In this speech, Sylvia struggles with the words with which to confront her male friend about her suspicion that he slept with her husband:

> SYLVIA: I did think it hurtful and disturbing that you should choose...
> I found it disturbing that you would... knowing that you have a flat,
> that you have your own flat, that you would choose...
>
> Alexi Kaye Campbell, *The Pride* (2008)

PARALIPSIS (pa-ruh-*lip*-sis) from the Greek meaning 'passing over'. Also spelled PARALEIPSIS.

A refusal to continue or an admission of not knowing what to do or say; a conscious version of APOSIOPESIS above. A typical example would involve a character actually saying 'I don't know what to say to you' or asking 'what do you want me to say?'

In this example Mrs Fainall chooses not to dignify her husband's mistress with a term, leaving us to imagine what was she going to say – Whore? Trull? Jezebel?:

> MRS FAINALL: Go, you and your treacherous – I will not name it –
> but starve together, perish!
>> William Congreve, *The Way of the World* (1700)

METASTASIS (met-*ass*-tuh-sis) from the Greek meaning 'change of place'.
1) To skate over something quickly to avoid talking about it.

In the extract below, Harper tries to explain to her daughter that her father might have paedophilic tendencies:

> HARPER: I'm not saying that he's a a a. But I don't know what he was
> thinking in that moment and I don't know that he would never think
> those thoughts again.
>> Simon Stephens, *Harper Regan* (2008)

2) To hurl an insult back in the face of the insulter.

Here's a wonderful example in which Lord Foppington and his younger brother, Thomas Fashion, are vying for Miss Hoyden's affections; she favours the latter and warns him thus:

> MISS HOYDEN: Pray, my lord, don't let him whisper too close, lest he
> bite your ear off.
> LORD FOPPINGTON: I am not altogether so hungry as your ladyship
> is pleased to imagine.
>> John Vanbrugh, *The Relapse* (1696)

AFFECTATION

SORAISMUS (sor-rah-*iz*-mus) from the Greek meaning 'piling up'.
To mix languages, usually to achieve a sense of affectation or pretension.

The characters themselves will usually think they are being witty, erudite or fashionable, though they may not be viewed as such by other characters or the audience. Various languages are commonly reached for:

Latin Phrases such as *per se*, *ad infinitum* and *carpe diem* are still relatively common. Here is a less common and slightly absurd one, meaning 'married life':

> CANON THROBBING: I thought before I embarked on the choppy waters of the *vita coniugalis* I'd better have the vessel overhauled.
> Alan Bennett, *Habeas Corpus* (1973)

Italian During the Renaissance, all things Italian were in fashion, so it was the preferred language to quote, such as the Italian proverb meaning 'Too much hope deceives' in this example:

> VASQUES: Foolish woman, thou art now like a fire-brand that hath kindled others and burnt thyself. *Troppo sperar inganna*, thy vain hope hath deceived thee, thou art but dead.
> John Ford, *'Tis Pity She's a Whore* (c1629)

French This was particularly popular in the Restoration, due to all things French being so fashionable – it is particularly favoured by the ladies and the fops. In modern times, it has become the preserve of the **Camp** camp, natural heirs to the fops, as here:

> PRIOR: I did my best Shirley Booth this morning, floppy slippers, housecoat, curlers, can of Little Friskies; 'Come back, Little Sheba, come back...' To no avail. Le chat, elle ne reviendra jamais, jamais...
> Tony Kushner, *Angels in America* (1991)

SYNCOPE (*sink*-uh-pee) from the Greek meaning 'cut short'.
To drop letters in a word or to shorten a word's pronunciation.

This can either be through affectation – as when George in Edward Albee's *Who's Afraid of Virginia Woolf?* (1962) explains 'It's just a private joke between li'l ol' Martha and me' – or due to accent:

> PAM: Fred's coming 'ome next week.
> LEN: 'Ome?
> PAM: 'Is ol' lady won't 'ave 'im in the 'ouse.
> Edward Bond, *Saved* (1965)

DIASTROPHOLOGIA (dy-*ast*-ruh-fuh-*lodj*-ee-uh) from the Greek meaning 'distorted or perverted words'.
This is our newly-coined term for the distortion of words to create an affectation.

Dramatic Adventures in Rhetoric

Here are George and Martha again, indulging in their baby-talk, a thin veneer covering their contempt for each other:

> MARTHA: Well, then, you just trot over to the barie-poo...
> GEORGE: *(taking the tone from her)* ...and make your little mommy a gweat big dwink.
>
> Edward Albee, *Who's Afraid of Virginia Woolf?* (1962)

Or here the tortured vowels of the fop, as proscribed by the playwright:

> LORD FOPPINGTON: Prithee, Tam, tell me one thing: did nat your heart cut a caper up to your mauth, when you heard I was run through the bady?
>
> John Vanbrugh, *The Relapse* (1696)

This can be extended into intended speech impediments, such as this fearsome lisp:

> R.B. MONODY: It'th the inthufferable mannerth of that blackhaired thlut that one findth tho offenthive.
>
> Rodney Ackland, *Absolute Hell* (1988)

Or the soft 'R' of Sir Frederick Blount, who – we are told in the play by Lady Franklin – 'objects to the letter R as being too wough and therefore dwops its acquaintance':

> SIR FREDERICK BLOUNT: I am vewy fond of twavelling. You'd like Wome; bad inns, but vewy fine wuins.
>
> Edward Bulwer-Lytton, *Money* (1840)

A trifle un-PC, but a comical gift for an actor.

Chapter 5 Debate

OSTENSIBILE: Signora, we do not understand your painting.
GALACTIA: It is a painting of a battle at sea.
OSTENSIBILE: It is a slaughter at sea.
GALACTIA: A battle is a slaughter.
OSTENSIBILE: No, it is the furtherance of political ends by violent means.
GALACTIA: I showed the violence.
OSTENSIBILE: But not the ends. So it is untruthful. The ends were the freedom of the seas, the affirmation of the Christian faith, the upholding of a principle.
GALACTIA: How do you paint the upholding of a principle?
OSTENSIBILE: You show it by the nobility of the participants.

Howard Barker, *Scenes from an Execution* (1984)

Reasoned argument and debate, in so far as we understand it as the art of persuasion, are at the very heart of rhetoric in the fields of politics and law. In drama, it is only one of its many facets. The devices in this chapter include forms of attack and defense, coercion and questioning – as well as, of course, balanced argument.

These are perhaps the most overtly persuasive of the devices we cover in this book, and are the ones which at times through the ages have given rhetoric a bad name. Powerful speeches, both by leaders and their enemies, by governments and their opposition, have swayed the people from one side to another, all through the power of language and the structures of rhetoric. It is easy to imagine how the great orators – whether benign or evil – have swept the masses along using these potent devices, and thereby been able to propagate their ideas. It is equally easy to imagine how a mistrust of such language has crept in.

In the realm of the theatre such mistrust is irrelevant, since it becomes a tool with which to conjure character, intention and plot. As playwrights, actors or directors, there is great pleasure to be had in exploring and subsequently honouring these balanced arguments and strongly reasoned stand-points. Do you need any more persuasion?

REASONING

SYLLOGISM (*sil*-uh-jiz-um) from the Greek meaning 'with reasoning'.
An argument that states if two claims are true, then so is the conclusion.

Examine this mischievous example:

> UNDERSHAFT: He knows nothing; and he thinks he knows everything.
> That points clearly to a political career.
>
> George Bernard Shaw, *Major Barbara* (1905)

ENTHYMEME (en-thim-*eem*) from the Greek meaning 'reasoning' or 'invention'. A partially stated SYLLOGISM which omits one of the claims or the conclusion.

Here, Gwendolen addresses Jack, who she believes is called Ernest. He asks whether she would still love him if he had another name – 'I think Jack, for instance, a charming name'. She replies:

> GWENDOLEN: I have known several Jacks, and they all, without exception, were more than usually plain.
>
> Oscar Wilde, *The Importance of Being Earnest* (1895)

The conclusion – that if he was called Jack then she would consider him plain – is omitted, but firmly suggested.

ANAPODOTON (*an*-uh-*pod*-uh-ton) from the Greek meaning 'corresponding with'. When the concluding part of a logical statement is left unsaid, but is strongly inferred, either to save face or to avoid an unpleasant truth. It is akin to APOSIOPESIS, but logic completes the unspoken thought.

Think of proverbial phrases that are so well known they do not require their second half, such as 'If looks could kill... [they probably will]', 'If the cap fits... [wear it]' or 'where there's a will... [there's a way]'.

Here's a tactful example:

> MEADLE: First a mild stroke, followed by a worse stroke, and then, if that doesn't do the job... (*he gestures*)
>
> Simon Gray, *Quartermaine's Terms* (1981)

DELIBERATIO (del-*ib*-uh-*rah*-tee-oh) from the Latin meaning 'consideration'. To work through two or more ways of proceeding before acting on one.

Many of the soliloquies in Shakespeare – Hamlet, Richard II and Iago in *Othello* – each involve famous examples of this device. Even Launcelot Gobbo, the clown in *The Merchant of Venice* (c.1597), indulges in it (Act II Scene ii). Here, however, is Charles

Courtly in deliberation. He is trying to win the love of Grace, who is currently engaged to his father, Sir Harcourt Courtly:

> CHARLES COURTLY: I must first ascertain what are the real sentiments of this riddle of a woman. Does she love me? I flatter myself. And even if she does, ought I to pursue this affair further? My father's rival! As a dutiful son, I should feel concerned for his happiness; so I am; for I feel assured if Grace Harkaway becomes his bride, he will forever be miserable. It is therefore my duty as a loving son, clearly, to save my father. Yes, I'll be a sacrifice and marry her myself.
>
> Dion Boucicault, *London Assurance* (1841)

BALANCE

DIALYSIS (dy-*al*-iss-iss) from the Greek meaning 'through separation'.
The presentation of a choice using 'either... or...' in order to lead to a conclusion.

Here is a double example, in which Berinthia persuades her friend Amanda to accept the advances of Loveless, because such a 'Man of Brains' is only likely to find one woman whom he can truly love:

> BERINTHIA: Either she is not to be had at all – though that seldom happens, you'll say – or he wants those opportunities that are necessary to gain her. Either she likes somebody else much better than him, or uses him like a dog, because he likes nobody so well as her.
>
> John Vanbrugh, *The Relapse* (1696)

DIRIMENS COPULATIO (*di*-ri-mens cop-you-*lah*-tee-oh) from the Latin meaning 'interrupting union'.
To mention a balancing or opposing fact to prevent an argument being one-sided (see also ANTISAGOGE 2 below).

Harriet in George Etherege's *The Man of Mode* (1676) warns her over-eager lover Dorimant 'though I wish you devout, I would not have you turn fanatic', thereby warning him not to overdo it.

This device often uses the figure 'not only... but also...' or its equivalent. In this example another character's extreme sense of secrecy is weighed up:

> RHONDA: Also, of course, he's fanatical about secrecy. So this makes him also, not only lascivious, not only a scuzzbag as you might say, but also very security-conscious.
>
> David Hare, *The Secret Rapture* (1988)

PROCATALEPSIS (*proh*-cat-uh-*lep*-sis) from the Greek meaning 'anticipation'. The anticipation of an objection by addressing it in advance. This is also known as **PREBUTTAL**.

Here, Mrs Erlynne responds to Lord Windermere's disapproval of her not wanting to make herself known to her long-estranged daughter:

> MRS ERLYNNE: Oh, don't imagine I am going to have a pathetic scene with her, weep on her neck and tell her who I am, and all that kind of thing. I have no ambition to play the part of a mother.
>
> Oscar Wilde, *Lady Windermere's Fan* (1892)

DEFENCE

PROECTHESIS (proh-*ekth*-iss-iss) from the Greek meaning 'seizing in advance'. To defend your own or another's actions by giving reasons or making excuses for them.

When he is challenged about his behaviour, the supremely manipulative title character in Joe Orton's *Entertaining Mr Sloane* (1964) claims 'It's my upbringing. Lack of training. No proper parental control'. Lady Bracknell in Wilde's *The Importance of Being Earnest* (1895), meanwhile, explains away the eccentricity of her brother-in-law, the General, as arising from 'the Indian climate, and marriage, and indigestion, and other things of that kind'. And here Susanna, a married woman, uses the teachings of the church to defend her love for Rafe:

> SUSANNA: We pledged our love. That is no sin. He said love one another...
> RAFE: He said do not covet your neighbour's wife!
> SUSANNA: Covet? We don't covet... we love! Hate is the sin... not love!
> RAFE: We are condemned if we don't confess...
> SUSANNA: We're destroyed if we do!
>
> Peter Whelan, *The Herbal Bed* (1996)

RESTRICTIO (res-*trik*-tee-oh) from the Latin meaning 'limitation' or 'restraint'. To make an exception to something already stated, as in 'present company excepted'.

Benedick in Shakespeare's *Much Ado About Nothing* (c.1598) goads Beatrice with the certainty that he is 'loved of all ladies, only you excepted'. Gabriella in David Edgar's *Pentecost* (1994) views a mural that may be an unknown Giotto, saying 'No-one knows about this. Present company excluded'. And here's a splendid variation:

MARTHA: I meet fifteen new teachers and their goddam wives... present company outlawed, of course...*(HONEY nods, smiles sillily)*... and I'm supposed to remember *everything*.

Edward Albee, Who's Afraid of Virginia Woolf? (1962)

TRAIECTIO IN ALIUM (try-*ek*-tee-oh in *al*-ee-um) from the Latin meaning 'pushing onto another'.
To shift responsibility onto someone else.

In this example, Geoffrey, running late and expecting guests at any moment, blames his wife:

GEOFFREY: O.K. I get the message. O.K. There is no help or co-operation to be expected from you tonight, is that it? All systems shut down again, have they? All right. All right. It won't be the first time – don't worry. *(He returns to his hunt for bottles)* I mean it's not as if you're particularly famous as a gracious hostess, is it? It hasn't been unheard of for you to disappear to bed in the middle of a party and be found reading a book.

Alan Ayckbourn, Absurd Person Singular (1972)

ATTACK

INVECTIVE from the Latin meaning 'abusive' or 'censorious'.
A harsher version of TRAIECTIO IN ALIUM – blame with abuse, if you like. INVECTIVE was one of the classical rhetorical exercises known as the *progymnasmata* (see Chapter 1).

In this example, Edmund blames his father for his mother's morphine addiction:

EDMUND: I know damned well she's not to blame! And I know who is! You are! Your damned stinginess! If you'd spent money for a decent doctor when she was sick after I was born, she'd never have known morphine existed!

Eugene O'Neill, Long Day's Journey Into Night (c.1940)

BDELYGMIA (del-*ig*-mee-uh) from the Greek meaning 'nastiness' or 'abomination'.
An expression of hatred or contempt.

We think this example speaks for itself!

> – You pig-fucking cock-sucking bastards. You sister-fucking blaspheming child-murdering mindless fuck-faced killers. I spit on your graves and on the graves of your mothers and fathers and curse all future generations.
>
> Martin Crimp, *Attempts On Her Life* (1997)

ANTIRRHESIS (an-ti-*ree*-sis) from the Greek meaning 'against the speech'.
To reject a statement or argument due to its ridiculousness or wrongness.

In this example, Pylades – in Kit Brookman's contemporary re-imagining of the Orestes myth – reflects on how religion is often called upon to lend specious justification to partaking in conflict:

> PYLADES: For some reason war always has to be holy – like war is terrible, it's terrible, everyone knows it's terrible, everyone agrees it's terrible, but *this* war, *our* war, this one is necessary. What a load of shit.
>
> Kit Brookman, *Small and Tired* (2013)

REDUCTIO AD ABSURDUM (red-*uck*-tee-oh ad ab-*sir*-dum) from the Latin meaning to 'reduce to the absurd'.
1) To emphasize the truth of an argument by rubbishing its alternative.

Here, Archbishop Cranmer is trying to persuade Sir Thomas More to sign an act agreeing that the King's marriage to Katherine of Aragon is religiously unlawful:

> CRANMER: But that you owe obedience to your King is not capable of question. So weigh a doubt against a certainty and sign.
> MORE: Some men think the Earth is round, others think it flat; it is a matter capable of question. But if it is flat, will the King's command make it round? And if it is round, will the King's command flatten it? No, I will not sign.
>
> Robert Bolt, *A Man for All Seasons* (1960)

2) To follow an argument through to an extreme conclusion, in order to demonstrate its absurdity.

Here, a teacher, who has been accused by a pupil of having a lesbian affair, confronts the child's grandmother, who has withdrawn the girl from the school and encouraged other parents to do the same:

MARTHA: (*Suddenly, with violence*) Were we supposed to lie down and
smile while you took up a gun and looked around for people to kill?
Lillian Hellman, *The Children's Hour* (1934)

Incidentally, there is an extension of this device called **REDUCTIO AD HITLERUM**,
coined by the philosopher Levi Strauss, in which someone attempts to dismiss an
opponent's opinion by comparing it to a point of view held by Adolf Hitler or the Nazi
Party. This is an example in which two characters are debating the merit of a contemporary
art exhibition:

– Well I have to say I think that's an extraordinary remark which I
would not expect to hear outside of a police state...
– Oh *please*...
– ... and which – no, I'm sorry, I'm sorry, this has to be said – which
appears to be an attempt to reinstate the notion of *Entartete Kunst* ...
– Oh rubbish. What an absurd / over-reaction.
– ... the so-called 'degenerate art' prohibited – rubbish? I don't
think so – prohibited by the Nazis.
Martin Crimp, *Attempts On Her Life* (1997)

CONCESSIO (con-*sess*-ee-oh) from the Latin meaning 'concession' or 'allowance'.
To agree with someone on a point, then to twist it to make an opposing point.

Here, Belinda tries to defend Mr Heartfree to her cousin:

LADY FANCIFUL: I told you he'd be rude, Belinda.
BELINDA: Oh, a little bluntness is a sign of honesty, which makes me
always ready to pardon it.
John Vanbrugh, *The Provok'd Wife* (1697)

APORIA (ap-*or*-ree-uh) from the Greek meaning 'without passage' and so 'confusion'.
1) To attempt to discredit the opposing view by casting doubt on it.

In this example, Knox quizzes the codebreaker Alan Turing on one of his theories:

KNOX: Forgive me for asking a crass and naïve question – but what is
the point of devising a machine that cannot be built in order to prove
that there are certain mathematical statements that cannot be proved?
Hugh Whitemore, *Breaking the Code* (1986)

2) A feigned expression of doubt in order to get a reaction from another character or the audience.

Here the recently widowed Quentin feels it is wrong to love Holga, but clearly does not want to let her go. It is as if he wants his balanced expression of doubt to provoke a reaction of affirmation in the listener:

> QUENTIN: I'm not sure, you see, if I want to lose her, and yet it's outrageous to think of committing myself again.
>> Arthur Miller, *After The Fall* (1964)

ENUMERATIO (en-*yoo*-muh-*rah*-tee-oh) from the Latin meaning a 'counting up'. To detail parts, causes, effects or consequences to make a point more forcibly (see also LIST).

It is most often just a LIST with a simple summation. The more forceful the summation, the stronger the ENUMERATIO:

> RUTH: You had four strong Martinis before dinner – a great deal too much Burgundy at dinner – heaven knows how much Port and Kummel with Dr Bradman while I was doing my best to entertain that mad woman – and then two double brandies later – I gave them to you myself – of course you were drunk.
>> Noël Coward, *Blithe Spirit* (1941)

CORRECTION

CORRECTIO (cor-*rek*-tee-oh) from the Latin meaning literally 'making straight'. To correct a word, phrase or idea to make a point (see also DISTINCTIO below) – usually someone else's, though it can be your own.

In this example, Marlow passes judgement on his intended, Miss Hardcastle, whom he now realizes he has wooed both as herself and disguised as a barmaid:

> MARLOW: What at first seemed rustic plainness, now appears refined simplicity. What seemed forward assurance, now strikes me as the result of courageous innocence, and conscious virtue.
>> Oliver Goldsmith, *She Stoops to Conquer* (1771)

DISTINCTIO (dis-*tink*-tee-oh) from the Latin meaning 'difference' or 'distinction'. The explicit reference to the particular meaning of a word to avoid ambiguity, although ironically this draws attention to the alternative.

In this example, the governess is concerned that her book might be thought racey, since 'abandoned' means uninhibited as well as given up. She is quick to clarify her meaning:

> MISS PRISM: The manuscript was unfortunately abandoned. I use the word in the sense of lost or mislaid.
>
> Oscar Wilde, *The Importance of Being Earnest* (1895)

EPEXEGESIS (ep-*ek*-si-*jee*-sis) from the Greek meaning 'explanation' or 'clarification'. A form of AMPLIFICATION in which an idea or argument is clarified by the addition of further words or phrases.

The addition of a single word represents this device at its simplest, as when Prospero in Shakespeare's *The Tempest* (1611) describes the spirits as having 'melted into air, into thin air'. Alternatively, a whole phrase can be added, as in this example, in which Brian is talking of the comedian Benny Hill's behaviour towards his scantily-clad co-stars:

> BRIAN: I was always gratified to learn, indeed the girls were often at pains to stress, that at all times he behaved like a perfect gentleman.
>
> Terry Johnson, *Dead Funny* (1994)

EPANORTHOSIS (*ep*-an-orth-*oh*-sis) from the Greek meaning 'correction'. To re-phrase something immediately in order to qualify it.

Bill in Stephen Poliakoff's *Playing With Trains* (1989) claims 'My parties tend not to be successes. Disasters in fact'. This device can be used to achieve various effects:

Intensification, as in this discussion of children's coffins:

> SEBASTIAN. It's the baby ones that always get me.
> MICHAEL: Yes, that is sad.
> SEBASTIAN: Sad? It's fucking tragic.
>
> Tanika Gupta, *Sanctuary* (2002)

Or **Justification**, as in this example from the same play:

> MICHAEL: I did as I was told to protect my wife and child.
> KABIR: You murdered children.
> MICHAEL: I killed to survive.
>
> Tanika Gupta, *Sanctuary* (2002)

This device is commonly heralded by a negative:

> TELFER: But with our friend's horses champing their bits, I am compelled
> – nay, forced – to postpone this toast to a later period of the day.
>
> Arthur Wing Pinero, *Trelawny of the 'Wells'* (1898)

QUESTIONING

RHETORICAL QUESTION

Also known as **EROTESIS** (air-roh-*tee*-sis) from the Greek meaning 'questioning'.
A question not expecting or requiring an answer, including such common examples as 'Do you expect me to believe that?' or – with a shrug – 'What can you do?' Here is a famous example from Shakespeare, in which the point is forcefully made:

> SHYLOCK: If you prick us, do we not bleed? If you tickle us, do we not laugh? If you poison us, do we not die? And if you wrong us, shall we not revenge?
>
> William Shakespeare, *The Merchant of Venice* (c.1597)

EPIPLEXIS (ep-ee-*plek*-sis) from the Greek meaning 'strike upon' or 'rebuke'.
A common form of RHETORICAL QUESTION in which someone asks someone else a question, already knowing the answer, in order to reprimand or shame them.

In this example, Lord Goring persuades Lady Chiltern not to be so unforgiving of her husband's former political indiscretion:

> LORD GORING: You love Robert. Do you want to kill his love for you? What sort of existence will he have if you rob him of the fruits of his ambition, if you take him from the splendour of a great political career, if you close the doors of public life against him, if you condemn him to sterile failure, he who was made for triumph and success?
>
> Oscar Wilde, *An Ideal Husband* (1895)

HYPOPHORA (hy-*pof*-or-ruh) from the Greek meaning 'suggestion' or 'rescue'.
To ask someone a question and to answer it oneself.

Here's a pleasingly simple example:

> MRS MOLLOY: Why does everybody have adventures except me, Minnie? Because I have no spirit, I have no gumption.
> Thornton Wilder, *The Matchmaker* (1954)

This device is often deployed using ANADIPLOSIS or CONDUPLICATIO, as in this example:

> ANGELICA: Would anything but a madman complain of uncertainty? Uncertainty and expectation are the joys of life.
> William Congreve, *Love for Love* (1695)

COUNTER-QUESTION
To answer a question *with* a question.

Here, Barnabus Goche, a 17th-century Vicar-General, explores the idea that the plague is indicative of God's will:

> GOCHE: And why does our merciful Lord send this new shivering plague over the seas to us, creeping across a cold land... to add to the summer plagues, the smallpox and the fevers we already have? Isn't it that this rising tide of death is to punish us for our infecting pestilence of sin? Isn't he saying that death itself is preferable to the death of the spirit?
> Peter Whelan, *The Herbal Bed* (1996)

Between two characters the COUNTER-QUESTION is often a rebuff to the first question, as in this exchange about capitalists:

> HECTOR: Who are we that we should judge them?
> CAPTAIN SHOTOVER: What are they that they should judge us?
> George Bernard Shaw, *Heartbreak House* (1919)

RATIOCINATIO (*rat*-ee-oh-sin-*ah*-tee-oh) from the Latin meaning 'reasoning' or 'consideration'.
To ask yourself the reason for your words or actions.

In drama, this device is most often used in a soul-searching soliloquy, such as this:

> ANGELO: What dost thou? Or what art thou, Angelo?
> Dost thou desire her foully for those things
> That make her good?
>
> William Shakespeare, *Measure for Measure* (1603)

PYSMA (*piz*-muh) from the Greek meaning 'question'.
To ask a lot of questions together, which require as many separate answers.

There is a lovely example in Act III Scene ii of Shakespeare's *As You Like It* (c.1600), in which Rosalind asks Celia ten questions and demands that Celia answers them, impossibly, 'in one word'. Here is another example in which Miss Treherne is utterly confused following the farcical contrivances of a play full of proposals, engagements, marriages and – crucially – money:

> MISS TREHERNE: What am I? Am I single? Am I married? Am I a widow? Can I marry? Have I married? May I marry? Who am I? Where am I? What am I? What is my name? What is my condition in life? If I am married, to whom am I married? Why am I his widow? What did he die of? Did he leave me anything? If anything, how much, and is it saddled with conditions? Can I marry again without forfeiting it? Have I a mother-in-law? Have I a family of step-children, and if so, how many, and what are their ages, sexes, sizes, names and dispositions?
>
> W.S. Gilbert, *Engaged* (1877)

HOMOIOAPOKRISIS (hom-*oy*-oh-ap-*ock*-riss-iss) from the Greek meaning 'same answer'.
To ask a lot of questions that all require the *same* answer. There seems not to be a name for this common device, so we have coined this term ourselves.

Here is an example in which the single answer is supplied:

> HELLENA: Have I not a world of youth? A humour gay? A beauty passable? A vigour desirable? Well shaped? Clean limbed? Sweet breathed? And sense enough to know how all these ought to be employed to the best advantage? Yes.
>
> Aphra Behn, *The Rover* (1677)

COERCION

COHORTATIO (*co*-hor-*tah*-tee-oh) from the Latin meaning 'exhortation'.
A form of AMPLIFICATION expressly used to move the hearer to strong emotion, such as pity, indignation, fury or – as in the following example – disgust.

Big Daddy describes an unpleasant experience in Morocco:

> BIG DADDY: She had a naked child with her, a little naked girl with her, barely able to toddle, and after a while she set this child on the ground and give her a push and whispered something to her. This child came toward me, barely able t' walk, come toddling up to me and – Jesus, it makes you sick t' remember a thing like this! It stuck out its hand and tried to unbutton my trousers!
>
> Tennessee Williams, *Cat on a Hot Tin Roof* (1955)

COMPROBATIO (*com*-proh-*bah*-tee-oh) from the Latin meaning 'approval'.
To flatter another character to get them on your side or, at least, win their confidence.

In this example, Valentine is trying to flatter the lawyer, Trapland, to whom he owes money:

> VALENTINE: Drink to me my friend Trapland's health. An honester man lives not, nor one more ready to serve his friend in distress, tho' I say it to his face.
>
> William Congreve, *Love for Love* (1695)

SYNCHORESIS (sin-kor-*ree*-sis) from the Greek meaning 'concession' or 'agreement'.
To give other characters permission to judge you, as in this example:

> IAGO: Now sir, be judge yourself
>   Whether I in any just term am affined
>   To love the Moor.
>
> William Shakespeare, *Othello* (c.1604)

This can also apply to the audience. In the Renaissance and the Restoration, it was common for a Prologue or Epilogue to give the audience permission to judge the play, the efforts of the actors and the characters they portray. Here, though, is a more modern example:

KATE: How many times have I told you not to leave your things around the house?

EUGENE: A hundred and nine.

KATE: What?

EUGENE: You said yesterday, "I told you a hundred and nine times not to leave your things around the house."

BLANCHE: Don't be fresh with your mother, Gene!

EUGENE: *(to audience)* Was I fresh? I swear to God, that's what she said to me yesterday.

Neil Simon, Brighton Beach Memoirs (1983)

PHILOPHRONESIS (*fil*-oh-fron-*ee*-sis) from the Greek meaning 'kind treatment'. To suppress anger in favour of more gentle and reasonable speech.

Here, a father addresses his sickly son:

TYRONE: You'll obey me and put out that light or, big as you are, I'll give you a thrashing that'll teach you – ! (*Suddenly he remembers EDMUND's illness and instantly becomes guilty and shamefaced.*) Forgive me, lad. I forgot – You shouldn't goad me into losing my temper.

Eugene O'Neill, Long Day's Journey Into Night (c.1940)

ANTANAGOGE (an-*tan*-uh-*godj*-ee) from the Greek meaning 'bring against'. To place a good point next to a bad one, or a compliment next to a criticism, to soften the blow.

On the occasion of his retirement, the Headmaster in Alan Bennett's *Forty Years On* (1968) says 'it is a sad occasion, but it is a proud occasion too' – a classic piece of sentimental spin. Judith in Noël Coward's *Hay Fever* (1925), having been kissed by her house guest Richard Greatham, instantly imagines it is a full-blown affair. She frets about how her writer husband will react, but rationalizes it thus: 'They say suffering's good for writers, it strengthens their psychology.' And here is Captain Hook talking of his nemesis, the crocodile:

HOOK: The brute liked my arm so much, Smee, that he has followed me ever since, from sea to sea, and from land to land, licking his lips for the rest of me.

SMEE: *(looking for the bright side)* In a way it is a sort of compliment.

J.M. Barrie, Peter Pan (1904)

ANTISAGOGE (an-*tiss*-uh-*godj*-ee) from the Greek meaning 'compensation'.
1) To promise a reward for goodness or a punishment for wickedness.

Here, Amanda's son, Tom, has failed to pay the electricity bill and they have been cut off (frankly, he gets off lightly!):

> AMANDA: Tom, as a penalty for your carelessness you can help me
> with the dishes.
>
> Tennessee Williams, *The Glass Menagerie* (1944)

2) To state one side of an argument, then the other (see also DIRIMENS COPULATIO above); the distinction we have drawn is that DIRIMENS COPULATIO is concerned primarily with fairness and balance, whereas ANTISAGOGE is more of a counter-assertion; possibly more antagonistic.

Here, however, is a relatively mild example:

> HELEN: He's a megalomaniac. The man's paranoid. He's cracked.
> DONALD: He's certainly very enthusiastic.
>
> Alan Ayckbourn, *Ten Times Table* (1978)

PROTROPE (pro-*troh*-pee) from the Greek meaning 'persuasion' or 'urging on'.
To incite someone to action through promises or threats.

In this example of the latter, the redoubtable dresser, Norman, catches young actress Irene coming out of the lead actor's dressing room:

> NORMAN: I'm waiting.
> IRENE: For what?
> NORMAN: A graphic description of events. Out with it. Or I shall
> slap your face. Hard.
>
> Ronald Harwood, *The Dresser* (1980)

APOPHASIS (ap-*pof*-uh-sis) from the Greek meaning 'denial'.
1) To draw attention to something by saying you will not mention it.

Here is a particularly pleasing example, in which the taboo subject left unsaid is America:

> KING: I agree with you, Mr Pitt, on everything apart from the place
> we mustn't mention. (*He gives PITT a sidelong look. PITT says
> nothing.*) We didn't see eye to eye over that, but we agreed

to draw a veil over it. And I'm only mentioning it now just to show that I haven't mentioned it.

Alan Bennett, *The Madness of George III* (1991)

2) To pretend to deny something as a way of implicitly affirming it.

Here is a terrific example from two great wits, whose use of language is almost unsurpassed:

MILLAMANT: What would you give to free yourself from loving me?
MIRABEL: I would give a great deal for you not to know I cannot help myself.

William Congreve, *The Way of the World* (1700)

SUMMARY

ANACEPHALAEOSIS (*an*-uh-*sef*-al-ee-*oh*-sis) from the Greek meaning a 'summary' or 'comprehension'.
A recapitulation of the facts; a summary.

Egeon at the beginning of Shakespeare's *The Comedy of Errors* (1594) gives the Duke (and thereby the audience) a full account of how he and his family were separated. Conversely, at the end of his *Pericles* (1607), the hero runs through the story of the whole play as his family are reunited. Staying in the realm of Shakespeare, but coming to more modern times, here are Hamlet's friends:

ROSENCRANTZ: The position as I see it, then. We, Rosencrantz and Guildenstern, from our young days brought up with him, awakened by a man standing on his saddle, are summoned, and arrive, and are instructed to glean what afflicts him and draw him on to pleasures, such as a play, which unfortunately, as it turns out, is abandoned in some confusion owing to certain nuances outside our appreciation – which, among other causes, results in, among other effects, a high, not to say, homicidal, excitement in Hamlet, whom we, in consequence, are escorting, for his own good, to England. Good. We're on top of it now.

Tom Stoppard, *Rosencrantz and Guildenstern Are Dead* (1967)

METABASIS (met-*ab*-uh-sis) from the Greek meaning 'transition'.
A concise summary of what has happened or of what has been said, and of what will consequently occur.

KAREN: You don't want to go.

CARDIN: No, I don't want to go. This was my place, where I was born, where I wanted to be. You wanted to stay here, too. Well, to hell with all that. We can't stay. So we're going to a place where we can live, and where I've got a good friend who understands, and will help us.

Lillian Hellman, The Children's Hour (1934)

PRAISE

EULOGY from the Greek meaning a 'good word'.
A formal speech in praise of someone, usually at a funeral or wake.

In this example, a prisoner extols the virtues of a fellow captive, who has disappeared and is presumed dead:

EDWARD: He was gentle. He was kind. He could be cruel, when he was afraid, and while he was often afraid, as we all are afraid, he was not often cruel. He was brave, he could protect himself, and me, and you. He was beautiful to look at. I watched him as he slept one night I couldn't sleep. He moved that night through his sleep like a man not dreaming of what life had in store for him. He was innocent. Kind, gentle. Friend. I believe it goes without saying, love, so I never said. He is dead. Bury him. Perpetual light shine upon him. May his soul rest in peace. Amen.

Frank McGuinness, Someone Who'll Watch Over Me (1992)

ENCOMIUM (en-*coh*-mee-um) from the Greek meaning 'praise'.
Praising someone or something, but not usually to the extent of a whole speech.

Here's a well-known example, interestingly praise after a fall from grace:

OPHELIA: O, what a noble mind is here o'erthrown!
    The courtier's, soldier's, scholar's, eye, tongue, sword,
    Th' expectancy and rose of the fair state,
    The glass of fashion and the mould of form,
    Th' observed of all observers, quite, quite down!

William Shakespeare, Hamlet (c.1601)

PANEGYRIC (pan-uh-*ji*-rik) from the Greek meaning 'for the whole assembly'.
A formal public speech in praise of a person or a thing.

Dramatic Adventures in Rhetoric

Staying with Shakespeare, here's an extract from an extended PANEGYRIC in which the Archbishop of Canterbury extols the hoped-for virtues of the baby Princess Elizabeth at her christening:

> CRANMER: This royal infant – heaven still move about her! –
> Though in her cradle, yet now promises
> Upon this land a thousand thousand blessings,
> Which time shall bring to ripeness. She shall be –
> But few now living can behold that goodness –
> A pattern to all princes living with her,
> And all that shall succeed.
> > William Shakespeare and John Fletcher, *Henry VIII* (1613)

Chapter 6 Structure

KING: She, on his left side, craving aid for Henry,
He, on his right, asking a wife for Edward.
She weeps, and says her Henry is deposed;
He smiles, and says his Edward is installed.

William Shakespeare, *Henry VI Part Three* (1591)

In this chapter we introduce the devices which create the structure of our thoughts and language. They give flight to our most complex ideas, and form the patterns of our speech. They are the mainstay of our communicative skills, and allow us to create an absolute clarity of argument. Within the realm of drama such clarity of expression is crucial, in order for our stories and ideas to be conveyed to an audience without ambiguity (unless, of course, ambiguity is what is required).

We range within this chapter from the basic constructs of such devices as ANTITHESIS, with which you are probably familiar – though not perhaps in all its forms – to the perfection of PARALLELISM and the complexities of HYPERBATON and its friends. However unusual these might seem, you will soon see that the structures they embody are ones we use every day in even our simplest conversations. This is why this family of rhetorical devices is key in dramatic writing; it is absolutely *how* we talk to each other.

ANTITHESIS

ANTITHESIS from the Greek meaning 'setting against'.
The juxtaposition of ideas that are in opposition to each other, using balanced or parallel words or phrases.

Direct Opposites These are very common; think of such pairings as 'true and false', 'day and night', 'good and evil', 'hot and cold', 'lost and found', 'young and old'... the list goes on and on.

Jerry in Harold Pinter's *Betrayal* (1978) accosts Emma with 'I should have blackened you, in your white wedding dress'; a wonderful conflict of the metaphorical and the literal. Barabas in Christopher Marlowe's *The Jew of Malta* (c.1592) accuses the Governor of the island with 'Your extreme right does me exceeding wrong'; the ANTITHESIS is brilliantly bolstered by the ALLITERATION of 'right' and 'wrong', and the PARACHESIS of 'extreme' and 'exceeding'. And here, Goche, the Vicar-General, is speaking to John Hall, a doctor – conveying their differences in a succinct ANTITHESIS:

> GOCHE: I understand the urgency you have to care for the body.
> Please understand the urgency I have to care for the soul.
> > Peter Whelan, *The Herbal Bed* (1996)

In Opposition It is a common mistake to think of ANTITHESIS as only being opposites, which it often is, of course, as we have seen above. However, it is more useful to think of it as two things held *in opposition* to each other. Consider the MAXIM 'finders keepers, losers weepers' – 'finders' and 'losers' are, of course, direct opposites, but 'keepers' and 'weepers' are not, although they *are* in opposition to each other and therefore antithetical.

Brutus in Shakespeare's *Julius Caesar* (1599) says 'Not that I loved Caesar less, but that I loved Rome more'; 'less' and 'more' are direct opposites, whereas Ceasar and Rome are held in opposition – all part of his careful exactitude in a dangerous political moment. Philo in *Antony and Cleopatra* (1606) describes Antony as being 'The triple pillar of the world, transformed / Into a strumpet's fool'; two wonderfully opposing images, though not direct opposites. And in this example Nick, a young biology lecturer, makes a comparison between himself and the older George, a lecturer in history – old vs young, humanities vs sciences, past it vs potential:

> NICK: *You've* got history on *your* side... I've got biology on mine.
> History, biology.
> > Edward Albee, *Who's Afraid of Virginia Woolf?* (1962)

A clear ANTITHESIS of one thing in opposition to another is a **Single Antithesis**, but antitheses can operate in multiples, and in combinations of direct opposites and things in opposition.

Double This description of Charity employs two pairs of direct opposites:

> BIANCA: There is no virtue can be sooner missed
> > Or later welcomed.
> > > Thomas Middleton, *Women Beware Women* (1621)

Whereas, in the following example, both the adjectives and nouns of the ANTITHESIS are in opposition:

> CANTILUPE: ...the hells of this world are paved, don't you think, less
> with good intentions than with high ideals.
> > Harley Granville Barker, *Waste* (1907)

Triple Here is a three-way ANTITHESIS, with two direct opposites ('occasionally' vs 'always' and 'a little' vs 'immensely') and one in opposition ('over-dressed' vs 'over-educated'):

> ALGERNON: If I am occasionally a little over-dressed, I make up for it by being always immensely over-educated.
>> Oscar Wilde, *The Importance of Being Earnest* (1895)

And here are three in opposition:

> COLLINS: I commend your endeavour to oppose the baneful influence of vice with the harmonising arts of civilisation.
>> Timberlake Wertenbaker, *Our Country's Good* (1988)

Quadruple Here's a four-way ANTITHESIS, in which Gerald addresses his wife, Susan:

> GERALD: Said by anybody else, that could be interpreted as quite an affectionate remark. Spoken by you, it sounds like an appalling accusation.
>> Alan Ayckbourn, *Woman in Mind* (1987)

Quintuple And a five-way – notice the pivot word 'than' which separates the two halves of the ANTITHESIS:

> MRS LOVEIT: The man who loves above his quality does not suffer more from the insolent impertinence of his mistress than the woman who loves above her understanding does from the arrogant presumptions of her friend.
>> George Etherege, *The Man of Mode* (1676)

Sextuple And finally a six-way antithetical comparison between rakes and fops:

> BERINTHIA: These have brains; the beau has none. These are in love with their mistress; the beau with himself. They take care of her reputation; he's industrious to destroy it. They are decent; he's a fop. They are sound; he's rotten. They are men; he's an ass.
>> John Vanbrugh, *The Relapse* (1696)

Comparative Antithesis There is always an element of comparison in an ANTITHESIS, but the following is an example of the blatantly comparative:

> TOM: In high school Laura had been as unobtrusive as Jim had been astonishing.
>> Tennessee Williams, *The Glass Menagerie* (1944)

Chapter 6 Structure

ANTITHESIS need not only be concerned with language; it can stretch into the very nature of the stories we are telling. You can have **Antithesis of Characters:** endless stories have goodies and baddies of some sort, and think of the good and evil angels in Marlowe's *Doctor Faustus*. You can also have the **Antithesis of Time:** think of plays that are set in both the past and the present, like J.B. Priestley's Time Plays. You can have an **Antithesis of Setting:** Shakespeare's *The Winter's Tale* is a case in point, with the ANTITHESIS between the brooding, emotionally stultified kingdom of Sicilia, in opposition to the light, playful world of Bohemia.

In Renaissance drama, it is common to have a rich **Antithesis of Thematic Imagery**. In no play is it more apparent than in Shakespeare's *Romeo and Juliet* (1595), in which the over-riding themes of black and white, day and night, and dark and light are verbal echoes of the opposition between the Capulets and Montagues. Here is Romeo when he first sets eyes on Juliet:

> ROMEO: O, she doth teach the torches to burn bright!
> It seems she hangs upon the cheek of night
> As a rich jewel in a Ethiop's ear –
> Beauty too rich for use, for earth too dear!
> So shows a snowy dove trooping with crows
> As yonder lady o'er her fellows shows.

ANTITHESIS is very often pointed up by combining with rhetorical devices from the acoustic family (see Chapter 2).

ALLITERATIVE ANTITHESIS

This is when ALLITERATION is used to point up the words in opposition to each other. Many classic examples have become well established: 'heaven or hell', 'virtue or vice', 'friend or foe', 'love or loathe', 'pleasure or pain', 'make or mar', 'hurt or heal', 'boom or bust', 'help or hinder', and 'like it or lump it' to name a few.

There is often a self-satisfied quality to characters who use this device. Consider Mrs Levi in Thornton Wilder's *The Matchmaker* (1954), who says that money is 'like the sun we walk under; it can kill or cure'. The Judge in Reginald Rose's *Twelve Angry Men* (1956) informs the jury that it is their 'duty to try and separate the facts from the fancy'. And here a black political campaigner is defending white right-wing journalists:

> KWAKU: None of them were writing in right-wing rags that black kids
> are more interested in mugging than mathematics.
> Kwame Kwei-Armah, *Statement Of Regret* (2007)

SIBILANT ANTITHESIS

This is when SIBILANCE is combined with ANTITHESIS. Once again there are some classic examples, such as 'sink or swim', 'saints or sinners' and 'sacred or sinful'. Here's a nice one employing the 'sh' sound:

> PERICLES: Who has a book of all that monarchs do,
>   He's more secure to keep it shut than shown.
> William Shakespeare and George Wilkins, *Pericles* (1607)

ASSONANT ANTITHESIS

This is when ASSONANCE is used to point up the words in opposition, such as in the phrase 'from the cradle to the grave'; the words 'cradle' and 'grave' share the same long 'A' sound. It is more subtle than Alliterative Antithesis, though no less effective.

Mrs Hitchcock in John Arden's *Serjeant Musgrave's Dance* (1959) faces their circumstances with 'if we can't have a laugh, we'll starve!' Giovanni, the incestuous brother in John Ford's *'Tis Pity She's a Whore* (c.1629), asks 'What cure shall give me ease in these extremes?' And here's a two-against-one ANTITHESIS of the positive 'rise' and 'thrives' in opposition to the negative 'declines':

> MARTIUS: They'll sit by th' fire and presume to know
>   What's done i' th' Capitol, who's like to rise,
>   Who thrives and who declines.
> William Shakespeare, *Coriolanus* (1608)

PARACHESIC ANTITHESIS

This is when combined sounds are repeated to point up antithetical words. It is most common at the beginning of words, as in the phrase 'thick or thin'.

Amy in David Hare's *Amy's View* (1997) berates her mother with 'your principles turn out to be much more like prejudice'; her point is forcefully made with the repeated 'pr' sound. In John Webster's *The White Devil* (1612) Flamineo asks how he will be saved 'from the galleys, or the gallows?' – both are punishments, but the 'galleys' signify a life of slavery and the 'gallows' death. And here the aging suitor Gremio wittily bests his young rival by chucking a Parachesic Antithesis back in his face:

> TRANIO: Greybeard, thy love doth freeze.
> GREMIO: But thine doth fry.
> William Shakespeare, *The Taming Of The Shrew* (c.1591)

Repeated combinations of sounds at both the beginning and end of words also occur, as in the memorable phrase 'nature versus nurture'. Fag in Sheridan's *The Rivals* (1775) asks for 'A little less simplicity, with a grain or two more sincerity'; his reprimand made more pert by the shared sounds of the antithetical words, as well as their SIBILANCE.

Teach in David Mamet's *American Buffalo* (1975), meanwhile, colloquially advises Don that this life is 'kickass or kissass'. And here is a more gentle reprimand:

> NORMAN: The time has come, if you don't mind my saying so,
> to stop waxing poetical and to wax a bit more practical.
> Ronald Harwood, *The Dresser* (1980)

HOMOIOTELEUTONIC ANTITHESIS
This often occurs, and is when the ends of antithetical words share the same combination of sounds, such as the phrase 'make or break'.

Nancy in Bryony Lavery's *Frozen* (1998) says 'I don't know whether to be sad or glad'; the simple rhyme of the antithetical words points up her emotional inertia. Martin Luther in John Osborne's *Luther* (1961) wittily responds to the papal decree demanding his excommunication with 'papal decretals are the devil's excretals'. And here is a lovely rhymed example:

> HIPPOLITO: He that did lately in disguise reject thee
> Shall, now thou art thyself, as much respect thee.
> Thomas Middleton, *The Revenger's Tragedy* (1607)

SYNOECIOSIS (sin-*ee*-see-*oh*-sis) from the Greek meaning 'binding together'.
Also spelt SYNECIOSIS and SYNAECIOSIS.
A form of ANTITHESIS which is paradoxical in nature. Some definitions claim it as an alternative name for an OXYMORON (see under WIT).

Henry in Tom Stoppard's *The Real Thing* (1982) dismisses his daughter Debbie's declaration that free love is free of propaganda as 'flawless but wrong. A perfect dud.' And here Claudio shames his bride on her wedding day:

> CLAUDIO: But fare thee well, most foul, most fair! Farewell,
> Thou pure impiety and impious purity!
> William Shakespeare, *Much Ado About Nothing* (c.1598)

QUALIFICATION

AMPLIFICATION from the Latin meaning 'making large'.
The expansion of a word or idea (see also EPEXEGESIS).

Most commonly an idea is launched, then elaborated on, as in this example, in which Bill is talking of his forward-thinking daughter:

BILL: You will notice she even has to wear her school uniform in a perverse way – little anarchic flourish.

Stephen Poliakoff, Playing With Trains (1989)

The word 'perverse' is expanded into and qualified by 'little anarchic flourish'.

AMPLIFICATION is usually achieved by repeating the idea and adding to it, in various ways:

Repeat, then Expand Such as when Mary in T.S. Eliot's *The Family Reunion* (1939) says 'The spring is very late in this northern country, / Late and uncertain...'. Here's another:

MAN: I wish I was dead. I wish I was dead because I don't care a damn about anything any more.

Athol Fugard with John Kani & Winston Ntshuna,
Sizwe Bansi Is Dead (1972)

Expand, then Repeat This can be as small an addition as a single adjective, such as when Teddy in Harold Pinter's *The Homecoming* (1965) describes his home as being 'like a urinal. A filthy urinal'. Commonly the expansion can also be a run of adjectives:

BRINDSLEY: It's all going to be a disaster. An A1, copper-bottomed, twenty-four-carat disaster!

Peter Shaffer, Black Comedy (1965)

Expansion Sandwiched Within Repeat This is a favourite of Shakespeare. Think of Othello's '...'twas strange, 'twas passing strange; / 'Twas pitiful, 'twas wondrous pitiful'. This form of the device accentuates the added word; we listen for the new information, rather than dwelling on the repeated words:

WILLY: Lick the world! You guys together could absolutely lick the civilized world.

Arthur Miller, Death of a Salesman (1949)

Expand, Repeat, then Qualify The AMPLIFICATION can continue into a qualification of the idea. Shakespeare's Henry V addresses his troops as 'We few, we happy few, we band of brothers'. And here's a more modern example:

LOUIS: That's just liberalism, the worst kind of liberalism, really, bourgeois tolerance...

Tony Kushner, Angels in America (1991)

SCESIS ONOMATON (*skee*-sis on-*om*-uh-ton) from the Greek meaning 'placement of words'.
1) Emphasizing an idea using a run of synonymous words or phrases (see also SYNONYM).

In this example, the effect is strongly accentuated by the use of POLYSYNDETON:

> BILL: I'm tired of being watched by you, and observed and scrutinized and assessed and guessed about.
> John Osborne, *Inadmissible Evidence* (1964)

2) A sentence omitting a verb, as in this common comparative structure in which the verb 'is' is omitted:

> RAY: The greater the deception
>   The greater the risk
> David Harrower, *Blackbird* (2005)

METANOIA (met-an-*oy*-yuh) from the Greek meaning 'after-thought' or 'change of mind'. To qualify a statement by retracting it and restating it in a different way (see also CORRECTIO in Chapter 5).

In the following example the retraction is implicit, but clear – an attempt to be more positive, and therefore persuasive. Dundas is urging Prime Minister William Pitt to make an effort in wooing his supporters in the run-up to an election:

> DUNDAS: It would help our situation if you endeavoured to be less distant. More convivial.
> Alan Bennett, *The Madness of George III* (1991)

It is perhaps most often deployed with a negative. Here the German physicist passes comment on persuading the Allies to give up their research into nuclear fusion:

> HEISENBERG: It's a hope. Not even a hope. A microscopically fine thread of possibility.
> Michael Frayn, *Copenhagen* (1998)

HYPOTAXIS (hy-poh-*tak*-sis) from the Greek meaning 'arrangement beneath'. The arrangement of clauses so that one is subordinate to another (the opposite of PARATAXIS).

Here, Mrs Mortar declares how she believes single women view those who become engaged to be married:

> MRS MORTAR: Every woman, no matter what she says, is jealous when another woman gets a husband.
>
> Lillian Hellman, *The Children's Hour* (1934)

INSERTION

HYPERBATON (hy-*per*-buh-ton) from the Greek meaning 'stepping over' or 'transposition'. 1) The separation of words that belong together, often to emphasize a key word.

Dr Chasuble in Oscar Wilde's *The Importance of Being Earnest* (1895) greets Miss Prism with 'You are, I trust, well'; the polite enquiry seems all the more pleasant and sincere by his particular turn of phrase. In the following example Mary is rather more circumspect about her husband's drinking:

> MARY: He has such a good excuse, he believes, to drown his sorrows.
>
> Eugene O'Neill, *Long Day's Journey Into Night* (c.1940)

Names are often used in this way, as when Dr Wicksteed in Alan Bennett's *Habeas Corpus* (1973) concludes 'So even you, Percy, are human' – the key word is delayed by the insertion of the name, thereby accentuating the point. Similarly, this warning is made more intense by the device:

> BEATRICE: Take heed, De Flores, of forgetfulness,
>   'Twill soon betray us.
>
> Thomas Middleton & William Rowley, *The Changeling* (1622)

2) When words within a sentence are placed in an unusual order to create an effect (see also ANASTROPHE).

The Duchess of York in Shakespeare's *Richard III* (c.1593) says to the homicidal king 'Bloody thou art; bloody will be thy end'; the altered word order accentuates the key word 'bloody'. And here the unusual word order creates a proverbial, even biblical feel:

> CORRIE: Six days does not a week make.
>
> Neil Simon, *Barefoot In The Park* (1965)

PARENTHESIS from the Greek meaning 'put in beside'.
A word or phrase inserted as an aside (a form of HYPERBATON).

This can have various effects, such as **Explanation:**

> SIR PETER TEAZLE: I had not been involved in matrimony a fortnight, before her father, a hale and hearty man, died.
>
> Richard Brinsley Sheridan, *The School for Scandal* (1777)

Or **Qualification:**

> ARTHUR: I'm afraid she's not – just in case you thought otherwise – the daughter of a rich man.
>
> Terence Rattigan, *The Winslow Boy* (1946)

Or **Confirmation:**

> MR HARDACHE: When I think of that innocent young man – you did say he was innocent, Rose? – alone in his cell.
>
> Edward Bond, *Restoration* (1981, revised 2006)

Or **Apology:**

> CISSIE: Mick and Sammy and Dave Goldman – and that bloody fool, if you'll excuse the expression, Sonny Becks.
>
> Arnold Wesker, *Chicken Soup With Barley* (1958)

Or **Digression** – a change of subject or lapse in concentration before returning to the original subject, as in this example:

> MAX: I made Jessie put her feet up on a pouffe – what happened to that pouffe, I haven't seen it for years – she put her feet up on the pouffe and I said to her, Jessie, I think our ship is going to come home.
>
> Harold Pinter, *The Homecoming* (1965)

SENTENTIAL ADVERB from the Latin meaning 'thoughtful addition to the word'. An adverbial word or phrase, usually interrupting syntax, used to lend emphasis to the subject. This is another form of HYPERBATON and a specific kind of PARENTHESIS.

> JOYCE: An artist is the magician put among men to gratify – capriciously – their urge for immortality.
>
> Tom Stoppard, *Travesties* (1993 edition)

HYSTEROLOGIA (*hist*-uh-ruh-*lodj*-ee-uh) from the Greek meaning 'afterthought'. When a qualifying phrase is inserted between a preposition and its object:

> MAZZINI: But nothing happened, except, of course, the usual poverty and crime and drink that we are used to.
>> George Bernard Shaw, *Heartbreak House* (1919)

TMESIS (t-*mee*-sis) from the Greek meaning 'cut'.
When a word or set phrase is split by an intervening word or phrase for emphasis – often involving swearing!

Split Words Jacko in Pam Gems' *Piaf* (1978) rates Piaf's appearance as 'Fan-bloody-tastic!' Izzy in Polly Stenham's *That Face* (2007) declares that the victim of her bullying is 'un-fucking-conscious'.

Split Set Phrases Hally in Athol Fugard's *'Master Harold'...and the Boys* (1982) weighs up where he can go as an alternative to hanging out with Sam and Willie, offering cynically 'Home-sweet-fucking-home'. Johnny in Terrence McNally's *Frankie and Johnny in the Clair de Lune* (1987) challenges Frankie with 'What the pardon-my-French fuck are you talking about?' Modern playwrights often use this device to create a naturalistic flow of dialogue, allowing a second character to do the interrupting, as in this example:

> RICHARD: It's one more nail...
> BRIAN: I know.
> RICHARD: ...in the coffin of music hall.
>> Terry Johnson, *Dead Funny* (1994)

Pre-established Phrase Split By this, we mean a phrase that is spoken, then repeated with a split. It can be as simple as:

> HARRY: To hell with you! *(The man is motionless, silent)* To hell, sweetheart, with you.
>> John Whiting, *Marching Song* (1954)

Or it can involve a more complex division, as in this exchange, in which Paul not only splits his own phrase 'I am more', but also John's 'a rubber stamp':

> JOHN: I thought you were a rubber stamp.
> PAUL: I am more, I am much much much more than a rubber as you put it stamp.
>> Mark Ravenhill, *The Cut* (2006)

APOSTROPHE from the Greek meaning 'turning away'.
To turn from general address to a specific person (usually absent) or an intangible entity, such as Honour or Reputation, or – as in this example – the gods:

> ANTONY: For Brutus as you know was Caesar's angel.
> Judge, O ye gods, how dearly Caesar loved him.
> William Shakespeare, *Julius Caesar* (1599)

Even an inanimate object can be addressed:

> MRS DARLING: Dear night-lights that protect my sleeping babes, burn clear and steadfast tonight.
> J.M. Barrie, *Peter Pan* (1904)

LENGTH OF PHRASE

PARALLELISM from the Greek meaning 'side by side'.
The repetition of the same grammatical structure in consecutive phrases or sentences, often involving ANTITHESIS or various forms of REPETITION (see Chapter 8).

Consider this character's ardent insistence:

> WORTHY: Behold a burning lover at your feet, his fever raging in his veins! See how he trembles, how he pants! See how he glows, how he consumes!
> John Vanbrugh, *The Relapse* (1696)

When this structure is shared between two characters, there is distinct sense of REPARTEE:

> WORTHY: You've a great deal of courage, madam, to venture into the walks where you were so lately frightened.
> MELINDA: And you have a quantity of impudence to appear before me, that you have so lately affronted.
> George Farquhar, *The Recruiting Officer* (1706)

Parallel Imagery (see also Comparative Parallels under SIMILE): Menenius in Shakespeare's *Coriolanus* (1608) says of the eponymous warrior 'There is no more mercy in him than there is milk in a male tiger'. Leo in David Edgar's *Pentecost* (1994) has flown using the national airline of an unspecified south-eastern European country, saying it 'is to civil aviation what Van Gogh was to cosmetic surgery'. And here's a rather unusual one:

VAL: ...in the same way that a plant takes oxygen and nutrients and uses the process of photosynthesis to turn sunlight into energy, I take customers and employees and use the process of hard fucking work to produce cash.

Dennis Kelly, *Love and Money* (2006)

ISOCOLON (eye-soh-*coh*-lon) from the Greek meaning 'equal parts'.
A form of PARALLELISM in which phrases or sentences are more evidently of the same length and formation, usually involving some form of REPETITION.

OXFORD: Not a sun but I thought of you, not a laugh but I heard yours, not a game but I saw you play it, not a pageant but I remembered your hurrah.

Anthony Minghella, *Two Planks And A Passion* (1984)

There is often an element of conscious cleverness in this device (see also EPIGRAM):

JACK: When one is in town one amuses oneself. When one is in the country one amuses other people.

Oscar Wilde, *The Importance of Being Earnest* (1895)

Once again, where two characters are involved there is a strong sense of REPARTEE:

ELYOT: Feminine intuition, very difficult.
AMANDA: Feminine determination, very praiseworthy.
Noël Coward, *Private Lives* (1930)

PARISOSIS (pa-ree-*soh*-sis) from the Greek meaning 'making equal'.
When clauses or sentences have equal lengths in terms of syllables. This is most common in verse drama, of course, due to the strictures of the metrical line:

LORENZO: Sister, what means this melancholy walk?
BEL-IMPERIA: That for a while I wish no company.
LORENZO: But here the prince is come to visit you.
BEL-IMPERIA: That argues that he lives in liberty.
BALTHAZAR: No madam, but in pleasing servitude.
Thomas Kyd, *The Spanish Tragedy* (c.1592)

Yet again it commonly involves elements of REPETITION and a strong sense of REPARTEE when it occurs between two characters:

YOUNG BELLAIR: He thinks himself the pattern of modern gallantry.
DORIMANT: He is indeed the pattern of modern foppery.
George Etherege, *The Man of Mode* (1676)

It is interesting to spot this device in contemporary writing, where it is far subtler. Consider Isobel in David Hare's *The Secret Rapture* (1988), who states 'We've been years together. We know each other's ways'; each sentence has the same number of syllables, echoing perhaps her simple statement of fact. And in this example two medical test patients bond and become attuned to each other's rhythms:

TRISTAN: I'm climbing the fucking walls.
CONNIE: I'd kill for a cigarette.
TRISTAN: I snuck out once for a fag.
Lucy Prebble, *The Effect* (2012)

HYPOZEUXIS (hy-poze-*yook*-sis) from the Greek meaning 'under the yoke'. Subsequent clauses in a sentence that each have independent subjects and verbs.

In David Mamet's *American Buffalo* (1975) Don pithily states that 'Action talks and bullshit walks'. Mrs Hardcastle in Oliver Goldsmith's *She Stoops to Conquer* (1771) says 'My bureau has been broke open, the jewels taken out, and I'm undone!' And here are five in a row:

SARAH: People come and people go, wars destroy, accidents kill and plagues starve –
Arnold Wesker, *Chicken Soup With Barley* (1958)

BREVITY

BRACHYLOGY (brak-*il*-uh-jee) from the Greek meaning literally 'short word'. A general term for brevity of expression, of which the following devices are types.

ELLIPSIS (el-*lip*-sis) from the Greek meaning a 'falling short' or 'omission'. To leave out extraneous or repetitious words for economy of speech. It usually involves not repeating a required word or phrase, leaving it silently understood. This is extremely common in everyday speech, and therefore appears frequently in dramatic writing.

Most often, of course, **Nouns** are replaced by pronouns or other alternatives – as in this example, in which the nouns 'interests' and 'truth' are not repeated, but replaced respectively by the words 'others' and 'it':

MARTIN: Some interests are furthered by finding the truth, others by destroying it.

John Osborne, Luther (1961)

Less commonly, a noun is not repeated at all, as when Fabritio in Middleton's *Women Beware Women* (1621) says 'Th' art a sweet lady, sister, and a witty'; 'lady' is not repeated, but is clearly understood. The 7th Juror in Reginald Rose's *Twelve Angry Men* (1956) remarks 'I'm tellin' ya, this is the craziest'; the omission of the noun 'thing' emphasizes the adjective 'craziest'. The missing out of a noun is a very common trait in Restoration plays, as being an affectation of the period. Here both characters omit the word 'servant':

MR SNAKE: Mr Surface, your most obedient.
JOSEPH SURFACE: Sir, your very devoted.

Richard Brinsley Sheridan, The School for Scandal (1777)

Equally a nominal *phrase* is often not repeated, again for concision; it is a very common colloquial form. In the following example the phrase 'half of my life was' is not repeated:

NIJO: The first half of my life was all sin and the second all repentance.

Caryl Churchill, Top Girls (1982)

Very often **Verbs** are not repeated, as when Lady Fulbank in Aphra Behn's *The Lucky Chance* (1686) declares 'How happy had I been, how prosperous he!' – the 'had been' is not repeated, but is clearly understood. Susan in Alan Ayckbourn's *Woman in Mind* (1987) replies to Gerald's 'We've agreed that we mustn't prejudge' with the wonderfully terse 'I didn't and I have'; her economy of phrase matches her acerbic mood. A verbal *phrase* can equally be left unrepeated, as 'exist without a soul' is in the following example. Again, this commonly occurs in colloquial English:

MR STATE: A business can no more exist without a soul than a human being can.

Harley Granville Barker, The Madras House (1910)

ASYNDETON (ass-*in*-duh-ton) from the Greek meaning 'without bond'. To leave out conjunctions (the opposite of POLYSYNDETON).

The Parson in John Arden's *Serjeant Musgrave's Dance* (1959) claims that he 'cannot be seen to countenance idleness, pauperism, beggary'; the lack of conjunctions strengthens his point, by making its delivery punchy and direct.

This device is not purely about concision however. Consider the following example if it were written with 'and's linking every phrase (POLYSYNDETON). It would create a very different energy – a weariness possibly, as opposed to the active energy of the ASYNDETON:

> LEO: Now, building, construction, engineering, architecture... these
> have effects.
>
> David Greig, *The Architect* (1996)

ECPHONESIS (ek-fon-*ee*-sis) from the Greek meaning to 'sound out loud' or 'exclamation'. A single word or short phrase with an exclamation mark.

Single Words Pizarro in Peter Shaffer's *The Royal Hunt of the Sun* (1964) bolsters the courage of his men saying that the Inca King 'must see gods walk on earth. Indifferent! Uncrushable!' – the single, polysyllabic words are urgent and defiant. Mercutio in Shakespeare's *Romeo and Juliet* (1595) taunts Romeo with 'Humours! Madman! Passion! Lover!' – each one a rhythmic, teasing poke. And consider the effect of this declaration:

> MICHAEL: We will stamp the filth of the Tutsi cockroaches out of our
> country once and for all. Vermin! Rats! Snakes!
>
> Tanika Gupta, *Sanctuary* (2002)

This device was a great favourite of the Restoration playwrights, who enjoyed such expletives as 'Pho!', 'Pshaw!', 'Zounds!' and 'Egad!' They would also have characters utter a single noun to convey their feelings at extreme moments, as in this example:

> MRS MARWOOD: Disclose all to your wife – confess to her what has
> passed between us.
> MR FAINALL: Frenzy!
>
> William Congreve, *The Way of the World* (1700)

Speaking of extreme moments, we couldn't resist including an extract from the final moments of Michael Frayn's farce, *Noises Off* (2000 version). Here, the performance of *Nothing On* – the play within the play – is collapsing around the increasingly desperate cast. Language becomes abbreviated to barking one-word observations, meaningless to all but the speaker:

> VICKI: Bag! Bag! Bag!
> ROGER: Sardines! Sardines!
> VICKI: Bag! Bag! Bag!
> ROGER: Sardines! Sardines!
> VICKI: Bag! Bag! Bag!

Phrases This device can also include a succinct phrase, such as when four characters in an earlier Michael Frayn play, *Alphabetical Order* (1975), exclaim 'What a mess!' one after another, at the sight of the chaos in their newspaper cuttings library. Freda in J.B. Priestley's *Dangerous Corner* (1932), meanwhile, calls her radio-obsessed friends 'Dance fiends!' with a playful sense of HYPERBOLE.

The playwrights of the Restoration often use the specific form of a nominal HENDIADYS (see below) in deploying this device, as when Dorimant in George Etherege's *The Man of Mode* (1676) condemns Mrs Loveit's response to Sir Fopling Flutter's advances as 'Grimace and affectation!' A fop in piratical form, Captain Hook in J.M. Barrie's *Peter Pan* (1904) uses such expletives as 'Obesity and bunions', 'Brimstone and gall' and ''Sdeath and oddsfish'. And here's a fun piece of PARALLELISM between two characters, the servant matching his master:

> FASHION: Death and furies! 'Tis impossible!
> LORY: Fiends and spectres! Sir, 'tis true.
> > John Vanbrugh, *The Relapse* (1696)

HENDIADYS (hen-*dy*-uh-diss) from the Greek meaning 'one through two'.

Two words joined by a conjunction, in which neither is subordinate to the other, but work together to convey a single idea. There is a rhythm and balance to this device, celebrating each word as equal, rather than making one qualify the other.

Nouns This device is most usually deployed as two nouns joined by a conjunction, such as the commonly used 'life and soul' or 'airs and graces'.

Gwendolen in Oscar Wilde's *The Importance of Being Earnest* (1895) describes Mr Worthing as being 'the very soul of truth and honour'. Wilde could very easily have written either 'truthful honour' or 'honourable truth', but he chose the HENDIADYS, which seems more robust and unassailable.

This device can equally use 'or' instead of 'and' to join the two entities, as in this example:

> BLANCHE: I'll *steal* before I let a daughter show that man one ounce
> of ingratitude or disrespect.
> > Neil Simon, *Brighton Beach Memoirs* (1983)

Shakespeare is a huge fan of HENDIADYS. Think of Macbeth's 'sound and fury', Hamlet's 'enterprises of great pitch and moment' and Portia describing the 'awe and majesty' of monarchy. And here is Edgar imagining himself as Poor Tom:

> EDGAR: And with presented nakedness outface
> The winds and persecutions of the sky.
> > William Shakespeare, *King Lear* (c.1606)

HENDIADYS can, however, be used in other grammatical forms too:

Adjectives We often use pairs of adjectives such as 'nice and cosy', 'just and proper' and 'fine and dandy', in which one adjective could be replaced by a qualifying adverb (for instance 'nicely cosy'), but instead HENDIADYS is used.

Michael in Brian Friel's *Dancing at Lughnasa* (1990) speaks of his Uncle Jack looking 'radiant and splendid in his officer's uniform'. Salieri in Peter Shaffer's *Amadeus* (1979) describes God's eyes in a painting in his childhood church as making 'bargains, real and irreversible'.

Noël Coward was particularly inventive in this form. Judith in *Hay Fever* (1925) accuses her argumentative son, Simon, of being 'precocious and tiresome'. His sister, Sorel, condemns him for becoming 'far too blasé and exclusive'. The ghost Elvira in *Blithe Spirit* (1941) berates her living ex-husband for being 'smug and supercilious'; and here's his second wife:

> RUTH: ...we've both been married before – careless rapture at this
> stage would be incongruous and embarrassing.

Verbs When verbs are used – such as when the Prince in *Hamlet* (c.1601) says 'to grunt and sweat under a weary life' – one verb could be subordinated to the other by using an adverb instead (grunt sweatily), but once again HENDIADYS is often preferred.

Harriet in George Etherege's *The Man of Mode* (1676) berates men for always being 'willing to flatter and comply with the rich'. And here's a more modern example:

> MARY: I was so bashful all I could do was stammer and blush like a
> little fool.
>
> Eugene O'Neill, *Long Day's Journey Into Night* (c.1940)

Adverbs Even these can be used as HENDIADYS, since one could be subordinate to another by using an adjectival phrase. In the following example, Michael Frayn could have written 'patiently quiet' or 'quietly patient', but he chooses HENDIADYS:

> BRANDT: It's waiting so quietly and patiently, the earth down there.
>
> Michael Frayn, *Democracy* (2003)

HENDIADYS is often combined with the acoustic family of devices (see Chapter 2).

ALLITERATIVE HENDIADYS
Consider these common examples, using nouns: 'fame and fortune', 'health and happiness' and 'peace and prosperity'. Or using verbs: 'beg or borrow', 'chop and change' and 'rock 'n' roll'. Or using adjectives: 'rough and ready', 'great and good' and 'fast and furious'. It is often deployed with TAUTOLOGY too, as in the nouns 'rack and ruin' and

'rules and regulations', the verbs 'tried and tested', 'weep and wail' and 'twist and turn', or the adjectives 'hale and hearty' and 'first and foremost'.

Here are some fine examples from plays using nouns: the arms manufacturer Undershaft in George Bernard Shaw's *Major Barbara* (1905) describes himself as 'a profiteer in mutilation and murder'; there is a certain gloating satisfaction in the effect. Elyot in Noël Coward's *Private Lives* (1930) berates Victor for being 'all fuss and fume'; wonderfully belittling. The marvellous Bob Acres in Richard Brinsley Sheridan's *The Rivals* (1775) deploys Alliterative Hendiadys as a character trait – using such terrific expletives as 'Odds whips and wheels!', 'Odds blushes and blooms!', 'Odds bullets and blades!' and 'Odds fire and fury!'.

Deploying this device with verbs, Liz in John Osborne's *Inadmissible Evidence* (1964) tells off Bill, with whom she is having an affair, with 'You beggar and belittle yourself just to get out of the game'; her point driven home by the HENDIADYS and its plosive ALLITERATION. And here is a defiant example:

> MRS FAINALL: My youth may wear and waste, but it shall never rust in my possession.
>> William Congreve, *The Way of the World* (1700)

Using adjectives, Alan Turing in Hugh Whitemore's *Breaking the Code* (1986) refers to the work as 'An impossibly lengthy and laborious process'; the combined devices somehow make the procedure seem longer and more burdensome. Consider the self-effacing quality of the ALLITERATION in this example:

> DYSART: I settled for being pallid and provincial, out of my own eternal timidity.
>> Peter Shaffer, *Equus* (1973)

SIBILANT HENDIADYS
This appears often. Think of 'signed and sealed' and 'safe and sound'.It is also used as ONOMATOPOEIA to achieve a sense of whispered secrecy or intimacy, as in this example from John Dryden, in which Cleopatra cradles the dying Antony:

> CLEOPATRA: We're now alone, in secrecy and silence; And is not this like lovers?
>> John Dryden, *All for Love* (1677)

ASSONANT HENDIADYS
This seems even more common than its alliterative cousin above. Consider phrases like 'smash and grab', 'keen and eager', 'free and easy' 'high and dry', 'high and mighty',

'hot and bothered', 'down and out', 'blood and thunder', 'cut and thrust' and 'rough and tumble'.

The doleful lawyer Graves in Edward Bulwer-Lytton's *Money* (1840) condemns the newspapers as being 'Daily calendars of roguery and woe'; nothing much has changed there then! Berlin, in David Greig's *Europe* (1994), meanwhile, claims he likes the political far right because 'It's dumb and blunt'; the repeated 'U' sounds echoing the sense. And here, Tamburlaine has asked a young virgin what she can perceive at the tip of his sword; she is unable to answer:

> TAMBURLAINE: Your fearful minds are thick and misty then,
> For there sits Death.
>
> Christopher Marlowe, *Tamburlaine the Great: Part One* (1587)

PARACHESIC HENDIADYS

This occurs often enough too. These repeated combinations of sounds most often occur at the beginning of words, such as in the pairings of 'prim and proper', 'pride and prejudice', 'spick and span', 'kith and kin', 'vim and vigour' and 'forgive and forget'.

Amidst the complicated mesh of love in T.S. Eliot's *The Cocktail Party* (1949), Celia wonders anxiously whether they are all 'unloving and unlovable'; the awful realization economically put in this ornately rhetorical form.

Less commonly, PARACHESIS occurs in the middle of words. For instance Kate Middleton in Mike Bartlett's *King Charles III* (2014) claims she is meant to be 'A male-created bland and standard wife'; the repeated 'and' sound somehow echoes the sentiment and even her attitude towards it. Meanwhile, Stephen in David Hare's *A Map of the World* (1983) says that right-wing politicians always have 'Form and decorum' on their side; the repeated 'or' sound is wonderfully hollow and plummy, representative of the upper classes that form the conservative right perhaps. This is worth exploring for the actor, though always within the bounds of taste!

PARACHESIS often occurs as repeated sounds at both the beginnings and ends of words, as in the phrases 'brain versus brawn' and 'flora and fauna'. Mrs Foresight in Congreve's *Love for Love* (1695) accuses the forward Mr Scandal of being 'impertinent and impudent'. And here's a consciously clever (and rather sexist) one describing the feminine influence on politics:

> CONSTANTINE: ...the nursery cotton wool of prettiness and pettiness.
>
> Harley Granville Barker, *The Madras House* (1910)

HOMOIOTELEUTONIC HENDIADYS

This is understandably common, due to the memorable rhyming of the paired words.

Classics include 'fair and square', 'moan and groan', 'loud and proud', 'hustle and bustle', 'wear and tear', 'nearest and dearest', 'odds and sods', 'flotsam and jetsam' and 'doom and gloom'.

Exasperated by her husband, Ruth in Lorraine Hansberry's *A Raisin in the Sun* (1959) exclaims 'you'll be fussing and cussing round here like a mad man!' Hatch in Edward Bond's *The Sea* (1973) miserably says to the villagers 'I tried to save you from your foolishness and selfishness' and promptly starts to cry; the two words seem splashily to herald his tears. And here's an example from Shakespeare:

> LADY PERCY: Never, O never, do his ghost the wrong
> To hold your honour more precise and nice
> With others than with him!
>
> William Shakespeare, *Henry IV Part Two* (c.1598)

HENDIATRIS (hen-*dy*-uh-triss) from the Greek meaning 'one through three'. Three words joined by conjunctions, in which none is subordinated to another, but work together to convey a single idea. Other definitions often blur this device with the TRICOLON (see Chapter 7) when in fact it is just a *form* of TRICOLON.

Even more rhythmic than HENDIADYS above, it should still be possible to put the three parts of a HENDIATRIS another way, with one or two of the words restated as qualifiers. Consider the classic description of snow as 'deep and crisp and even', which could be restated as 'deeply and crisply even' or 'evenly crisp and deep' or as one of several other permutations.

Stephen in David Hare's *A Map of the World* (1983) warns Mehta with 'You must endure dictatorship and bloodshed and barbarity'. Dearth in J.M. Barrie's *Dear Brutus* (1917) berates his daughter for speaking out of turn, saying 'It is wicked and stupid and naughty'. Both examples use the device to hammer home the point, strongly rhythmic and insistent. Here's another adjectival example, in which Roxanna warns her work-obsessed father:

> ROXANNA: You'll probably go to seed, become flabby and destructive and boring.
>
> Stephen Poliakoff, *Playing With Trains* (1989)

Here are two other pleasing effects using this device: in the first, from Stephen Jeffreys' *The Libertine* (1994), the Earl of Rochester compliments the actress Elizabeth Barry on a comic performance with 'You were light and larky and true'; the sprung rhythm of the device reflecting what it describes. Whereas the monosyllabic weight of the three words in the following example create the opposite effect:

CASCA: I have seen
Th' ambitious ocean swell and rage and foam,
To be exalted with the threatening clouds.

William Shakespeare, *Julius Caesar* (1599)

This seems to be a favourite device of John Osborne's. Jimmy in *Look Back in Anger* (1956) claims that 'One of us is mean and crazy and stupid'. Steinbauer, dressed in drag in *A Patriot for Me* (1965), quotes his horrified priest as saying 'You're a soldier, a man of courage and honour and virtue'. And here's Archie Rice:

ARCHIE: She was poor and lonely and oppressed like nobody you've ever known.

John Osborne, *The Entertainer* (1957)

HENDIATETRIS (hen-*dy*-uh-*tet*-riss) from the Greek meaning 'one through four'. Four words joined by conjunctions, in which none is subordinated to another, but work together to convey a single idea (see also POLYSYNDETON).

Sir Percy woefully summarizes having an affair with a younger woman, in Alan Bennett's *Habeas Corpus* (1973), as a 'A fantasy of frustration and loneliness and sadness and despair'. These could be restated as 'frustrated loneliness and sad despair' or as 'frustrated, lonely, sad despair' or as 'lonely frustration and desperate sadness'... (we could go on) – but the separating of each entity in the HENDIATETRIS allows each to stand alone, at the same time as building a particular and complex image. Consider this, too – Hickey's description of his long-suffering wife, Evelyn:

HICKEY: It was written all over her face, sweetness and love and pity and forgiveness.

Eugene O'Neill, *The Iceman Cometh* (1939)

EXCESS

CLIMAX from the Greek meaning 'ladder' or 'flight of stairs'.
Words, phrases or sentences arranged in ascending power. A host of other rhetorical devices are used to achieve CLIMAX! These include all kinds of REPETITION and the rhythmic structural devices, such as AMPLIFICATION, SCESIS ONOMATON, PARALLELISM and TRICOLON.

Consider this LIST tumbling towards the threat against Bellinda's reputation, which is – after all – everything in the Restoration:

DORIMANT: I vow revenge, resolve to pursue and persecute you more impertinently than ever any loving fop did his mistress, hunt you i' the Park, trace you i' the Mall, dog you in every visit you make, haunt you at the plays and i' the drawing room, hang my nose in your neck, and talk to you whether you will or no, and ever look upon you with such dying eyes, till your friends grow jealous of me, send you out of town, and the world suspect your reputation.

George Etherege, *The Man of Mode* (1676)

More than one character can, of course, help to create a climactic effect. In this extraordinary extract, two nuclear physicists and the wife of one of them discuss how nuclear fission could be used to create a nuclear bomb. Note how the numerical growth is matched by the METAPHORICAL avalanche:

BOHR: What happens in fission? You fire a neutron at a uranium nucleus,
it splits, and it releases energy.
MARGRETHE: A huge amount of energy. Yes?
BOHR: About enough to move a speck of dust. But it also releases two or three more neutrons. Each of which has the chance of splitting another nucleus.
MARGRETHE: So then those two or three split nuclei each release energy in their turn?
BOHR: And two or three more neutrons.
HEISENBERG: You start a trickle of snow sliding as you ski. The trickle becomes a snowball...
BOHR: An ever-widening chain of split nuclei forks through the uranium, doubling and quadrupling in millionths of a second from one generation to the next. First two splits, let's say for simplicity. Then two squared, two cubed, two to the fourth, two to the fifth, two to the sixth...
HEISENBERG: The thunder of the gathering avalanche echoes from all the surrounding mountains...

Michael Frayn, *Copenhagen* (1998)

AUXESIS (orx-*ee*-sis) from the Greek meaning 'growth' or 'increase'.
Words, phrases or sentences organized to create a climactic effect; a more formally structured CLIMAX. This device tends to use more obvious structures, such as forms of REPETITION, like the GRADATIO in this speech:

> SIR JOHN VESEY: On the strength of his services I got a pension of four hundred pounds a year; on the strength of four hundred pounds a year I took credit for eight hundred pounds; on the strength of eight hundred pounds a year I married your mother with ten thousand pounds; on the strength of ten thousand pounds I took credit for forty thousand pounds and paid Dicky Gossip three guineas a week to go about everywhere calling me 'Stingy Jack'.
>
> Edward Bulwer-Lytton, *Money* (1840)

POLYSYNDETON (*pol*-iss-*in*-duh-tun) from the Greek 'many bonds'.
The repeated use of conjunctions, usually for emphasis (see also HENDIATETRIS above).

With 'And' This is how this device occurs most commonly:

> BRINDSLEY: She was beautiful and tender and considerate and kind and loyal and witty and adorable in every way!
>
> Peter Shaffer, *Black Comedy* (1965)

His gushing account is reflected in his over-use of the conjunctions. It is not usually deployed as excessively as this. Generally, it is used simply to create a simple LIST:

> CLIVE: This whole continent is my enemy. I am pitching my whole mind and will and reason and spirit against it to tame it...
>
> Caryl Churchill, *Cloud Nine* (1979)

Or even used as a narrative link, with the sense of one thing leading to another:

> ARIEL: Little kids are gonna follow me around and they're gonna know my name and what I stood for, and they're gonna give me some of their sweets in thanks, and I'm gonna take those sweets and thank them and tell them to get home safe, and I'm gonna be happy.
>
> Martin McDonagh, *The Pillowman* (2003)

With 'Or' This can be as simple as when Justice Overdo in Ben Jonson's *Bartholomew Fair* (1614) asks Quarlous 'Do you want a house or meat or drink or clothes?' Or the more compelling and excessive:

> GOOPER: I don't give a goddam if Big Daddy likes me or don't like me or did or never did or will or will never!
>
> Tennessee Williams, *Cat on a Hot Tin Roof* (1955)

With 'Nor' In addition, it can be made negative, of course:

KATHRYN: Her kitchen's no comparison with mine. Nor her cooks. Nor her hangings. Nor her bed.

Anthony Minghella, *Two Planks And A Passion* (1984)

PARATAXIS (pa-ruh-*tak*-sis) from the Greek meaning 'placing side by side'.

Successive independent clauses with or without conjunctions (the opposite of HYPOTAXIS).

With Conjunctions Consider this case of pre-affair nerves:

MURIEL: I have three children and I'm very happy and I have a wonderful life and I have no business being in a hotel room in New York at three o'clock in the afternoon with a man I haven't seen since Tavern on the Green seventeen years ago – *(He kisses her on the lips.)*

Neil Simon, *Plaza Suite* (1968)

Without Conjunctions As in this example:

MAX: We'd walk into a place, the whole room'd stand up, they'd make way to let us pass.

Harold Pinter, *The Homecoming* (1965)

LIST from the Old English meaning a 'border' or 'strip'.

Self-explanatory (see also ENUMERATIO). Cicely Berry holds that a LIST is never just a shopping list, but a run of individual items or qualities in which to invest.

It can be as simple as a catalogue of nouns, as with this liver-shivering example:

ROBIN: If thou't go but to the tavern with me, I'll give thee white wine, claret wine, sack, muskadine, malmesey, and whippincrust. Hold, belly, hold.

Christopher Marlowe, *Doctor Faustus* (c.1589)

Or a series of adjectives to describe one noun, as in this declaration, in which John assigns attributes to his wife – moving from negative to positive as the LIST grows, in this, the penultimate line of the play. Sadly (spoiler alert!) she is not convinced by his appeal:

JOHN: You are the most maddening, wilful, capricious, wrongheaded, delightful, and enchanting woman man was ever cursed with having for a wife.

W. Somerset Maugham, *The Constant Wife* (1926)

Or it can be altogether more complex and insistent, as in this example:

> ROSALIND: I set him every day to woo me: at which time would I, being
> but a moonish youth, grieve, be effeminate, changeable, longing and
> liking, proud, fantastical, apish, shallow, inconstant, full of tears, full of
> smiles, for every passion something and for no passion truly anything,
> as boys and women are for the most part cattle of this colour...
>
> William Shakespeare, *As You Like It* (c.1600)

SYSTROPHE (*sis*-truh-fee) from the Greek meaning a 'gathering together'.
The listing of many qualities of someone or something without providing a definition –
leaving the listener to make the connections and draw a conclusion.

In this example, the Steward is peddling facts about Sir Thomas More, but offering
no conclusion:

> STEWARD: I mean I could have told him any number of things about
> Sir Thomas – that he has rheumatism, prefers red wine to white, is
> easily sea-sick, fond of kippers, afraid of drowning.
>
> Robert Bolt, *A Man for All Seasons* (1960)

BOMPHIOLOGY (*bom*-fee-*ol*-uh-jee) from the Greek meaning 'booming words'.
Excessive bragging or self-aggrandizement, with the sense that it is true but exaggerated.
Perhaps surprisingly, it was a device actually practised in classical times; an early form of
shameless self-promotion.

Here a TV producer – despite his claims to the contrary – boasts about the guests he
is able to secure for his show:

> DOMINIC: People are begging to appear on our show...
> AMY: I know...
> DOMINIC: I don't even write to them! Painters! Writers! Musicians!
> Truly. I'm not boasting. I'm not. We don't even have to approach
> them. Really. You'd be astonished. We've reached the point where
> nearly always *they* approach *us*.
>
> David Hare, *Amy's View* (1997)

RODOMONTADE (*rod*-uh-mon-*tard*) from the name Rodomonte, an arrogant and
boastful character who features in two epic poems of the Italian Renaissance, *Orlando
Innamorato* and its sequel *Orlando Furioso*.

Vain or pretentious boasting, with a sense too that it is unfounded (as opposed to BOMPHIOLOGY above).

Here, the titular hero of the play arrogantly imagines the reaction on the day he is hanged:

> CHRISTY: And won't there be crying out in Mayo the day I'm stretched upon the rope, with ladies in their silks and satins snivelling in their lacy kerchiefs, and they rhyming songs and ballads on the terror of my fate?
>
> J.M. Synge, *The Playboy of the Western World* (1907)

VERBOSITY

LOGORRHOEA (log-uh-*ree*-ah) from the Greek meaning 'flow of words'.
The polite word for verbal diarrhoea! By its very nature, lengthy.

See Philip's nervous rant about smoking in Christopher Hampton's *The Philanthropist* (1970), Carr's ramblings of memory in Tom Stoppard's *Travesties* (1993 edition) or Louis' neurotic tirades in Tony Kushner's *Angels In America* (1991). Here, however, is a mere extract from what is perhaps the most extreme example of this device in drama. Without punctuation or, indeed, clear sense, it is at once unsettling and bizarrely poetic:

> LUCKY: ...but time will tell and suffers like the divine Miranda with those who for reasons unknown but time will tell are plunged in torment plunged in fire whose fire flames if that continues and who can doubt it will fire the firmament that is to say blast hell to heaven so blue still and calm so calm with a calm which even though intermittent is better than nothing but not so fast...
>
> Samuel Beckett, *Waiting for Godot* (1955)

MACROLOGIA (*mak*-ruh-*lodj*-ee-uh) from the Greek meaning 'long speech'.
Speech full of over-description and superfluous words – often employing REPETITIONS, SYNONYMY and TAUTOLOGY.

In the following example, the playwright deftly uses this elaborate device to give a glimpse into the character – in rehearsals, one would need to decide whether Deeley's use of language springs from a desire to be precise, or to unsettle:

> DEELEY: I use the word globe because the word world possesses emotional political sociological and psychological pretensions and

resonances which I prefer as a matter of choice to do without, or
shall I say to steer clear of, or if you like to reject.
Harold Pinter, Old Times (1971)

PLEONASM (*plee*-on-az-um) from the Greek meaning 'more than enough'.
The use of superfluous or redundant words, which would not affect the sense if they
were omitted. They are merely a sort of verbal punctuation.

Consider 'I mean', 'basically' and 'let's face it' in this example from Alan Ayckbourn,
the master of such acutely observed writing:

> DIANA: I mean, I know I'm running myself down but Paul basically,
> he's got much more go – well, I mean let's face it, he's much cleverer
> than me. Let's face it. Basically.
Alan Ayckbourn, Absent Friends (1974)

The PLEONASM is often deployed by playwrights as a character trait. Mistress Quickly
in Shakespeare's *The Merry Wives of Windsor* (c.1598) punctuates much of what she says
with the affirming phrase 'I warrant you'. Another character who indulges in PLEONASM
is Boniface, who repeatedly uses the phrase 'as the saying is' with absolutely no regard
to meaning, as here:

> BONIFACE: Well, daughter, as the saying is, have you brought Martin
> to confess? CHERRY: Pray, father, don't put me upon getting
> anything out of a man; I'm but young, you know, father, and I don't
> understand wheedling.
> BONIFACE: Young! Why, you jade, as the saying is, can any woman
> wheedle that is not young? Your mother was useless at five-and-
> twenty. Not wheedle! Would you make your mother a whore, and
> me a cuckhold, as the saying is?
George Farquhar, The Beaux' Stratagem (1707)

SYNCHISIS (*sin*-kiss-iss) from the Greek meaning 'gushing together', and so
'confusion'. Sometimes spelled SYNCHYSIS.
1) Confused or clumsy word order or sentence structure, usually fuelled by anger or
confusion.

In dramatic writing such clumsiness of expression results in the appearance of fractured
thoughts. It is always interesting to consider whether a character's thoughts are being
completed or self-interrupted.

Here, a character is embarrassed by his own un-PC remark:

> BRUCE: I know I just said it but – I shouldn't have – I was – humouring
> – I was, you know – it's a no-no.
> > Joe Penhall, *Blue/Orange* (2000)

2) We have found evidence of this confused sentence structure gaining a more formalized shape with an interlocked word order in the pattern A-B-A-B, as in this example:

> ADA: ...you have eyes and tongue to see and talk...
> > Arnold Wesker, *I'm Talking About Jerusalem* (1960)

It is the 'eyes' (A) that 'see' (A), and the 'tongue' (B) that 'talks' (B), but the two phrases have been interwoven, creating a rather quaint effect (see also ANASTROPHE below).

This version of the device can be extended into GRAMMATICAL SYNCHISIS, which seems far more common. It is when parts of speech are used in the A-B-A-B pattern, lending a strong sense of PARALLELISM.

In Ben Jonson's *Volpone* (1605-6) the protagonist wisely pronounces 'To be a fool born is a disease incurable'; the inversion of the normal word order points up the synchisic structure of noun/adjective, noun/adjective. When Hester in Athol Fugard's *Hello and Goodbye* (1965) says 'Four walls that rattled and a roof that leaked!' – the sentence is again structured A-B-A-B, although this time with noun/verb, noun/verb. And consider this beautifully antithetical line:

> LADY MACDUFF: All is the fear and nothing is the love.
> > William Shakespeare, *Macbeth* (1606)

ANACOLUTHON (*an*-uh-col-*ooth*-on) from the Greek meaning 'not following'. An abrupt change in grammatical construction within the same sentence, often with a superceding point. It starts as one sentence, then ends as another – a clumsy form of AMPLIFICATION – which creates a very colloquial and immediate effect.

Consider this example, which turns into a question mid-way:

> ALISTAIR: He reckons it gives him the right to sneer at us 'cause he's what, honest, decent, hardworking?
> > Laura Wade, *Posh* (2012)

AUREATION (or-ree-*ay*-shun) from the Latin meaning 'golden', and therefore 'highly ornamented'.

The use of Latinate or polysyllabic words to 'heighten' diction for a character. This usually belongs in the mouths of well-educated characters or insufferable and pretentious pedants.

Hugh in Brian Friel's *Translations* (1981) talks of 'truths immemorially posited'; the latinate words are unsurprising in the mouth of a man who runs a 'hedge school' in Ireland. Miss Pert abuses the lawyer Mr Meddle in Dion Boucicault's *London Assurance* (1841), who responds with 'Don't calumniate my calling, or disseminate vulgar prejudices'; angular words, pretentiously used. Bennett, the communist butler in Tom Stoppard's *Travesties* (1993 edition), describes the Russian Revolution as 'a revolution of classes contraposed by the fissiparous disequilibrium of Russian society'; hilarious in its desiccated exactitude (we're at it now!).

This device lends itself to a surprising number of possible effects. Consider the dangerous sarcasm of this example:

> LENNY: Do you detect a certain logical incoherence in the central affirmations of Christian theism?
>> Harold Pinter, *The Homecoming* (1965)

Or the pompous pretensions of the Bishop in mistaking a porn shoot for the Women's Institute 'shooting their Advent Calendar':

> BISHOP: Ample ladies of unimpeachable morals, their salient features artfully occluded.
>> Alan Bennett, *People* (2012)

Or the affronted dignity of Adolphus Spanker, who is under the misapprehension that his wife, Lady Gay, is having an affair, and so takes issue with her calling him 'Dolly' – her usual pet name for him:

> ADOLPHUS SPANKER: Pardon me, Lady Gay Spanker, I conceive your mutilation of my sponsorial appellation highly derogatory to my *amour propre*.
>> Dion Boucicault, *London Assurance* (1841)

SESQUIPEDALIANISM (*ses*-kwi-ped-*ail*-ee-an-iz-um) from the Latin meaning 'a foot and half long'.
Long-winded language characterized by the use of long words – grandiloquent, if you will (see also AUREATION above).

Here's a wonderful example from a Justice of the Peace:

TAPPERCOOM: The whole thing's a lot of amphigourious
                Stultiloquential fiddle-faddle.
            Christopher Fry, *The Lady's Not For Burning* (1948)

And here the lawyer's reputation for incomprehensibility seems not to have changed over the centuries:

LAWYER: Most literated judges, please your lordships
          So to connive your judgements to the view
          Of this debauched and diversivolent woman,
          Who such a black concatenation
          Of mischief hath effected, that to extirp
          The memory of't must be the consummation
          Of her and her projections.
            John Webster, *The White Devil* (1612)

ARCHAISM (*ar*-kay-iz-um) from the Greek meaning 'ancient'.
The use of an old-fashioned or obsolete word or grammatical form.

A classic is that cliché of wedding speeches: 'It behoves me...' Elements of ALLUSION and EUPHEMISM abound in this device.

    Chief Whip Mellish in James Graham's *This House* (2012) refers to the Labour Party's meagre majority as possibly creating 'the shortest government that e'er bloody lived'; his ironic use of the Shakespearean 'e'er' for 'ever' places their situation in a mock historical context. The Oedipus figure Eddy in Steven Berkoff's *Greek* (1980) uses a more extreme cod-Shakespearean vernacular when he claims 'a villain hard faced doth distribute a bit of sense with bars of iron'. A 'hard-faced villain' would be the more normal word order, as would 'iron bars' instead of 'bars of iron'; he also uses 'doth', the old form of 'does'. And here cod-Biblical language is employed in response to 'Thou shall not kill' in a playful mock TV debate:

BRI: Except when it shall come to pass that thy trade routes shall be
in jeopardy.
         Peter Nichols, *A Day In The Death Of Joe Egg* (1967)

ANASTROPHE (an-*ass*-truh-fee) from the Greek meaning 'turning back'.
The inversion of normal word order, often to appear quaint or old-fashioned, such as 'Unaccustomed as I am to public speaking...' – another cliché of wedding speeches.

There is often a feeling of PARODY with this device, when a character uses cod-Biblical or cod-Shakespearean language. Lady Chiltern in Oscar Wilde's *An Ideal Husband* (1895) warns 'That great inheritance throw not away – that tower of ivory do not destroy'. George in Edward Albee's *Who's Afraid of Virginia Woolf?* (1962) taunts his guests Nick and Honey with such pronouncements as 'Blondie and his frau out of the plain states came'; his barely-hidden derision heightened by the quaint sentence structure. The most common usage, however, is to create an effect of pedantry or pretension:

> HEADMASTER: We have forgotten since how strong and fresh and pure was in those days the first sensation of speed.
>
> Alan Bennett, *Forty Years On* (1968)

Another common use of this device is when foreign characters speak pidgin English. Einstein, the German doctor in Joseph Kesselring's *Arsenic and Old Lace* (1941), says such things as 'It's like comes true a beautiful dream'. Alternatively, a character who speaks a vernacular *influenced* by a foreign language, such as the New York Jewish turn of phrase that Eddie uses in Neil Simon's *Lost In Yonkers* (1990) when he explains 'He cried in my bedroom. Not like a man, like a child he cried'.

Chapter 7 The Rule of Three

FRIAR: Acknowledge what thou art,
            A wretch, a worm, a nothing; weep, sigh, pray
            Three times a day, and three times every night.
                        John Ford, *'Tis Pity She's a Whore* (c.1629)

The Rule of Three – or TRICOLON, as it is more formally called – crops up in all walks of life – here, there and everywhere, you might say. We love jokes involving threes (an Englishman, a Scotsman and an Irishman went into a pub...). There are three primary colours, three dimensions, three states of being. Three Musketeers, Three Stooges, Three Graces. Bad luck comes in threes, yet third time is lucky. You score a hat trick, but three strikes and you're out. We give each other three cheers, yet three's a crowd. We have musical trios, film trilogies and painted triptychs. We strive for Faith, Hope and Charity; play Paper, Scissors, Stone; listen to our cereal go Snap, Crackle, Pop! It's everywhere!

We are introduced to the TRICOLON early in our lives by way of children's rhymes (think of 'Easy as ABC', 'Do Re Mi' and 'Three Blind Mice'). It also abounds in fairy tales – three wishes, three knocks at the door, three balls attended by Cinderella – and it is structurally important in such stories as *Three Little Pigs*, *Three Billy Goats Gruff* and *Goldilocks and the Three Bears*.

The history of politics and oratory is littered with threes, from Caesar's alleged declaration following his swift victory in the Pontic War – 'Veni, vidi, vici' (I came, I saw, I conquered) – to the French national motto 'Liberté, Égalité, Fraternité' (Liberty, Equality, Fraternity); from President Lincoln's Gettysburg address, at which he envisaged 'government of the people, by the people, for the people', to more recent pronouncements, such as Tony Blair's famous call for 'Education, education, education'.

Consider also Christianity, at the heart of which is the Holy Trinity. The faithful speak of 'One church, one faith, one Lord', and contemplate the three temptations of Christ, and the Parable of the Good Samaritan – in which a priest and a Levite pass by an injured man, but it is the third man, the Samaritan, who stops to help. And, of course, there are the Three Wise Men.

No one has come up with a definitive reason as to where our apparent obsession with threes comes from, though there are many theories. It certainly appears that we find things more memorable grouped in this way. There is also a distinct and pleasing rhythm to the TRICOLON, which plays a major part in why it is so rhetorically potent.

Unsurprisingly, the world of drama is similarly awash with threes – as this chapter will show. So prevalent is this device that, while it obviously belongs to the wider topic of Structure covered in Chapter 6, we decided it deserved a whole chapter to itself. So, roll your sleeves up and get stuck in. Or perhaps we should say 'Ready? Steady? Go!'

THE TRICOLONIC FAMILY

TRICOLON (try-*coh*-lon) from the Greek meaning 'in three parts'.
A phrase, sentence or speech comprising three parts in parallel. It can also provide a structural device for a whole scene or even an entire play – think of the three-act structure of the 'well-made' play.

There are two predominant variations:

1) Three separate and equal entities, such as 'lock, stock and barrel', 'eat, drink and be merry', or 'wine, women and song'.

Words This can be as simple as three adjectives describing one noun, as when Amanda in John Vanbrugh's *The Relapse* (1696) denounces Loveless as a 'base, ungrateful, perjured villain!' Or it can be three verbs, as when Sir, the actor-manager in Ronald Harwood's *The Dresser* (1980), refuses to cancel a performance of *King Lear*, saying 'Can't. Mustn't. Won't.' Or even three adverbs, as when Cheviot in W.S. Gilbert's *Engaged* (1877) proclaims 'I love that girl, madly, passionately, irresistibly'.

Perhaps most common, however, are sets of three nouns, as in King Henry's 'Cry God for Harry, England and Saint George!' in Shakespeare's *Henry V* (c.1599), or this double-whammy:

> AUNG: Americans are the Romans – power, armies, strength.
> The English are the Greeks – ideas, civilization, intellect.
> David Hare, *Plenty* (1978)

Phrases These are very often deployed with PROZEUGMA – as in this example, in which the word 'after' governs each of the three parts of the TRICOLON (for more examples, see under **With WIT**, below):

> HIPPOLITO: My lord, after long search, wary inquiries,
> And politic siftings, I made a choice of yon fellow.
> Thomas Middleton, *The Revenger's Tragedy* (1607)

Sentences These often involve a strong element of PARALLELISM, as here:

> JACK: Your vanity is ridiculous, your conduct an outrage, and your presence in my garden utterly absurd.
> Oscar Wilde, *The Importance of Being Earnest* (1895)

Even Longer Structures These usually display various forms of REPETITION (see Chapter 8), like the ANAPHORA in this example:

> PETRUCHIO: Say that she rail, why then I'll tell her plain
> She sings as sweetly as the nightingale.
> Say that she frown, I'll say she looks as clear
> As morning roses newly washed with dew.
> Say she be mute and will not speak a word,
> Then I'll commend her volubility,
> And say she uttereth piercing eloquence.
>
> William Shakespeare, *The Taming of the Shrew* (c.1591)

2) Two entities followed by a third that supercedes the other two, as in 'Ready? Steady? Go!' mentioned above.

Words Maire in Brian Friel's *Translations* (1981) declares 'I don't want Latin. I don't want Greek. I want English' – two negatives superceded by a positive, as well as the shift from dead languages to a living one. This version seems most common using three adjectives, as when Fitzroy in Alan Bennett's *The Madness of George III* (1991) says of the King 'His curiosity is benevolent, undirected. And infinite'; the punctuation upholds the separateness of the third adjective.

Here is another example using nouns, as well as pleasing ALLITERATION: Margaret teases Beatrice, who is newly in love with Benedick:

> BEATRICE: By my troth, I am exceeding ill. Heigh-ho!
> MARGARET: For a hawk, a horse, or a husband?
>
> William Shakespeare, *Much Ado About Nothing* (c.1598)

Phrases These are usually formed, once again, using PROZEUGMA (for more examples, see under **With WIT**, below). Here, Lydia responds to her lover who has just shed his disguise:

> LYDIA: I am so astonished! and so terrified! and so overjoyed!
>
> Richard Brinsley Sheridan, *The Rivals* (1775)

Sentences Again, this often includes an element of PARALLELISM. Observe how John Proctor defends his wife in court:

> PROCTOR: There are them that cannot sing, and them that cannot weep
> – my wife cannot lie.
>
> Arthur Miller, *The Crucible* (1953)

Even Longer Structures Enjoy the satisfying rhythmic pay-off in this example:

> CELIA: I can't bear cooking: and I cook. I can't bear working: and
> I work. *(She smiles)* And I can't bear Philip: and I'm marrying him.
> Christopher Hampton, The Philanthropist (1970)

ASCENDING TRICOLON

A TRICOLON in which each successive word or phrase grows in length.

Perhaps the most famous example of this is Antony's 'Friends, Romans, countrymen' in Shakespeare's *Julius Caesar* (1599). This simple construction – one syllable, followed by two, then three – bears the effects of the assassination of Caesar, emanating outwards from the personal to the civic and onwards to the national: concentric rings of political repercussion. How different would it have been had he said 'Countrymen, Romans, friends' (a DESCENDING TRICOLON – see below)?

Words Again, this device can be deployed using nouns, as when Barabas, the titular protagonist of Marlowe's *The Jew of Malta* (c.1592), refers to his riches as 'My gold, my fortune, my felicity'; the words grow in length as he moves from his actual gold, through the double meaning of 'fortune' as both wealth and good luck, to the full breadth of his luck and happiness in 'felicity'. Consider the mounting absurdity in this appraisal of General Pizarro:

> DE CANDIA: They say in the Indies he traded his immortal part to
> the Devil.
> ESTETE: For what, pray? Health? Breeding? Handsomeness?
> Peter Shaffer, The Royal Hunt of the Sun (1964)

Similarly, adjectives grow in intensity when deployed as an ASCENDING TRICOLON, as when Dr Wicksteed in Alan Bennett's *Habeas Corpus* (1973) admires a girl dressed as a boy as 'a fresh, lovely, passionate creature'; as the syllables increase, so perhaps do his amorous intentions. Conversely Jerome, in Alan Ayckbourn's *Henceforward* (1987), describes his wife as a 'selfish, vindictive, unforgiving bitch'; his spitting venom fuelled by the growing words, leading to the harsh monosyllabic 'bitch'.

Phrases In this example – following the governing PROZEUGMA of 'They cry a woman's...' – each subsequent phrase grows in length, echoing the increasing ages:

> DORIMANT: They cry a woman's past her prime at twenty, decayed at
> four and twenty, old and unsufferable at thirty.
> George Etherege, The Man of Mode (1676)

Sentences Here, we move wittily from mirth to serious thought as the phrases expand:

PHILLIP: We will laugh, we may be moved, we may even think a little.
Timberlake Wertenbaker, Our Country's Good (1988)

DESCENDING TRICOLON

A TRICOLON in which each successive word or phrase decreases in length. Where an ASCENDING TRICOLON usually burgeons or diverges, a DESCENDING TRICOLON often homes in or focuses. Consider the classic instruction at the beginning of a race: On your marks! Get Set! Go!

Words In this example, Edgar addresses his blinded father, Gloucester, whom he has led to an imaginary cliff edge from which Gloucester now thinks he has thrown himself. The three light things, to which Edgar likens him, become somehow lighter with the reduction of syllables:

> EDGAR: Hadst thou been aught but gossamer, feathers, air
> So many fathom down precipitating,
> Thou'dst shivered like an egg.
William Shakespeare, King Lear (c.1606)

Phrases Consider the matter-of-fact, self-satisfied rhythm of this example, somehow matching the simplicity of the fare:

> CORNELIUS: Rudolph, bring us gentlemen two glasses of beer, a loaf of bread and some cheese.
Thornton Wilder, The Matchmaker (1954)

The narrowing effect of this device encourages some clever usage by playwrights: Sweets in Jez Butterworth's *Mojo* (1995) refuses to open the bar with 'We can't mate. Love to. Can't.' – the terrific economy and curtness of this gives a real sense of the character closing the subject. Or how about this strong appeal, which moves from one plane of reference between the colleagues to another; from the drily academic through the inspirational to the personal, thereby making the sense of blame more acute:

> BRUCE: You're not going to show me any support here, are you? As my supervisor? As a mentor? A friend?
Joe Penhall, Blue/Orange (2000)

'BEETHOVEN' TRICOLON

This is a TRICOLON followed by a fourth entity that somehow supercedes or 'caps' the previous three, named by us after the famous opening bar – da da da DA – of the composer's Fifth Symphony.

Once again, Shakespeare provides us with a famous example: Jacques, in the 'seven ages of man' speech in *As You Like It* (c.1600), describes old age as 'Sans teeth, sans eyes, sans taste, sans everything'; the pitiful physical failings of human decline are trumped by the all-encompassing final phrase. Another glorious one appears in Edward Albee's *Who's Afraid of Virginia Woolf?* (1962), when George asks Nick if he likes this brutal – and brutally concise – declension: 'Good, better, best, bested.'

Words In the following example the 'but' allows the superceding shift – if it was 'and', it would merely be a list of four adjectives:

> JEAN: It's shoddy, it's parochial, it's old-fashioned, but it's British.
> Timberlake Wertenbaker, *Three Birds Alighting on a Field* (1991)

Phrases Here, King George III succinctly displays his knowledge of animal husbandry:

> KING: Hay is the means of maintenance of the cow, grass of the sheep, oats of the horse, and pigs will eat anything.
> Alan Bennett, *The Madness of George III* (1991)

Sentences In this example, a manservant threatens to reveal everything:

> RAZOR: I have heard all, I have seen all, I understand all, and I'll tell all.
> John Vanbrugh, *The Provok'd Wife* (1697)

Summation TRICOLONS are often used in summaries. They are often short and clean, though sometimes can be long and baroque, as in this example, in which each part of the TRICOLON is a TRICOLON of its own:

> BONIFACE: She cures rheumatisms, ruptures, and broken shins in men; green-sickness, obstructions, and fits of the mother, in women; the king's evil, chincough, and chilblains, in children: in short, she has cured more people in and about Lichfield within ten years than the doctors have killed in twenty.
> George Farquhar, *The Beaux' Stratagem* (1707)

DOUBLE TRICOLON

Another coinage by us: a TRICOLON whose three parts each comprise two parts – AA-BB-CC. This form usually displays strong PARALLELISM, and often each pair is antithetical.

In this example, Sir Tunbelly appraises his daughter, Hoyden:

> SIR TUNBELLY CLUMSY: This I must say for her, what she wants in art, she has by nature; what she wants in experience, she has in breeding;

and what's wanting in her age, is made in her constitution.

John Vanbrugh, *The Relapse* (1696)

TRICOLONIC INTERBREEDING

More than any other rhetorical device, the TRICOLON interbreeds indiscriminately with other devices. Below we have chosen the more common 'marriages', but it would seem that virtually every device can display tricolonic structure in some form.

With SOUND

TRICOLONIC ALLITERATION

Three alliterative words in close proximity.

In Christopher Marlowe's *Edward II* (c.1592) the King decries his enemy Mortimer's forces as 'A ranker rout of rebels there never was'; his derision made more acute by the ALLITERATION. Similarly the King in Mike Bartlett's *King Charles III* (2014) imagines Prince William and Kate ruling the country as 'A pretty plastic picture with no meaning'; the plosive 'P's are viciously expressive. Pinchwife in William Wycherley's comedy *The Country Wife* (1675) describes his beautiful new bride Margery as merely 'wholesome, homely, and huswifely' in order to deter prospective adulterer Horner. And here's a disdainful example, talking of Lord Glossmore:

> LADY FRANKLIN: Whose grandfather kept a pawnbroker's shop, and who, accordingly, entertains the profoundest contempt for everything popular, *parvenu*, and plebeian.
>
> Edward Bulwer-Lytton, *Money* (1840)

This combined device often draws on the plosive sounds (as above), which, along with the tricolonic rhythm, can be very forceful. Alsemero in Middleton and Rowley's *The Changeling* (1622) refers to Piracquo's murder as a 'brave bloody blow'. This combination is useful for a good insult too, as when Mrs Hitchcock in John Arden's *Serjeant Musgrave's Dance* (1959) calls Musgrave a 'gormless great gawk!' And how about this gloriously cynical viewpoint:

> HELEN: All the pimps, prostitutes and politicians in creation trying to cash in on eternity...
>
> Shelagh Delaney, *A Taste of Honey* (1958)

TRICOLONIC SIBILANCE

The deployment of three 'S' sounds in close proximity.

Dramatic Adventures in Rhetoric

In Shakespeare's *Henry VI Part One* (1592) Joan La Pucelle – better known as Joan of Arc – belittles the long list of titles of her recently slaughtered enemy, the English warrior Talbot, with 'Here's a silly stately style indeed!' Mrs Sullen in Farquhar's *The Beaux' Stratagem* (1707) advises her sister 'If ever you marry, beware of a sullen, silent sot'. Or this camply-put question:

> DANIEL: Are you cooking something simply sensational?
> Kevin Elyot, *My Night with Reg* (1994)

TRICOLONIC ASSONANCE
The deployment of three of the same vowel sounds in close proximity.

These seem more emotive, as when Cheviot in W.S. Gilbert's *Engaged* (1877), expressing his love for the widow Mrs Macfarlane, utters 'I see, I feel, I speak'; the long 'E's echo his yearning. Conversely, Sandra in Jonathan Harvey's *Beautiful Thing* (1993) explodes at her son's friend, Leah, with 'You twisted little bitch!' – the sharp, bitter 'I's combine with the harsh 'T's to create a vicious sound (see CACOPHONY). And note the punch of these three short 'U's (look away if you are of a delicate sensibility):

> TUPOLSKI: ...the person who wrote this story is a sick fucking scummy cunt.
> Martin McDonagh, *The Pillowman* (2003)

TRICOLONIC PARACHESIS
The deployment of combinations of sounds in threes.

Hamm in Samuel Beckett's *Endgame* (1957) belittles Clov, saying 'you'll be like a little bit of grit in the middle of the steppe'; the image somehow more little and gritty because of the echoed 'IT' sound. Clifton in Kwame Kwei-Armah's *Elmina's Kitchen* (2003) complains about his estranged son, saying 'Man should be glad not mad to see him fadder'. Consider the implicit mockery of the 'PR's here:

> NANCY: Somebody's been in here...
> maybe Bob...
> to primp and preen in private!
> Bryony Lavery, *Frozen* (1998)

TRICOLONIC HOMOIOTELEUTON
Words in close proximity with the same endings.

This is very common, due to the memorability of the rhymes; think of such phrases as 'snug as a bug in a rug', or the commonly used euphemism for newspaper announcements of births, marriages and deaths: 'hatches, matches and dispatches'.

In Eugene O'Neill's *The Iceman Cometh* (1939) Hope dismisses the British Army as a 'Lousy Limey army!' – the repeated ending adding to the belittlement. Johnny in Jez Butterworth's *Jerusalem* (2009) playfully calls a piss-up in his woodland home a 'Bucolic Alcoholic Frolic'. And here's a splendid early Restoration example:

> SIR FEEBLE FAINWOOD: When I was a young fellow I would not let the young wenches look pale and wan, but rouse 'em and touse 'em and blowze 'em, till I put a colour in their cheeks.
>
> Aphra Behn, *The Lucky Chance* (1686)

With IMAGERY

TRICOLONIC PROGRESSIO

To use three metaphorical comparisons to make a point.

In this example, when asked Sir Percy's name – which she does not know – the romantically motivated Connie evades the question with:

> CONNIE: His name is curtains billowing wide on a summer night. His name is a special secret rose pressed in an old book. His name is the name of all lovers down the ages who have cried their challenge to the wild night and dared to cast themselves away on the frail bark of love.
>
> Alan Bennett, *Habeas Corpus* (1973)

TRICOLONIC HYPERBOLE

A three-part exaggeration, either numerically or through imagery.

Any device that relies on overstatement of any kind seems drawn to the TRICOLON. For instance, when accused of unfaithfulness at her own wedding, the innocent Hero in Shakespeare's *Much Ado About Nothing* (c.1598) utters 'Refuse me, hate me, torture me to death!' – the three parts building to the hyperbolic image of 'torture me to death'. Conversely, in this overwhelmingly beautiful piece of overstatement, Mary asks her grandmother how much she loves her, and receives this reply, in which the TRICOLON is made all the more potent by the repetition of 'all the':

> MRS TILFORD: As much as all the words in all the books in all the world.
>
> Lillian Hellman, *The Children's Hour* (1934)

TRICOLONIC COMPOUNDS
Three pairs of compound words in close proximity.

In Ben Jonson's *Bartholomew Fair* (1614) Winwife refers to 'A wife here with a strawberry-breath, cherry-lips, apricot-cheeks'; a lovely fruity concoction. In Sean O'Casey's *Juno and the Paycock* (1924) Boyle disparages the 'hymn-singin', prayer-spoutin', craw-thumpin' Confraternity men!' And here is a wonderful indictment of our secular age, jam-packed with PARACHESIS and ALLITERATION too:

> HEADMASTER: In our crass-builded, glass-bloated, green-belted world Sunday is for washing the car...
> Alan Bennett, *Forty Years On* (1968)

With WIT

TRICOLONIC ZEUGMA
One word or phrase used to 'yoke' three others together.

The ZEUGMA family very often combine with the TRICOLON. Consider this lovely PROZEUGMA:

> ANTONY: I thought how those white arms would fold me in,
> And strain me close, and melt me into love.
> John Dryden, *All for Love* (1677)

Lady Fanciful in John Vanbrugh's *The Provok'd Wife* (1697) scornfully examines Belinda, saying 'What a nose she has, what a chin, what a neck!' – a clear MESOZEUGMA with 'she has' governing all three body parts. Chance in Tennessee Williams' *Sweet Bird of Youth* (1959) sums up his lost dreams with 'I wanted, expected, intended to get something better'; the three verbs leading to the DIAZEUGMA of 'something better'. And how about this example of an ASCENDING TRICOLONIC PROZEUGMA, in which one verb governs the three tiers of the theatre, each phrase growing in length and the sound of the audience becoming louder as we climb higher in the auditorium:

> CHORUS: Waiting for the rustling in the stalls, the titter in the dress circle, the laughter and catcalls in the gallery.
> T.S. Eliot, *The Family Reunion* (1939)

With DEBATE

TRICOLONIC BDELYGMIA
A three-part expression of hatred or contempt.

Here, Professor Higgins makes clear his feelings for his professional rival, Professor Nepean:

> HIGGINS: What! That imposter! that humbug! that toadying ignoramus!
> George Bernard Shaw, *Pygmalion* (1912)

TRICOLONIC EPEXEGESIS

Adding three words or phrases to clarify an idea or argument.

In this ASCENDING example, a priest is talking about his inner-city parishioners:

> LIONEL: They're furious. At their lives. At the system. At where they find themselves.
> David Hare, *Racing Demon* (1990)

And here is a strong PARALLELISM, in which each of the three phrases has its own clarifying sub-clause:

> BALTHAZAR: His men are slain, a weakening to his realm,
>   His colours seized, a blot unto his name,
>   His son distressed, a corsive to his heart.
> Thomas Kyd, *The Spanish Tragedy* (c.1592)

TRICOLONIC EPANORTHOSIS

A three-part re-phrasing of something.

This can be deployed either for **Intensification**, as in this example about a man dropping litter:

> UNA: It was the man, the person doing that.
>   Because he hasn't been, been
>   schooled
>   educated
>   *civilised* enough.
> David Harrower, *Blackbird* (2005)

Or **Justification**, as here, with a supporter of England's World Cup bid passionately declaring his enthusiasm:

> ASHOK: ... the best team will win! Not only *will* they win, not only do they *deserve* to win, they have a *right* to win.
> William Gaminara, *The Three Lions* (2013)

TRICOLONIC RHETORICAL QUESTIONS
Three questions in succession not requiring an answer.

At the start of Stephen Jeffreys' *The Libertine* (1994) the Earl of Rochester claims the audience will not like him. Due to his dangerous charisma they, of course, *adore* him – but during the course of the play they watch him descend into ruin through drink. The final line of the play has the dissolute Earl asking them the same question three times: 'Do you like me now? Do you like me now? Do you like me now?' – full of self-loathing and disgust.

Three different, consecutive questions are equally common. The valet Waitwell, disguised as Sir Rowland in Congreve's *The Way of the World* (1700), woos the desperate Lady Wishfort with 'Am I here? Do I live and breathe? Do I love this pearl of India?' – his pressuring of her echoed in the growing length of the questions – a fine ASCENDING TRICOLON. How about this heavily rhetorical example:

> HUBERT: If lusty love should go in quest of beauty,
> Where should he find it fairer than in Blanche?
> If zealous love should go in search of virtue,
> Where should he find it purer than in Blanche?
> If love ambitious sought a match of birth,
> Whose veins bound richer blood than Lady Blanche?
> William Shakespeare, *King John* (1596)

TRICOLONIC EPIPLEXIS
To ask three questions in order to shame or reprimand someone.

In the example below, not only are there three sentences, but the first question is also in three parts, as Harry, an embittered American filmmaker, goads a former general recently released from prison:

> HARRY: Where is the triumphal drive through the streets, the heroic music, the garland of war? Where is the howling mob upping its sweaty nightcaps? Where are the young virgins casting themselves in front of your jeep?
> John Whiting, *Marching Song* (1954)

TRICOLONIC HYPOPHORA
To ask three questions and then answer them yourself, as here:

> FIRK: Shall I betray my brother? No! Shall I prove Judas to Hans? No! Shall I cry treason to my corporation? No!
> Thomas Dekker, *The Shoemaker's Holiday* (1599)

Or here's a more recent example, in which a man under police investigation claims that pornography drives technology:

> SIMS: The first photographs? Porn. The first movies? Porn. The most popular content when the Nether was called the Internet? Porn.
> Jennifer Haley, *The Nether* (2013)

With STRUCTURE

TRICOLONIC ANTITHESIS

Three pairs of things held in opposition to each other.

This is most common with a 'DOUBLE' TRICOLON, as in the following two examples. Here the irrepressible Sir John Falstaff is described:

> PISTOL: He woos both high and low, both rich and poor,
>   Both young and old, one with another, Ford.
> William Shakespeare, *The Merry Wives of Windsor* (c.1598)

And this is from a lecture on the criminal mind:

> AGNETHA: the distinctions
>   between right and wrong
>   between the speakable and unspeakable
>   between the forgivable and the unforgivable...
> Bryony Lavery, *Frozen* (1998)

TRICOLONIC AMPLIFICATION

A three-part expansion of a thought or idea.

This example, in which Berowne is talking of a sonnet he has sent to Rosaline, boasts two TRICOLONS, both with PARALLELISM, and the second one incorporates a glorious AUXESIS of the adjective, comparative, and superlative; so perfect in so many ways:

> BEROWNE: The clown bore it, the fool sent it, and the lady hath it –
> sweet clown, sweeter fool, sweetest lady!
> William Shakespeare, *Love's Labour's Lost* (c.1595)

TRICOLONIC PARALLELISM

Three phrases or sentences bearing the same or similar structure.

This is a very common marriage, whether it be a combination of adjectives and nouns, as when Salieri in Peter Shaffer's *Amadeus* (1979) describes Mozart's trademark sounds as 'crushed harmonies – glancing collisions – agonizing delights'. Or a combination of nouns and verbs, as when Knox in Hugh Whitemore's *Breaking the Code* (1986) bewails our lot for living too long, since the 'faculties fade, the body disintegrates, the mind crumbles'. And here's one in three parallel *phrases*:

> ESTHER: She used to hum and feed us. Sing and dress us. Coo and scold us.
>
> Arnold Wesker, *I'm Talking About Jerusalem* (1960)

And one in three *sentences*, in this case ASCENDING:

> EVELYN: I am ambitious, and poverty drags me down! I have learning, and poverty makes me the drudge of fools! I love, and poverty stands like a spectre before the altar!
>
> Edward Bulwer-Lytton, *Money* (1840)

The playwrights of the Renaissance relished the use of PARALLELISM, and very often in TRICOLONIC form. Here's a complex example between two rival lovers:

> BALTHAZAR: O sleep mine eyes, see not my love profaned,
> Be deaf my ears, hear not my discontent,
> Die heart, another joy's what thou deserv'st.
> LORENZO: Watch still mine eyes, to see this love disjoined,
> Hear still mine ears, to hear them both lament,
> Live heart, to joy at fond Horatio's fall.
>
> Thomas Kyd, *The Spanish Tragedy* (c.1592)

TRICOLONIC HYPOZEUXIS

When each of three clauses in a sentence has its own subject and verb.

Here, following a train accident, Belvawney addresses his beloved, Belinda (in a pleasing ASCENDING TRICOLON):

> BELVAWNEY: The line is blocked, your parasol is broken and your butterscotch trampled in the dust.
>
> W.S. Gilbert, *Engaged* (1877)

TRICOLONIC POLYSYNDETON

Three things strung together with conjunctions.

In this example, the trio is emphasized by the use of two 'ands' (instead of a comma and one 'and'), thereby emphasizing the importance and togetherness of the three characters.

> SCHMIDT: It's we three who made this party electable! You and Willy and I.
> Michael Frayn, *Democracy* (2003)

Interestingly, ASYNDETON (see below) would also work, although the effect would be different: 'You, Willy, me.'

TRICOLONIC ASYNDETON
Three things strung together without conjunctions.

This is very popular; it is curt, rhythmic and punchy. Jimmy in John Osborne's *Look Back in Anger* (1956) claims to like Alison's friend Webster, saying 'He's got edge, bite, drive'; the three monosyllabic nouns bang home his admiration. Similarly, Ventidius in John Dryden's *All for Love* (1677) berates Antony for falling for Cleopatra, asking 'What's this toy / In balance with your fortune, honour, fame?' – a lovely imbalanced ANTITHESIS with the 'toy' grossly out-weighed by the enormous concepts of 'fortune, honour, fame'. And here, Amanda bewails to her son the lot of her daughter:

> AMANDA: It's terrible, dreadful, disgraceful that poor little sister has
> never received a single gentleman caller!
> Tennessee Williams, *The Glass Menagerie* (1944)

TRICOLONIC ECPHONESIS
Three words or short phrases in a row with exclamation marks.

In Thomas Holcroft's *A Tale of Mystery* (1802) Bonamo cries 'Oh, shame! Dishonour! Treachery!' in reaction to a scandalous letter. Lord Loam in J.M. Barrie's *The Admirable Crichton* (1902) condemns a recalcitrant servant with 'The ingrate! The smug! The fop!' And here Private Gar addresses his Public self about their overbearing father (a fine example of PARACHESIS too):

> PRIVATE: What the hell do you care about him. Screwballs! Skinflint! Skittery face!
> Brian Friel, *Philadelphia, Here I Come!* (1964)

TRICOLONIC PARATAXIS
Three successive independent clauses with or without conjunctions.

Here, Harper summarizes (see ANACEPHALAEOSIS) a programme on holes in the ozone layer she has heard on the radio:

> HARPER: Skin burns, birds go blind, icebergs melt. The world coming to an end.
>
> Tony Kushner, *Angels In America* (1991)

With REPETITION

Any form of REPETITION combined with the TRICOLON is a match made in heaven. Playwrights throughout the ages have used it – whether it be effusive, insistent or joyous, it is always an intensification.

TRICOLONIC REPETITION

Three words or phrases repeated in succession.

Words A single word can be repeated three times within a single sentence, as in this example, in which Esther describes her husband, who is defending Ireland from invasion, as:

> ESTHER: ...a neutral man in a neutral army protecting his neutral wife.
>
> Frank McGuinness, *Dolly West's Kitchen* (1999)

Phrases In John Webster's *The White Devil* (1612) Cornelia accuses Carlo with 'O you abuse me, you abuse me, you abuse me!' and Eleanor in Terry Johnson's *Dead Funny* (1994) wails 'I want a baby! I want a baby! I want a baby!'

A common variant of this is an addition to the third repetition, as when Maggie observes of Brick in Tennessee Williams' *Cat on a Hot Tin Roof* (1955) 'You look so cool, so cool, so enviably cool' (see also TRICOLONIC EPIZEUXIS below).

TRICOLONIC SYNONYMY

Three words or phrases in succession that have the same meaning.

The TRICOLON seems to lend intention to the choice of words – such as the phrase 'me, myself and I' – preventing the effect of the more accidental TAUTOLOGY.

Sir Cautious Fulbank in Aphra Behn's *The Lucky Chance* (1686) encounters Sir Feeble Fainwood in the dark and demands to know who he is with 'Speak – declare – pronounce', thereby utilizing a pleasing ASYNDETON. As does Chapuys in Robert Bolt's *A Man for All Seasons* (1960), when asked what his reaction would be if the Catholic Church agreed to Henry VIII's divorce from Katherine of Aragon. He replies that he would 'Approve, applaud, admire' – which also boasts a strong rhythm and frontal ASSONANCE.

In this example, Silvia is in disguise as Jack Wilful and is trying to be manly and evasive:

SILVIA: I live where I stand; I have neither home, house, nor habitation, beyond this spot of ground.

George Farquhar, *The Recruiting Officer* (1706)

When the REPETITION is impassioned, this may shade across into TRICOLONIC TAUTOLOGY. Within the context of a play, its writing and rehearsal process, it must be decided whether the three repetitions are made consciously or unconsciously by the character. Consider these: Mrs Malaprop in Sheridan's *The Rivals* (1775), when asked what the matter is, exclaims regarding a duel 'Why, murder's the matter! Slaughter's the matter! Killing's the matter!' And Attercliffe in John Arden's *Serjeant Musgrave's Dance* (1959), having just murdered his fellow deserter, declares 'that wipes the whole thing out, wiped out, washed out, finished'. Would you consider them to be SYNONYMY or TAUTOLOGY?

TRICOLONIC EPIZEUXIS
To say a single word three times in succession.

The combining of these two devices is very common. Think of the everyday impatience of 'okay, okay, okay' or the insistence of 'spend, spend, spend' – or The Beatles' 'yeah, yeah, yeah'!

Shakespeare was an especial fan of this combination. Remember Hamlet's reply when asked by Polonius what he is reading: 'Words, words, words.' Or Othello's desperate 'O, blood, blood, blood!' when he has murdered the hapless Desdemona. Or the three witches in *Macbeth* (1606) greeting the anti-hero with 'Hail! Hail! Hail!'

It can denote an energized **Glee**, as when the ambitious Marlene in Caryl Churchill's *Top Girls* (1982) declares 'I'm going up up up'. Or it can bring **Pressure** to bear, as when Roy Cohn in Tony Kushner's *Angels in America* (1991) insists that Joe takes a high-powered job, saying 'You must do this. You must must must'. Or simple **Invective**, as when Elyot insults Amanda in Noël Coward's *Private Lives* (1930) calling her a 'slattern, slattern, slattern, and fishwife' – with a nice 'BEETHOVEN' button.

It can also create an insistent sense of **Blame**, as when Amanda in Tennessee Williams' *The Glass Menagerie* (1944) berates her son, saying 'Self, self, self, is all that you ever think of!' Or when Jo in Shelagh Delaney's *A Taste of Honey* (1958) levels at her mother the accusation 'Drink, drink, drink, that's all you're fit for'. Or an explosive effect of **Bitterness**, as when Betty in J.B. Priestley's *Dangerous Corner* (1932) exposes her marriage with 'It's just nothing – pretence, pretence, pretence'.

Here are two particularly pleasing examples. The first boasts a wonderfully rhythmic ONOMATOPOEIA of distant drumming:

> THOMAS: O tedium, tedium, tedium. The frenzied
> Ceremonial drumming of the humdrum!
>> Christopher Fry, *The Lady's Not For Burning* (1948)

And the second a great trajectory of challenge-abuse-apology in one succinct line:

> PAUL: Healthy? Healthy? Healthy? Fuck you. Fuck you. Fuck you. Sorry.
> Sorry. Sorry.
>> Mark Ravenhill, *The Cut* (2006)

Also very common is an interrupted Tricolonic Epizeuxis, in the mode of Hamlet when he famously pronounces 'O villain, villain, smiling, damnèd villain!' of his murderous uncle Claudius. Or Richard III in his desperate cry 'A horse, a horse, my kingdom for a horse!' Or – and this is not from a play, but it is too good to pass up – when Kenneth Williams as Julius Caesar in the film *Carry On Cleo* wails 'Infamy! Infamy! They've all got it in for me!' – a delightful piece of WORDPLAY.

Here's another, incorporating a TRICOLON of adjectives:

> MÖHL: Yours is effort, effort, concerted, sustained, intelligent effort.
>> John Osborne, *A Patriot for Me* (1965)

TRICOLONIC PLOCE
The repetition of a single word separated by another word or words.

Anita in Simon Gray's *Quartermaine's Terms* (1981) utters 'it had all been done and done and done to death'. And here, Tilley, a First World War soldier, dismisses the misguided patriotism of an aristocratic woman's 'open letter to England', printed in a newspaper following the death of her son:

> SHAW: *(reading delightedly)* "Every woman of England should be
> proud and glad to give and give and give, even the flesh of her
> flesh and the blood of her blood – "
> TILLEY: And the tripe of her tripe.
>> Noël Coward, *Post-Mortem* (1930)

TRICOLONIC EPIMONE
The structural repetition of a key phrase three times.

In this example, Joseph Surface addresses Lady Teazle, wife to Sir Peter, who suspects her of having an affair:

> SURFACE: What is it makes you negligent of forms, and careless
> of the world's opinion? – why, the consciousness of your own

innocence. What makes you thoughtless in your conduct, and apt to run into a thousand little imprudences? – why, the consciousness of your own innocence. What makes you impatient of Sir Peter's temper, and outrageous at his suspicions? – why, the consciousness of your innocence.

Richard Brinsley Sheridan, The School for Scandal (1777)

TRICOLONIC ANAPHORA

Three successive phrases or sentences beginning with the same words.

This combination is extremely common. It can be the simple rhetoric of Cusins in Shaw's *Major Barbara* (1905) when he says 'Dare I make war on war? I dare. I must. I will.' Or the emphatic insistence of Mrs Wicksteed in Alan Bennett's *Habeas Corpus* (1973) when she commands 'Speak clearly, speak firmly, speak now'. Both examples utilize the minor ANAPHORA of repeating one word and changing a second word, which causes us to listen for what is changed, the new information.

This extends simply into a repeated word with an altered *phrase* following it each time, as when the 9th Juror in Reginald Rose's *Twelve Angry Men* (1956) discredits the testimony of an elderly witness, saying 'Nobody knows him, nobody quotes him, nobody seeks his advice'. And June in Alan Bennett's *People* (2012) states 'You don't want the Trust. You don't want the damp. You don't want the people'.

The obverse of this is when a *phrase* is repeated leading to a single altered word each time, as when Troy in August Wilson's *Fences* (1985) challenges Death with 'Bring your army. Bring your sickle. Bring your wrestling clothes'; the repeated 'bring your...' leads to the final word of each phrase with a strong insistence, like a gauntlet being thrown down each time. Similarly, Sheena in David Greig's *The Architect* (1996), doubting an architect's professional morals, says cynically 'Build them high, build them quick and build them cheap'.

Here's a two-character example, between the Prime Minister and his long-suffering PA – an exchange which includes a wonderful pay-off (see 'BEETHOVEN' TRICOLON above):

> PENNY: But it is a double room, double bed, double... everything.
> CAMERON: Double-booked by the sound of it.
> William Gaminara, The Three Lions (2013)

Moving still further on with this form, a phrase can be repeated followed by three different phrases, as in this lovely split between three characters:

> MRS ALLONBY: The secret of life is never to have an emotion that is unbecoming.

> LADY STUTFIELD: The secret of life is to appreciate the pleasure of being terribly, terribly deceived.
> MR KELVIL: The secret of life is to resist temptation, Lady Stutfield.
>
> Oscar Wilde, *A Woman of No Importance* (1893)

TRICOLONIC ANTISTROPHE

Three successive phrases or sentences that end with the same words.

Think of the famous admonition 'see no evil, hear no evil, speak no evil'. Or the ASCENDING legal declaration 'the truth, the whole truth, and nothing but the truth'.

Much like ANAPHORA above, ANTISTROPHE also has a variety of structural variants. It can be the repetition of one word preceded by three different words, as when Lord Illingworth in Oscar Wilde's *A Woman of No Importance* (1893) claims that you either have to 'feed people, amuse people or shock people' to get into the best society.

Alternatively, the repeated word can be preceded by altering *phrases*, as when Stella in Tennessee Williams' *A Streetcar Named Desire* (1947) utters defensively to her husband 'There weren't any papers, she didn't show any papers, I don't care about papers'; there is a wonderfully frustrated, staccato rhythm to this line, enabled by the ANTISTROPHE. Conversely, a single word can be altered before a repeated phrase, as when Blanche in the same play likens her brother-in-law, Stanley, to an animal, saying he 'Eats like one, moves like one, talks like one!'

Extending the form further, it can be a repeated phrase preceded by three differing phrases, as in this assertion:

> BENEDICT: One woman is fair, yet I am well; another wise, yet I am well; another virtuous, yet I am well.
>
> William Shakespeare, *Much Ado About Nothing* (c.1598)

This marriage of devices is often further combined with PROZEUGMA (as a way of achieving ELLIPSIS), as when Putana exclaims in John Ford's *'Tis Pity She's a Whore* (c.1629) 'We are all undone, quite undone, utterly undone!'

TRICOLONIC ANADIPLOSIS

1) The repetition, mid-phrase or -sentence, of the same word or words.

This example also boasts very strong PARALLELISM:

> LORD ARE: Your feet tapped when I promised you the opera! Your mouth watered when I promised you diamonds! Your knees shivered when I promised you the prince!
>
> Edward Bond, *Restoration* (1981, revised 2006)

2) The repetition of a phrase from the end of one clause at the beginning of the next.

If this occurs more than once in quick succession, it creates a form of GRADATIO (see below), as in this example:

> FIRST KNIGHT: From naught at first thou cam'st to little wealth,
> From little unto more, from more to most.
>> Christopher Marlowe, *The Jew of Malta* (c.1592)

TRICOLONIC GRADATIO

A progression in three steps, using repetition from one step to the next.

In the following example an old man bemoans the optimists of the world who are full of 'Faith and hope'. The third sentence boasts a TRICOLON of its own:

> DODGE: If it's not God then it's a man. If it's not a man then it's a woman. If it's not a woman then it's politics or bee pollen or the future of some kind.
>> Sam Shepard, *Buried Child* (1997 version)

TRICOLONIC SYMPLOCE

Three successive sentences that begin and end with the same words.

This is a combination of ANAPHORA and ANTISTROPHE. Usually a single changing word is flanked by repeated ones, as when Sir Anthony Absolute in Sheridan's *The Rivals* (1775) threatens his son Jack with 'I'll disown you, I'll disinherit you, I'll unget you!' – once again the repetitions serve to emphasize the altered words. In Mark Ravenhill's *The Cut* (2006), Stephen declaims 'There are systems of evil. There are acts of evil. There are people of evil'.

This form can be extended into whole sentences, as here:

> IRWIN: If you want to learn about Stalin, study Henry VIII.
> If you want to learn about Mrs Thatcher, study Henry VIII.
> If you want to learn about Hollywood, study Henry VIII.
>> Alan Bennett, *The History Boys* (2004)

Chapter 8 Repetition

ERIC: It'll do, won't it? The speech?
SOPHIE: It's super. Really super. *(Pause)* It's very powerful. *(Pause)*
The way you repeat things. Something *this* and something *that*...
ERIC: That's rhetoric.
SOPHIE: It's really effective.

Alan Ayckbourn, Ten Times Table (1978)

We all know what REPETITION is. From reciting a poem 'by rote' at school, to learning a language – or lines in a play – we are well-versed in it from an early age. Going over and over vocabulary or speeches aids remembrance, so we are well aware of how REPETITION is linked to memory. In rhetoric, too, REPETITION ensures an audience understands, appreciates and recalls a key point: very useful in politics – and, of course, in drama too.

In this, our final chapter, we encounter not only some simple examples of reiteration, but also more subtle or complex ones, such as PAREGMENON or SYMPLOCE. As a performer or director, one should always ask *why* a character repeats something – and also *how* that REPETITION may be expressed, finding fresh ways to restate one's case.

It is worth considering that any form of REPETITION is invariably an *intensifier*, an emphatic tool whereby an important point is made and a character's intentions are made clear, or the emotion at the heart of them is revealed. This is particularly worth noting in the realm of drama.

SIMPLE

REPETITION from the Latin meaning – surprise, surprise – 'repetition'.
The simple repetition of a word or phrase in close proximity.

Words The repetition of individual words invariably has an **Emphatic** effect, as when the title character in Ben Jonson's *Volpone* (1605-6) instructs those he is duping to 'toss your handkerchiefs cheerfully, cheerfully'. Or when, in a darker vein, Doctor Faustus in Marlowe's play of that name (c.1589) declares helplessly 'Tis magic, magic that hath ravished me!' – a fine tagline for the whole play. The intensification of the concept of 'magic' is achieved through this simple repetition.

Also, very commonly, a word is repeated and then added to (see AMPLIFICATION), as when the Colonel in John Osborne's *Look Back in Anger* (1956) sums up the failure of his daughter Alison's marriage with 'It was all so unfortunate – unfortunate and unnecessary'.

The recurrence of single words can create a strong sense of **Insistence**, as in this terrific example in which we get the word 'bastard' six times, and just when we expect a seventh, receive instead a more formal alternative:

> THERSITES: I am a bastard too; I love bastards: I am a bastard begot, bastard instructed, bastard in mind, bastard in valour, in every thing illegitimate.
>
> William Shakespeare, *Troilus and Cressida* (1602)

Many playwrights use REPETITION as a **Character Trait**. Take Lady Stutfield in Oscar Wilde's *A Woman of No Importance* (1893), who repeats words in virtually every line she speaks, saying such things as 'How very, very charming those gold-tipped cigarettes of yours are' or 'It must be terribly, terribly distressing to be in debt'. In the same play, the Archdeacon tends to repeat short phrases when talking about his sickly wife, including 'she has many resources in herself, many resources' and 'she's never morbid, never morbid'; creating a wonderfully resigned effect. In terms of character, this quirk of delivery is a gift to explore.

Phrases are similarly **Emphatic**. Susan in David Hare's *Plenty* (1978) declares 'In my experience it is best, it really is best if you always obey the rules'; the repeated words being separated by the intensifier 'really'. And here's Wilde again:

> LORD GORING: Your transaction with Robert Chiltern may pass as a loathsome commercial transaction of a loathsome commercial age.
>
> Oscar Wilde, *An Ideal Husband* (1895)

Repeated phrases often seem laced with more acute **Emotions**. The little girl Angie in Caryl Churchill's *Top Girls* (1982) expresses her excitement at receiving a new dress from her aunt, pronouncing it 'Beautiful, Beautiful' and demanding 'I want to wear it. I want to wear it'. Conversely, consider the desperate exasperation of:

> KATURIAN: I don't care if they kill me. I don't care. But they're not going to kill my stories. They're not going to kill my stories.
>
> Martin McDonagh, *The Pillowman* (2003)

It can, of course, be a device for **Buying Time**, in order to find the perfect word or phrase to express a thought, which creates a very naturalistic effect:

> RALPH: Those well-balanced lines of Mr Farquhar, they seemed to acquire a dignity, they seemed – they seemed to lose some of their corruption.
>
> Timberlake Wertenbaker, *Our Country's Good* (1988)

It can be **Evasive** too, like Sweets in Jez Butterworth's *Mojo* (1995), who states 'Could be me could be you. Could be me could be you'. There is a sense that he says this a lot, a non-committal refrain. Or it can denote **Comic Uncertainty**, as in this example, where Lucy has brought a coat:

> LUCY: I don't know whether it's my sort of thing. I don't know what my sort of thing *is*. Well, I suppose my sort of thing is the sort of thing I buy, so since I've bought it it must be my sort of thing.
> Michael Frayn, *Alphabetical Order* (1975)

ECHO from the Greek meaning 'reverberated sound' or, indeed, 'echo'.
The repetition of key words or phrases from earlier in the play.

It can be as simple as one character immediately echoing the word or words of another, including here the pleasing comic twist of the final echo becoming a question:

> SIR FOPLING: We'll sacrifice all to our diversion.
> MRS LOVEIT: All, all.
> SIR FOPLING: All.
> BELINDA: All?
> George Etherege, *The Man of Mode* (1676)

Alternatively it can be the very common form of repeating a phrase or sentence with a simple change of pronoun, as here:

> MRS ELTON: If that's the way you want it.
> HESTER: That's the way I want it.
> Terence Rattigan, *The Deep Blue Sea* (1952)

It can be **Ironic**, particularly when one character echoes the sentiments of another character at a crucial turn in their relationship, as in this example from Oscar Wilde's *An Ideal Husband* (1895):

> LORD GORING: You mustn't do that. It would be vile, horrible, infamous.
> MRS CHEVELEY: Oh! don't use big words. They mean so little.

Then, moments later, Lord Goring traps Mrs Cheveley with a trick bracelet she has stolen. He deliberately and triumphantly echoes the line she used on him:

MRS CHEVELEY: You brute! You coward!
LORD GORING: Oh! don't use big words. They mean so little.

It can also be **Thematic** (see EPIMONE), when a line is repeated several times during the course of a play. Norman in Ronald Harwood's *The Dresser* (1980) punctuates his dialogue with 'if you don't mind my saying so', using it to excuse telling a few home truths to his overbearing actor-manager boss. Cheviot in W.S. Gilbert's *Engaged* (1877) falls head over heels in love with every girl he meets, and proclaims each of them to be 'the tree upon which the fruit of my heart is growing; my Past, my Present, and my Future, my own To Come!' – each time we hear it, the more ludicrous it becomes.

It can be **Choric** too, as in Silvius, Rosalind, Orlando and Phebe's paean to love in Act V Scene ii of Shakespeare's *As You Like It* (c.1600) with its repeated chorus of affirmations. Or the Greek-style chorus of aunts and uncles in T.S. Eliot's *The Family Reunion* (1939) with its 'the knot be unknotted / The cross be uncrossed' motif. Or, of course, the famous refrain in Samuel Beckett's *Waiting For Godot*, which reverberates throughout the play:

ESTRAGON: Let's go.
VLADIMIR: We can't.
ESTRAGON: Why not?
VLADIMIR: We're waiting for Godot.
ESTRAGON: *(despairingly)* Ah!
Samuel Beckett, Waiting for Godot (1955)

Finally, we cannot leave this device without mentioning 'The Echo Scene' (Act V Scene iii) in John Webster's *The Duchess of Malfi* (1614), in which the ghost of the Duchess echoes the words of her husband and his friend. This is not an ECHO in the strict rhetorical sense, but a literal echo – and it is used to chilling and ironic effect.

SYNONYMY (sin-*on*-im-ee) from the Greek meaning 'of like meaning'.
The *conscious* use of different words or phrases with identical or similar meanings – usually with an emphatic effect; think of the phrase 'me, myself and I' (see also TAUTOLOGY below).

Kabir in Tanika Gupta's *Sanctuary* (2002) reassures Jenny about some shadily acquired turf, saying 'It is all above board, strictly legitimate'; the two phrases mean the same thing, the first a slang equivalent of the second. The REPETITION serves to emphasize the reassurance. Pinchwife in William Wycherley's *The Country Wife* (1675), meanwhile, acquires a letter from his wife to her lover, in which she refers to her husband as a 'man whom I loathe, nauseate and detest'; pretty clear sentiments in their OVERSTATEMENT. And here's an example of Don Armado's florid style; he is speaking to Costard:

DON ARMADO: By my sweet soul, I mean setting thee at liberty, enfreedoming thy person. Thou wert immured, restrained, captivated, bound.

William Shakespeare, *Love's Labour's Lost* (c.1595)

TAUTOLOGY (tort-*ol*-uh-jee) from the Greek meaning 'same word'.
In strictly rhetorical terms TAUTOLOGY is an argument that repeats the same thing insistently in various ways, without necessarily providing proof. In terms of playwriting, however, it is more useful to think of it in its more commonly understood form as being the use of words or phrases with identical or similar meanings – usually with a sense of *unnecessary* repetition.

Andrew in Howard Brenton and David Hare's *Pravda* (1986) says 'I'm printing this document in its whole entirety'; the word 'whole' is seemingly redundant, except that it adds emphasis and an element of OVERSTATEMENT. Lady Wishfort in Congreve's *The Way of the World* (1700) fears that if she sees Mr Mirabell she will 'turn to stone, petrify incessantly'; 'petrify', of course, means 'turn to stone'; and you can hardly do it 'incessantly' – once is enough! And here's a pleasing example in an Irish vernacular:

MAHON: Wasn't he the laughing joke of every female woman where four baronies meet...

J.M. Synge, *The Playboy of the Western World* (1907)

CLEVER

PAREGMENON (pa-*regg*-men-on) from the Greek meaning 'sitting beside'.
The juxtaposition of words that share their derivation. *Sense and Sensibility* is a classic example.

Kingston in David Hare's *Racing Demon* (1990) states that 'a committee may commission a report'; both words derive from the Latin *committere*, to send together. More subtly, Idrissa in Kwame Kwei-Armah's *Statement Of Regret* (2007) accuses Adrian with 'Your assumptions are presumptuous'; both words stemming from the Latin *sumere*, to take, here with differing prefixes. More subtly still, Constant in John Vanbrugh's *The Provok'd Wife* (1697) says 'No cloister ever enclosed so true a penitent'; both 'cloister' and 'enclosed' stem originally from the Latin *claudere*, to close.

There can be a conscious **Wit** in using such root-sharing words, as when Salvador Dali in Terry Johnson's *Hysteria* (1993) says 'Dali has no intentions, only intent'. There is a knowing, even smug quality to such WORDPLAY. And consider this hilarious description by Jimmy of his mother-in-law:

> JIMMY: She will pass away, my friends, leaving a trail of worms
> gasping for laxatives behind her – from purgatives to purgatory.
> > John Osborne, *Look Back in Anger* (1956)

POLYPTOTON (pol-ip-*toh*-ton) from the Greek meaning 'falling many times', and so 'regurgitating'.
The repetition of a word in a different part of speech or verbal tense within a sentence.

This is most commonly the combination of a verbal and a nominal form of the same word; think of such phrases as 'to begin at the beginning' or the 'pipers piping', 'drummers drumming' and 'dancers dancing' of the festive song *The Twelve Days of Christmas*.

Expectant mother Jo in Shelagh Delaney's *A Taste of Honey* (1958) claims 'I'm not planning big plans for this baby or dreaming big dreams'. And here is an example from Shakespeare:

> PRINCE HAL: I'll so offend to make offence a skill,
> > Redeeming time when men least think I will.
> > William Shakespeare, *Henry IV Part One* (c.1597)

Once again there is often a conscious sense of WORDPLAY with this device, as when Tom in Tennessee Williams' *The Glass Menagerie* (1944) complains that 'People go to the *movies* instead of *moving!*' Or this careful piece of politicking by Sir Thomas More:

> MORE: A dispensation was given so that the King might marry
> Queen Catherine, for state reasons. Now we are to ask the Pope to –
> dispense with his dispensation, also for state reasons?
> > Robert Bolt, *A Man for All Seasons* (1960)

Other grammatical combinations occur too. Nouns and adjectives are fairly common, as when Mosher in Eugene O'Neill's *The Iceman Cometh* (1939) says 'If I had any nerves I'd have a nervous breakdown'. Or this double-whammy:

> GUARDIANO: I perceive fools are not at all hours foolish,
> > No more than wise men wise.
> > Thomas Middleton, *Women Beware Women* (1621)

Equally, a combination of verbal tenses can occur, as when Lenin in Tom Stoppard's *Travesties* (1993 edition) proclaims 'We want to establish and we shall establish a free press'. And consider this example, which boasts three forms of the same verb:

ROSE: Times have changed from when you was young, Troy. People change. The world's changing around you and you can't even see it.
August Wilson, Fences (1985)

ANTANACLASIS (*an*-tan-uh-*klass*-iss) from the Greek meaning 'calling back again'. The repetition of a single word each time with a different meaning.

The King in Alan Bennett's *The Madness of George III* (1991) enthuses about agriculture, saying he could plough a furrow as 'straight as a ruler, done by a ruler'; playing on the two meanings of the word. Martha in Polly Stenham's *That Face* (2007) criticizes her father for lavishing presents on his new, Oriental wife, saying they are 'Exotic toys for your exotic toy'; literal playthings for a metaphorical one.

This device often combines with ELLIPSIS, so that a key word is not actually repeated; an implied ANTANACLASIS, if you like. In this example, in which country-bred Cecily addresses Gwendolen Fairfax – who is down from London – the word 'common' is not repeated, thereby veiling its insulting, though heavily implied, alternative meaning:

CECILY: Flowers are as common here, Miss Fairfax, as people are in London.
Oscar Wilde, The Importance of Being Earnest (1895)

ANTISTASIS (an-*ti*-stuh-sis) from the Greek meaning 'standing against'.
The repetition of a word in a new, especially contrary, sense. This device is often combined with ANAPHORA, ANTISTROPHE or CONDUPLICATIO (see below).

Roy Cohn in Tony Kushner's *Angels in America* (1991) says that the influential Mr Heller 'sitteth on the right hand of the man who sitteth on the right hand of The Man'; the capitalization creates a nice distinction between the head of the Justice department and the President. And here a convict in an Australian penal colony muses on the distinction between countryside and nation:

WISEHAMMER: Country can mean opposite things. It renews you with trees and grass, you go to rest in the country, or it crushes you with power: you die for your country, your country doesn't want you, you're thrown out of your country.
Timberlake Wertenbaker, Our Country's Good (1988)

EMPHATIC

EPIZEUXIS (ep-iz-*yook*-sis) from the Greek meaning 'yoked together'.
Also known as **GEMINATIO** (*jem*-in-*ah*-tee-oh) from the Latin meaning 'doubling' – as in the star sign Gemini, the twins.

The repetition of one word with no other word in between for emphasis (see also ECPHONESIS).

This can be a simple repetition of a word, such as when Emma in Harold Pinter's *Betrayal* (1978) says 'It's all all over'. Or the very common TRICOLONIC form (see also Chapter 7) – as in Mr M's 'Splendid! Splendid! Splendid!' in Athol Fugard's *My Children! My Africa!* (1989). Four is common too: Dodge in Sam Shepard's *Buried Child* (1997 version) mocks his wife and son's concern about his own mental health, saying 'Crazy. Crazy, crazy, crazy'.

More than four becomes quite extreme. Take Nell's wonderful entrance line in Caryl Churchill's *Top Girls* (1982) when she arrives at work, demanding 'Coffee coffee coffee coffee coffee'. Or in Ronald Harwood's *The Dresser* (1980) Sir's insistence that *King Lear* must be played with 'Pace, pace, pace, pace, pace, pace'. Or even Mosca's desperation in Ben Jonson's *Volpone* (1605-6) when trying to come up with a plan: 'Think, think, think, think, think, think, think!'

Such repetition is a gift *and* a challenge for an actor. Consider Pyper – in Frank McGuinness' *Observe The Sons of Ulster Marching Towards The Somme* (1985) – who declares his love for life and his city, 'I love my Ulster. Ulster. Ulster. Ulster. Ulster. Ulster. Ulster. Ulster. Ulster'. In Rodney Ackland's *The Pink Room* (1945) the play ends with the utterly broken club owner, Christine, uttering the word 'hell!' eight times. Then, in the re-named 1987 version, *Absolute Hell*, the word gains titular status and is uttered ten times at the end of the play.

Shakespeare loves this device. Isabella, for instance, demands 'justice, justice, justice, justice!' in *Measure for Measure* (1603). Capulet questions his daughter in *Romeo and Juliet* (1595) with 'How, how, how, how? Chopped logic! What is this?' And here is Lear's pitiful lament over Cordelia's body:

> KING LEAR: Why should a dog, a horse, a rat have life,
> And thou no breath at all? Thou'lt come no more;
> Never, never, never, never, never.
> William Shakespeare, *King Lear* (c.1606)

PLOCE (*ploh*-see) from the Greek meaning 'something plaited or woven'.
1) A general term for the repetition of a single word separated by another word or words, with the sense of the words becoming woven together (as opposed to DIACOPE below).

It can be as simple as when Attercliffe in John Arden's *Serjeant Musgrave's Dance* (1959) tries to calm the Pugnacious Collier with 'Steady, matey, steady'. Or it can be more emotive, as in this example, which Flamineo utters with his final breath:

FLAMINEO: This busy trade of life appears most vain,
Since rest breeds rest, where all seek pain by pain.
John Webster, *The White Devil* (1612)

2) This device also has a more specific usage when the response to the repeated word is altered by an intervening qualification (see also AMPLICATION).

Heisenberg in Michael Frayn's *Copenhagen* (1998) states 'The question is now resolved. Happily resolved'. And here's another:

JERRY: ...to offer a token, without blush, a token of one's unalloyed appreciation.
Harold Pinter, *Betrayal* (1978)

DIACOPE (dye-*ak*-uh-pee) from the Greek meaning 'cut through'.
The repetition of a word, after an intervening word or phrase, for emphasis. The Greek root helps define this device from PLOCE above: *that* is an interweaving, *this* is a division.

Repeated Word Afraid of losing the love she holds for Martin, Janet in Githa Sowerby's *Rutherford and Son* (1912) claims she is 'helpless to hold it – helpless!'

Repeated Phrase Mr Rice exclaims of his ex-wife Maria in Brian Friel's *Molly Sweeney* (1994) 'And so beautiful; my God, so beautiful'; the intervening phrase here is a definite intensifier.

Names, Titles and Epithets Very often the device is deployed with a character's name inserted, as when Sir Robert Chiltern in Oscar Wilde's *An Ideal Husband* (1895) beseeches his wife with 'Oh, love me always, Gertrude, love me always!' Or this passive-aggressive remark to another wife:

GEORGE: How did I try, Martha? How did I try?
Edward Albee, *Who's Afraid of Virginia Woolf?* (1962)

Similarly, the insertion can be the character's title, as when Ketch in Timberlake Wertenbaker's *Our Country's Good* (1988) recalls travelling players coming to his village, saying 'They were loved like the angels, Lieutenant, like the angels'. Alternatively, it can be a character's EPITHET, as with this character, who does it all the time:

LORD AUGUSTUS: You're excessively trivial, my dear boy, excessively trivial.
Oscar Wilde, *Lady Windermere's Fan* (1892)

EPIMONE (ep-*im*-uh-nee) from the Greek meaning a 'stay' or 'delay'.
The structural repetition of a word, phrase or question in order to make a point, usually with the effect that the listener – be it another character or the audience – will have changed their response to it between the first time it is stated and the last.

Famously Mark Antony uses it to great effect in his 'Friends, Romans, countrymen' speech in Shakespeare's *Julius Caesar* (1599). He returns repeatedly to Brutus' assertion that he and his co-conspirators are 'honourable men' and that Caesar was 'ambitious'. Each time the crowd become less convinced by these assertions, ultimately turning against Brutus.

Conversely, here's a lovely comic example:

> MRS HARDCASTLE: Was ever poor woman so beset with fools on the one hand, and thieves on the other?
> TONY LUMPKIN: I can bear witness to that.
> MRS HARDCASTLE: Bear witness again, you blockhead you, and I'll turn you out of the room directly. My poor niece, what will become of her? Do you laugh, you unfeeling brute, as if you enjoyed my distress?
> TONY LUMPKIN: I can bear witness to that.
> MRS HARDCASTLE: Do you insult me, monster? I'll teach you to vex your mother, I will.
> TONY LUMPKIN: I can bear witness to that.
>
> Oliver Goldsmith, *She Stoops to Conquer* (1771)

STRUCTURAL

CHIASMUS (kai-*az*-mus) from the Greek meaning 'crossed over', after the Greek letter χ (chi).
The reversal of the second of two parallel sets of words in the form A-B-B-A (see also ANTIMETABOLE below). Think of *The Three Musketeers'* declaration 'All for one, one for all', or the MAXIM 'when the going gets tough, the tough get going'.

There is a strong rhythmic quality to this device, perhaps most obvious in formal introductions, such as when Max in Dion Boucicault's *London Assurance* (1841) introduces 'Mr Hamilton, Sir Harcourt Courtly; Sir Harcourt Courtly, Mr Hamilton'. Equally rhythmic is a simple chiatic repetition, as when George in Ayub Khan-Din's *East Is East* (1996) berates his wife with 'you sit with Annie, talking, smoking, smoking, talking'.

Longer phrases are less rhythmic, but no less effective. Mary in Eugene O'Neill's *Long Day's Journey Into Night* (c.1940) claims that morphine 'hides you from the world and the world from you'. And Chance in Tennessee Williams' *Sweet Bird of Youth* (1959) says that 'To change is to live, Miss Lucy, to live is to change'.

Shakespeare loved this: think of the Witches' 'Fair is foul, and foul is fair' in *Macbeth* (1606); or Mercutio's 'If love be rough with you, be rough with love' in *Romeo and Juliet* (1595); or:

BEROWNE: Let us once lose our oaths to find ourselves,
             Or else we lose ourselves to keep our oaths.
        William Shakespeare, *Love's Labour's Lost* (c.1595)

The neatness and rhythm of CHIASMUS often gives this device an epigrammatic feel; hence its regular occurrence in dialogue with a witty aspect. Consider this interchange:

LOVELESS: My courage should disperse your apprehensions.
AMANDA: My apprehensions should alarm your courage.
        John Vanbrugh, *The Relapse* (1696)

It is often deployed with a 'pivotal' word or phrase, as in this example – discussing the kilt – in which 'makin' fun o' th'' acts as the pivotal phrase (the spelling is the playwright's):

FLUTHER: ...you'd wondher whether th' man was makin' fun o' th' costume, or th' costume was makin' fun o' th' man!
        Sean O'Casey, *The Plough and the Stars* (1926)

And here's a lovely three-way repetition to end on:

FAUSTUS: Bell, book and candle, candle, book and bell,
           Forward and backward, to curse Faustus to hell.
        Christopher Marlowe, *Doctor Faustus* (c.1589)

ANTIMETABOLE (*an*-ti-met-*ab*-uh-lee) from the Greek meaning 'swapping round'. A kind of CHIASMUS in which the form is stretched, and the balance of the repeated words or phrases – again in reverse order – is more loose, due to the linguistic context or the demands of grammar. Where, in these cases, it is not possible to make a direct repetition, a different verbal tense or part of speech is required to complete the thought.

For instance, when June in Alan Bennett's *People* (2012) says 'Doing the right thing isn't always the right thing to do', the participle 'doing' must change to the infinitive 'to do' for the line to make sense, though the A-B-B-A rhythm is still there. Or when Pinchwife in William Wycherley's *The Country Wife* (1675) proclaims 'He's a fool that marries, but a greater that does not marry a fool', the form of the verb has to change due to it being made negative. These small grammatical changes prevent the REPETITION from being pure, so we make the distinction between CHIASMUS, which is a pure repetition, and ANTIMETABOLE, which has a looser structure.

Adjectives often morph into nouns (and vice versa) when this device is used. Consider this:

> MARLOW: An impudent fellow may counterfeit modesty, but I'll be
> hanged if a modest man can ever counterfeit impudence.
>> Oliver Goldsmith, *She Stoops to Conquer* (1771)

As with CHIASMUS above, there is often a pivotal word that enables this structure. In the example above, the word 'counterfeit' is the pivot of each phrase.

ANAPHORA (an-*af*-or-ruh) from the Greek meaning 'carrying back'.
A succession of clauses or sentences beginning with the same word or phrase.

There can simply be one repetition, and it can either be of a single word or whole phrases.

Words Alan Turing in Hugh Whitemore's *Breaking the Code* (1986) explains 'Each problem – each decision – requires fresh ideas, fresh thought'; the repetitions of 'each' and 'fresh' hammer home the point with great clarity.

Phrases These can lead to either a differing word or phrase. Consider this example, in which Lady Teazle has just been revealed hiding behind a screen; the device points up delightfully the different reactions of her lover and her husband:

> SURFACE: Lady Teazle, by all that's wonderful!
> SIR PETER: Lady Teazle, by all that's damnable!
>> Richard Brinsley Sheridan, *The School for Scandal* (1777)

This is common between two characters, and creates an effect of REPARTEE or RAILLERY, as between this father and daughter:

> HUGH: Since when did you smoke?
> MIA: Since when did you care?
>> Polly Stenham, *That Face* (2007)

Three repetitions are very common (see also Chapter 7). Once again either a single word or a short phrase can be repeated.

Words Ben Nicholson in Lee Hall's *The Pitmen Painters* (2007) claims he envies the freedom of amateur painters, because they have 'No patrons, no public, no press'; the effect further enhanced by the ALLITERATION. Here's an interesting one, using prefixes to the same effect: Happy in Arthur Miller's *Death of a Salesman* (1949) boasts that he 'can outbox, outrun, and outlift anybody in that store'.

Phrases Once again, these can lead to either a differing word or phrase. Dan in Patrick Marber's *Closer* (1997) tries to win back Anna, saying 'I can't think, I can't work, I can't *breathe*'.

If three feels rhythmic, four begins to feel a little overbearing. Brandon in Patrick Hamilton's *Rope* (1929) likens Raglan to Keatley, whom he has just murdered, with 'Same age. Same height. Same colour. Same sweet and refreshing innocence'. Four repeated phrases become even more obviously insistent and persuasive:

> KING RICHARD: With mine own tears I wash away my balm,
> With mine own hands I give away my crown,
> With mine own tongue deny my sacred state,
> With mine own breath release all duteous oaths.
> William Shakespeare, *Richard II* (1595)

The Renaissance playwrights are unabashed in their use of such devices. These flights of rhetorical fancy are enabled by the heightened form of the verse. Look at this:

> BALTHAZAR: Yet might she love me for my valiancy,
> Ay, but that's slandered by captivity.
> Yet might she love me to content her sire,
> Ay, but her reason masters his desire.
> Yet might she love me as her brother's friend,
> Ay, but her hopes aim at some other's end.
> Yet might she love me to uprear her state,
> Ay, but perhaps she hopes some nobler mate.
> Yet might she love me as her beauty's thrall,
> Ay, but I fear she cannot love at all.
> Thomas Kyd, *The Spanish Tragedy* (c.1592)

This device is not limited to strength and insistence, however. The following example, though still making a strong point, is much gentler and utterly charming:

> MR HARDCASTLE: I love everything that's old: old friends, old times, old manners, old books, old wine; and, I believe, Dorothy *(taking her hand)*, you'll own I have been pretty fond of an old wife.
> Oliver Goldsmith, *She Stoops to Conquer* (1771)

ANTISTROPHE (an-*tiss*-truh-fee) from the Greek meaning 'turning back'.
Also known as **EPISTROPHE** (ep-*iss*-truh-fee) from the Greek meaning 'turning about'.
The repetition of a word or phrase at the end of successive clauses or sentences.

Words Sir Epicure Mammon in Ben Jonson's *The Alchemist* (1610) prepares to conquer Dol Common, saying 'She shall feel gold, taste gold, hear gold, sleep gold.'

Phrases Thomas More in Robert Bolt's *A Man for All Seasons* (1960) insists 'I do none harm, I say none harm, I think none harm'. Or this explanation of the characteristics that a man in love should display by Rosalind (dressed as a man) to Orlando:

> ROSALIND: A lean cheek, which you have not, a blue eye and sunken,
> which you have not, an unquestionable spirit, which you have not,
> a beard neglected, which you have not...
>> William Shakespeare, *As You like It* (c.1600)

Once again, there is a strong sense of REPARTEE when this device is shared between two characters:

> BELLMOUR: By heaven, I'll seize her even at the altar, and bear her
> thence in triumph.
> GAYMAN: Ay, and be borne to Newgate in triumph, and be hanged
> in triumph.
>> Aphra Behn, *The Lucky Chance* (1686)

ANADIPLOSIS (*an*-uh-dip-*loh*-sis) from the Greek meaning 'duplication'.

1) The repetition of a word or phrase in the middle of successive sentences.

Words Rita in Willy Russell's *Educating Rita* (1980) says 'I'm busy enough findin' meself, let alone findin' someone else'; the word 'findin' providing the pivot to each phrase.

Phrases Alison in John Osborne's *Look Back in Anger* (1956) explains to her father that 'You're hurt because everything is changed. Jimmy is hurt because everything is the same'; the repeated 'because everything is' clearly points up the ANTITHESIS of 'changed' and 'the same'. And consider the effect of the repetition of 'it must be a plot, because' in this delightful example:

> SCRUB: First, it must be a plot, because there's a woman in 't: secondly,
> it must be a plot, because there's a priest in 't: thirdly, it must be a
> plot, because there's French gold in 't: and fourthly, it must be a plot,
> because I don't know what to make on 't.
>> George Farquhar, *The Beaux' Stratagem* (1707)

Yet again, there is a sense of REPARTEE when it involves two characters:

> LORD ILLINGWORTH: We men know life too early.
> MRS ARBUTHNOT: And we women know life too late.
>> Oscar Wilde, *A Woman of No Importance* (1893)

2) The repetition of the last word or phrase of one clause at the beginning of the next (similar to CONDUPLICATIO below). This version of the device is often a form of AMPLIFICATION.

Words Once again, a single word can be picked up, as in this example:

> TROY: You can't tell me nothing about death. Death ain't nothing but a fastball on the outside corner.
> August Wilson, *Fences* (1985)

Phrases In this example, a maid relays the action of the trial she has been attending:

> VIOLET: Sir Robert standing there at the table with his wig on crooked and the tears running down his face – running down his face they were and not able to speak because of the noise.
> Terence Rattigan, *The Winslow Boy* (1946)

When two characters are involved, the feeling of REPARTEE is once more present:

> CHEVIOT: I am about to remove the weight of sorrow which hangs so heavily at your heart. Resume your fancy check trousers, I have consented to live.
> SYMPERSON: Consented to live? Why, sir, this is confounded trifling.
> W.S. Gilbert, *Engaged* (1877)

CONDUPLICATIO (cond-*yoo*-plik-*ah*-tee-oh) from the Latin meaning 'doubling'. The repetition of a key word or phrase from anywhere in the preceding sentence at the start of the next (see also ANADIPLOSIS above, of which it is a looser form). This too is a type of AMPLIFICATION.

Kate in Neil Simon's *Brighton Beach Memoirs* (1983) reprimands her sister Blanche with 'You have no right to talk to me like that. No right'; there is a certain indignation in the repetition. Here is an example in which a single word is picked up and expanded on (AMPLIFICATION):

> FLAMINEO: O justice! Where are their flatterers now? Flatterers are but the shadows of princes' bodies; the least thick cloud makes them invisible.
> John Webster, *The White Devil* (1612)

Once again, between two characters there is often a feeling of one-upmanship or REPARTEE:

> SCANDAL: The pleasures of last night, my dear, too considerable to be forgot so soon.
> MRS FORESIGHT: Last night! And what would your impudence infer from last night?
>
> William Congreve, *Love for Love* (1695)

GRADATIO (grad-*ah*-tee-oh) from the Latin meaning 'stepping up'.
An extended ANADIPLOSIS 2 or CONDUPLICATIO in which a point is made by building a series by steps.

King Henry in Shakespeare's *Henry V* (c.1599) woos Katherine saying 'If thou would have such a one, take me; and take me, take a soldier; take a soldier, take a king'; a clear and winning line of thought. It is worth noting that three linked phrases will only have two repetitions as steps. Here's an example with three steps, and a lovely descent from the 'whole world' down to a 'private purse':

> VOLPONE: Why, the whole world is but as an empire, that empire as a province, that province as a bank, that bank as a private purse, to the purchase of it.
>
> Ben Jonson, *Volpone* (1605-6)

And here's one with four steps, sporting a common question and answer format:

> BETTY: Why am I tied? Tied to be bled. Why am I bled? Because I was screaming. Why was I screaming? Because I'm bad. Why was I bad? Because I was happy.
>
> Caryl Churchill, *Vinegar Tom* (1976)

And finally, one with five steps:

> BALTHAZAR: Now in his mouth he carries pleasing words,
>   Which pleasing words do harbour sweet conceits,
>   Which sweet conceits are limed with sly deceits,
>   Which sly deceits smooth Bel-imperia's ears,
>   And through her ears dive down into her heart,
>   And in her heart set him where I should stand.
>   Thomas Kyd, *The Spanish Tragedy* (c.1592)

EPANALEPSIS (*ep*-an-al-*ep*-sis) from the Greek meaning 'repeating' or 'resuming'.
When the same word or phrase appears at the beginning *and* end of a sentence.

Words Paulina in David Greig's *The Architect* (1996) goads her husband with 'Say what you want to say'. When a single word is repeated in this way, there is often a strong sense of emphasis, as when Archie in John Osborne's *The Entertainer* (1957) explains away a naked tableau to his Vaudeville audience: 'Nudes, that's what they call them, lady, nudes'; the repetition at the end really drives the point home. Anxious to get the attention back on him, he almost bullies his audience.

It can also create a more colloquial tone, as when Jenny in Arnold Wesker's *Roots* (1959) denounces her daughter Beatie with 'Then you're not right in the head then'. Alternatively, there can be a conscious wit to it:

> MRS LINTOTT: Pillars of a community that no longer has much use
> for pillars.
>
> Alan Bennett, *The History Boys* (2004)

Phrases Dull Gret in Caryl Churchill's *Top Girls* (1982) describes a Brueghel painting as having 'Faces on things that don't have faces on'. Again, this device lends itself both to emphasis and to colloquialism, as when Harry in Timberlake Wertenbaker's *Our Country's Good* (1988) complains 'I didn't want to hang him, Ralph, I didn't'.

In the following example, in which Brick is talking of his 'love' for a fellow team-mate, there is a strong element of AMPLIFICATION:

> BRICK: It was too rare to be normal, any true thing between two
> people is too rare to be normal.
>
> Tennessee Williams, *Cat on a Hot Tin Roof* (1955)

SYMPLOCE (*sim*-ploh-see) from the Greek meaning 'interwoven'.
When several successive clauses boast the same first word or phrase and the same last word or phrase.

There is a strong effect of conviction and of persuasion with this device, making it heavily rhetorical. Kwaku in Kwame Kwei-Armah's *Statement Of Regret* (2007) urges 'People are talking about it, people are arguing about it'. Similarly, Thami in Athol Fugard's *My Children! My Africa!* (1989) asserts 'I don't listen to what he says and I don't do what he says'. And consider the strong insistence here:

> ELWOOD: All of my shopping I do online. All of my reading I do
> online. All of my news I get online. All of my television I watch online.
> All of my radio I listen to online.
>
> Simon Stephens, *Harper Regan* (2008)

Dramatic Adventures in Rhetoric

As ever, there is a strong feeling of REPARTEE when the device is shared between two characters, as in this example, boasting strong ANTITHESIS and Wilde's love of women besting men:

> LORD WINDERMERE: How hard good women are!
> LADY WINDERMERE: How weak bad men are!
>
> Oscar Wilde, *Lady Windermere's Fan* (1892)

Glossary of Rhetorical Devices

ADAGE A short memorable saying, often philosophical or ethical in tone. (page 95)

ADIANOETA A consciously ambiguous statement with a secondary negative meaning. (page 87)

ALLEGORY A story with two meanings, one literal and one symbolic. (page 66)

ALLITERATION When words in proximity begin with the same sound. (page 26)

ALLUSION A reference to another artistic or inspirational form. (page 60)

AMPHIBOLOGY An ambiguous grammatical sentence structure. (page 98)

AMPLIFICATION The expansion of an idea, by repeating it and adding to it. (page 144)

ANACEPHALAEOSIS A recapitulation of the facts; a summary. (page 136)

ANACOLUTHON A change in grammatical structure in the same sentence. (page 167)

ANADIPLOSIS 1 To repeat a word in the middle of successive sentences. (page 206)

ANADIPLOSIS 2 To repeat the last words of one sentence at the start of the next. (page 207)

ANALOGY The use of a similar or parallel example to clarify a point. (page 66)

ANAPHORA A succession of sentences beginning with the same words. (page 204)

ANAPODOTON When the conclusion of a logical statement is left unsaid. (page 122)

ANASTROPHE The inversion of normal word order. (page 169)

ANTANACLASIS The repetition of a single word with an altered meaning. (page 199)

ANTANAGOGE To place a good point next to a bad one to soften the blow. (page 134)

ANTAPODOSIS An extended SIMILE with several aspects to the comparison. (page 51)

ANTHROPOMORPHISM To describe non-human things in human terms. (page 58)

ANTICLIMAX An insignificant or disappointing conclusion to a sequence. (page 99)

ANTIMERIA (also spelled ANTHIMERIA) A word used in a different part of speech than usual. (page 107)

ANTIMETABOLE To reverse the order of repeated words. (page 203)

ANTIPHRASIS To use a word or short phrase ironically. (page 101)

ANTIRRHESIS To reject a statement as ridiculous or wrong. (page 126)

ANTISAGOGE 1 To promise a reward for goodness or a punishment for wickedness. (page 135)

ANTISAGOGE 2 To state one side of an argument, then the other. (page 135)

ANTISTASIS The repetition of a word in a new, especially contrary sense. (page 199)

ANTISTROPHE To repeat words at the end of successive sentences. (page 205)

ANTITHESIS The juxtaposition of contrasting ideas in a parallel way. (page 139)

ANTONOMASIA A word or phrase used to represent a person instead of their name. (page 81)

APHORISM A pithy saying embodying a general truth or astute observation. (page 95)

APOMNEMONYSIS To quote a higher authority to make a point. (page 68)

APOPHASIS 1 To draw attention to something by saying you will not mention it. (page 135)

APOPHASIS 2 To pretend to deny something as a way of affirming it. (page 136)

APOPLANESIS To avoid a tricky subject by digressing deliberately. (page 117)

APORIA 1 To attempt to discredit an opposing view by casting doubt on it. (page 127)

APORIA 2 A feigned expression of doubt in order to get a reaction. (page 128)

APOSIOPESIS An abrupt halt due to an inability to complete a thought. (page 117)

APOSTROPHE To turn from addressing a general audience to a specific person or thing. (page 150)

APPOSITION A qualifying noun or phrase next to the thing it qualifies. (page 74)

ARCHAISM The use of old or obsolete words, language or grammar. (page 169)

ASCENDING TRICOLON Three successive words or phrases that grow in length. (page 174)

ASSONANCE The repetition of identical vowel sounds in neighbouring words. (page 33)

ASTEISMUS Polite mockery, often to bat a word back with a new spin on it. (page 91)

ASYNDETON The omission of conjunctions. (page 153)

AUREATION The use of Latinate words to 'heighten' diction. (page 167)

AUXESIS Words, phrases or sentences organised to create a climactic effect. (page 161)

AXIOM A form of MAXIM that states a widely accepted principle for life. (page 94)

BADINAGE Light banter or ridicule between friends, usually affectionate. (page 90)

BATHOS A deliberate ANTICLIMAX used to comic or ironic effect. (page 100)

BDELYGMIA An expression of hatred or contempt. (page 125)

'BEETHOVEN' TRICOLON Three entities followed by a fourth that caps them. (page 175)

BOMPHIOLOGY Excessive bragging or bombastic speech. (page 164)

BRACHYLOGY A general term for brevity of expression. (page 152)

CACEMPHATON 1 A rude joke or double entendre. (page 91)

CACEMPHATON 2 Ugly sounds in words, often using PARIMION. (page 91)

CACOPHONY Ugly sounds in words, reflective of what they describe. (page 43)

CATACHRESIS An unlikely METAPHOR using a word abnormally. (page 56)

CHARIENTISMUS 1 To couch something unpleasant in positive terms. (page 114)

CHARIENTISMUS 2 To brush off a cruel remark with a joke. (page 115)

CHIASMUS The reversed repetition of words in the form A-B-B-A. (page 202)

CHREMAMORPHISM To assign humans with the attributes of objects. (page 59)

CLICHÉ A TRUISM that has become over-used. (page 96)

CLIMAX Words, phrases or sentences in ascending power. (page 160)

COHORTATIO A form of AMPLIFICATION to elicit a strong emotion. (page 133)

COMPOUNDS An inventive combination of words to create an image. (page 76)

COMPROBATIO To flatter the listener to get them on your side. (page 133)

CONCESSIO To agree with something, then twist it to make a point. (page 127)

CONDUPLICATIO To repeat key words from one sentence at start of the next. (page 207)

CONSONANCE The repetition of the same consonants within successive words. (page 31)

CORRECTIO To correct a word, phrase or idea to make a point. (page 128)

COUNTER-QUESTION To answer a question with another question. (page 131)

DELIBERATIO To work out possible courses of action before choosing one. (page 122)

DESCENDING TRICOLON Three successive words or phrases that decrease in length. (page 175)

DIACOPE To repeat a word or phrase after an intervening word or phrase. (page 201)

DIALYSIS The presentation of a choice using the figure 'either...or...'. (page 123)

DIAPHORA To use a single word as representative of a person. (page 80)

DIASTROPHOLOGIA Distortion in the pronunciation of words. (page 119)

DIAZEUGMA When a single subject has two or more verbs. (page 88)

DICTUM A MAXIM that has a formality of form. (page 95)

DIRIMENS COPULATIO To mention a balancing fact to prevent a one-sided argument. (page 123)

DISTINCTIO To state the particular meaning of a word to avoid ambiguity. (page 129)

DOGBERRYISM Alternative name for MALAPROPISM. (page 111)

DOUBLE TRICOLON A three-part entity, each part comprising two parts. (page 176)

DRAMATIC IRONY When an audience knows things the characters do not. (page 97)

ECHO To repeat key words or phrases from earlier in the play. (page 195)

ECPHONESIS A single word or short phrase ending in an exclamation mark. (page 154)

EFFICTIO A detailed description of someone's body. (page 74)

ELLIPSIS To leave out extraneous words for economy of speech. (page 152)

ENALLAGE The intentional misuse of grammar, usually for comic effect. (page 109)

ENARGIA A general term for any form of vivid description. (page 72)

ENCOMIUM A speech that commemorates a person or thing (page 137)

ENTHYMEME An informally stated SYLLOGISM. (page 122)

ENUMERATIO To detail causes or consequences to make a forcible point. (page 128)

EPANALEPSIS When the same word appears both at the beginning and end of a sentence. (page 208)

EPANORTHOSIS To re-phrase something immediately in order to qualify it. (page 129)

EPEXEGESIS Adding words or phrases to clarify an idea. (page 129)

EPIGRAM A clever, perfectly balanced statement. (page 106)

EPIMONE The structural repetition of a word or phrase to make a point. (page 201)

EPIPLEXIS To ask someone a question in order to reprimand or shame them. (page 130)

EPISTROPHE Another name for ANTISTROPHE. (page 205)

EPITHET A qualifying description or substitute for someone or something. (page 75)

EPIZEUXIS The repetition of a word with no other word in between. (page 199)

EPONYM To substitute a famous person's name for something attributed to them. (page 81)

EROTESIS Another name for a RHETORICAL QUESTION. (page 130)

ETHOPOEIA To put oneself into another's character to convey their feelings. (page 70)

EULOGY A formal speech in praise of someone, usually after their death. (page 137)

EUPHEMISM An inoffensive term for something unpleasant or indecent. (page 113)

EUPHONY A beauty of sound in the words, reflective of what they describe. (page 42)

EXEMPLUM To cite as an illustrative example a true or fictitious story. (page 67)

FORESHADOWING To mention something that subsequently occurs (page 70).

GEMINATIO Another name for EPIZEUXIS. (page 199)

GRADATIO To build a series by steps; an extended ANADIPLOSIS. (page 208)

HENDIADYS Two words joined by a conjunction to convey a single idea. (page 155)

HENDIATETRIS Four words joined by conjunctions to convey a single idea. (page 160)

HENDIATRIS Three words joined by conjunctions to convey a single idea. (page 159)

HOMOIOAPOKRISIS To ask many questions requiring the same answer. (page 132)

HOMOIOTELEUTON When parallel words have the same endings; often resulting in rhyme. (page 39)

HYPALLAGE The agreement of a word with one it does not logically qualify. (page 75)

HYPERBATON 1 The separation of words that belong together. (page 147)

HYPERBATON 2 When words in a sentence are in an unusual order. (page 147)

HYPERBOLE Emphasis through exaggeration. (page 57)

HYPERZEUGMA When each phrase in a sentence has its own verb. (page 88)

HYPOPHORA To ask someone a question and to answer it oneself. (page 130)

HYPOTAXIS A subordinate clause used to clarify the main clause. (page 146)

HYPOZEUGMA 1 When two or more words or phrases are governed by another word or phrase following them. (page 88)

HYPOZEUGMA 2 When two or more subjects are governed by one verb. (page 88)

HYPOZEUXIS When each clause in a sentence has its own subject and verb. (page 152)

HYSTEROLOGIA A qualifying phrase between a preposition and its object. (page 149)

INVECTIVE To abuse a person or idea, often with a sense of blame. (page 125)

IRONY A deliberate ambivalence between the literal and intended meaning. (page 96)

ISOCOLON When phrases are of corresponding structure and equal length. (page 151)

LEPTOLOGIA A deliberately evasive form of CIRCUMLOCUTION. (page 116)

LIST Exactly what you think it is! (page 163)

LITOTES 1 To state a positive by negating a negative. (page 108)

LITOTES 2 An understatement by denying the contrary. (page 109)

LOGORRHOEA Verbal diarrhoea! (page 165)

MACROLOGIA Speech full of over-description and unnecessary words. (page 165)

MALAPROPISM The unintentional misuse of similar sounding words. (page 110)

MARTYRIA To confirm something through previous experience. (page 70)

MAXIM A saying which states concisely what does or should happen in life. (page 94)

MEIOSIS A form of SARCASM in which someone or something is belittled. (page 100)

MESOZEUGMA When a word or phrase governs others on either side of it. (page 87)

METABASIS A brief statement of what has been said and what will follow. (page 136)

METALEPSIS Where one thing is referred to by something associated with it. (page 80)

METANOIA To qualify a statement by restating it in a different way. (page 146)

METAPHOR An image made when one word is applied to another with which it is not normally associated. (page 51)

METASTASIS 1 To skate over something quickly to avoid talking about it. (page 118)

METASTASIS 2 To hurl an insult back in the face of the insulter. (page 118)

METONYMY When one word stands for an idea with which it is associated. (page 78)

MIMESIS The direct imitation of someone either vocally or physically. (page 69)

MISNOMER The deliberate misuse of similar sounding words. (page 110)

NEOLOGISM A newly coined word. (page 106)

ONOMATOPOEIA When words imitate the sounds to which they refer. (page 44)

OVERSTATEMENT When something is described as more than it is. (page 98)

OXYMORON A condensed PARADOX. (page 102)

PANEGYRIC A formal public speech in praise of someone or something. (page 137)

PARABLE A story or extended METAPHOR used to teach a moral lesson. (page 67)

PARACHESIS The repetition of the same combination of sounds in neighbouring words. (page 37)

PARADIGM A clear example illustrating a pattern of human behaviour. (page 68)

PARADOX A seemingly true statement that creates a contradiction. (page 101)

PARALIPSIS (also spelled PARALEIPSIS) A refusal to continue or admission of not knowing what to say. (page 117)

PARALLELISM The consecutive repetition of the same sentence structure. (page 150)

PARAPROSDOKIAN An unexpected ending to a phrase or series. (page 103)

PARATAXIS Successive independent clauses with or without conjunctions. (page 163)

PAREGMENON The juxtaposition of words that share their derivation. (page 197)

PARENTHESIS A word or phrase inserted as an aside. (page 148)

PARIMION Extreme ALLITERATION. (page 32)

PARISOSIS When sentences have equal lengths in terms of syllables. (page 151)

PARODY A humorous, often exaggerated imitation of another literary style. (page 104)

PAROMOIOSIS The parallelism of sound between two clauses or sentences. (page 41)

PARONOMASIA Another name for PUN. (page 85)

PATHOS Language used to elicit a strong emotional response. (page 72)

PERIPHRASIS 1 To talk round a subject to avoid raising it. (page 115)

PERIPHRASIS 2 To substitute several words to avoid saying one particular word. (page 115)

PERSIFLAGE Another name for BADINAGE. (page 90)

PERSONIFICATION To give human characteristics to an inanimate object or animal. (page 58)

PHILOPHRONESIS To suppress anger in favour of reason. (page 134)

PLEONASM The use of superfluous or redundant words. (page 166)

PLOCE 1 A general term for the repetition of one word separated by another. (page 200)

PLOCE 2 The repetition of a word after a qualification alters the response to that word. (page 201)

POLYPTOTON The repetition of a word in different grammatical cases. (page 198)

POLYSYNDETON The repeated use of conjunctions, usually for emphasis. (page 162)

PRAGMATOGRAPHIA The description of an action or occurrence. (page 72)

PREBUTTAL Another name for PROCATALEPSIS. (page 124)

PROCATALEPSIS To anticipate an objection by addressing it in advance. (page 124)

PROECTHESIS To defend your own or another's actions. (page 124)

PROGRESSIO To use a series of comparisons to make a point. (page 55)

PROLEPSIS When a future event is presumed to have happened. (page 104)

PROSOPOGRAPHIA The detailed description of a person's face. (page 74)

PROTROPE To incite someone to action through promises or threats. (page 135)

PROVERB A concise and memorable statement of a well-established truth. (page 92)

PROZEUGMA When one word or phrase precedes two or more others that it governs. (page 87)

PUN 1 The use of similar sounding words for comic, clever or ironic effect. (page 85)

PUN 2 The juxtaposition of words or phrases to witty or clever effect. (page 86)

PYSMA To ask a lot of questions that require as many separate answers. (page 132)

RAILLERY Playful banter laced with anger or bitterness. (page 90)

RATIOCINATIO To ask oneself the reasons for your actions. (page 131)

REDUCTIO AD ABSURDUM 1 To prove an argument true by rubbishing its alternative. (page 126)

REDUCTIO AD ABSURDUM 2 To follow an argument to an extreme to prove its falsity. (page 126)

REDUCTIO AD HITLERUM To dismiss an opponent's opinion by comparing it to a view held by Hitler or the Nazis. (page 127)

REPARTEE An exchange of witty retorts, each one 'capping' the last. (page 89)

REPETITION The reiteration of a word or phrase in close proximity. (page 193)

RESTRICTIO To make an exception to something already stated. (page 124)

RHETORICAL QUESTION A question not requiring an answer. (page 130)

RODOMONTADE Pretentious boasting. (page 164)

SARCASM Harsh, bitter or witty derision, often overtly ironic. (page 99)

SCESIS ONOMATON 1 To emphasise an idea in a string of synonymous phrases. (page 146)

SCESIS ONOMATON 2 A sentence without a verb. (page 146)

SCHEMATISMUS To hide a meaning through evasive speech. (page 116)

SENTENTIA To apply a general truth to a situation by quoting a MAXIM. (page 94)

SENTENTIAL ADVERB An emphatic adverbial word or phrase. (page 148)

SESQUIPEDALIANISM Long-winded language full of long words. (page 168)

SIBILANCE A form of ALLITERATION using only 'S' sounds. (page 30)

SIMILE A comparison of unlike things to imply a resemblance, using 'like', 'as' or 'than'. (page 48)

SOLECISM The ignorant misuse of grammar. (page 112)

SORAISMUS To mix languages in order to appear urbane or affected. (page 118)

SPOONERISM The accidental switching of letters between key words. (page 111)

SYLLEPSIS A word applied differently to each of two or more others. (page 89)

SYLLOGISM An argument that states if two claims are true, then so is the conclusion. (page 121)

SYMPLOCE When successive clauses have the same first and last words. (page 209)

SYNAESTHESIA (also spelled SYNESTHESIA) When one sensation is described in the terms of another. (page 59)

SYNCHISIS 1 (also spelled SYNCHYSIS) Confused or clumsy word order. (page 166)

SYNCHISIS 2 (also spelled SYNCHYSIS) Interlocked word order with the pattern A-B-A-B. (page 167)

SYNCHORESIS To give others permission to judge you. (page 133)

SYNCOPE To shorten the pronunciation of a word. (page 119)

SYNCRISIS 1 A comparison achieved through parallel clauses. (page 56)

SYNCRISIS 2 When opposing things are compared; an antithetical METAPHOR. (page 56)

SYNECDOCHE A part for a whole or the whole for a part. (page 79)

SYNESIS The agreement of words according to logic, not grammatical form. (page 113)

SYNOECIOSIS (also spelled SYNAECIOSIS or SYNECIOSIS) A paradoxical form of ANTITHESIS. (page 144)

SYNONYMY The intentional use of different words with similar or identical meanings. (page 196)

SYSTROPHE Listing the many qualities of someone or something without providing a definition. (page 164)

TAPINOSIS To belittle someone by lessening their status. (page 101)

TAUTOLOGY Saying the same thing twice using different words. (page 197)

TAXIS To assign everything in its proper place. (page 71)

THANATOGRAPHIA The description of a death. (page 73)

TMESIS When a word or phrase is severed by an intervening word or phrase. (page 149)

TOPOGRAPHIA The detailed description of a real place. (page 73)

TOPOTHESIA The detailed description of an imagined or imaginary place. (page 73)

TRAIECTIO IN ALIUM To shift responsibility or blame onto someone else. (page 125)

TRICOLON A phrase, sentence or speech comprising three parts in parallel. (page 172)

TRUISM An obviously true and often hackneyed statement. (page 95)

UNDERSTATEMENT To represent something as less than it is to draw attention to it. (page 97)

WELLERISM To follow a well-known quotation with a witty remark. (page 105)

WORDPLAY Words used inventively, usually for clever or comic effect. (page 84)

ZEUGMA When two words are 'yoked' to one or more others; various forms. (page 87)

ZOOMORPHISM To imagine someone or something in terms of an animal. (page 59)

Glossary of Rhetorical Devices

Index of Playwrights and Plays Quoted

Appendix Further Reading

As we mentioned in our Introduction, there are umpteen books of varying levels of complexity available on the history and forms of rhetoric, as well as their usage in various fields, from politics to pop music, advertising to academia. While no list can hope to be comprehensive, the following selection are certainly well worth seeking out, if you are keen to continue your study of rhetoric.

Professor Max Atkinson, *Lend Me Your Ears: All You Need To Know About Making Speeches & Presentations* (Vermilion, 2004)
Atkinson uses the findings of recent scientific research, combined with the rules of classical rhetoric, to highlight the secrets of successful persuasion – although with a focus on public speaking, rather than performance.

Edward P.J. Corbett, and Robert J. Connors, *Classical Rhetoric for the Modern Student* (OUP USA, 1998)
A comprehensive and in-depth study of rhetoric from Ancient Greece to modern times, along with how best to present an argument. Not an easy read, but an informative one.

Mark Forsyth, *Elements of Eloquence: How To Turn The Perfect Phrase* (Icon Books, 2014)
A recent study of a range of rhetorical devices, drawing on pop lyrics, advertising slogans – and some plays.

Miriam Joseph, *Shakespeare's Use of the Arts of Language* (Paul Dry Books, Inc, 2013)
Sister Miriam Joseph presents the general theory of composition current in Shakespeare's England, then lays out those figures of speech in simple, understandable patterns, using examples to explain each one.

William M. Keith, and Christian O. Lundberg, *The Essential Guide to Rhetoric* (Bedford Books, 2008)
At only 80 pages long, this is a compact and informative guide to the elements of rhetoric, and how these relate to communicating.

Richard A. Lanham, *A Handlist of Rhetorical Terms* (University of California Press, 2013)
Lanham's book is undeniably comprehensive, but its register is also unabashedly academic. Aimed at students of English literature rather than of drama, it is perhaps not the most rehearsal-room friendly of books.

Sam Leith, *You Talkin' To Me? Rhetoric from Aristotle to Obama* (Profile Books, 2012)
How people have thought about, and been taught, rhetoric – from the earliest times to the modern day. Along the way, Leith draws on many examples, from pop music to politicians.

Dramatic Adventures in Rhetoric

Russ McDonald, *Shakespeare and the Arts of Language* (Oxford University Press, 2001)
An examination of Shakespeare's classical education and how it came to bear on his writing, along with an exploration of the changing modes of language in the Elizabethan age, and what effect this had on Shakespeare. McDonald then goes on to consider the progression of Shakespeare's use of rhetoric through his writing career.

Thomas O. Sloane, *Encyclopedia of Rhetoric* (Oxford University Press, 2001)
At almost 900 pages long, this is perhaps the most wide-ranging reference work available. But perhaps one to borrow from the library, rather than invest in.

Richard Toye, *Rhetoric: A Very Short Introduction* (Oxford University Press, 2013)
Part of OUP's extremely successful and informative pocket-sized series, this is – as its title suggests – a brief summary of the origins, development and what Toye calls the 'scaffolding' of rhetoric.

Brian Vickers, *In Defence of Rhetoric* (Clarendon Press, 2002)
A comprehensive and detailed account of the history of the rhetorical tradition, from its earliest beginnings in Greece to the present.

Acknowledgements

We are extremely grateful to the following authors and their publishers for granting permission to quote extracts from their plays:

Extracts from *Who's Afraid of Virginia Woolf* by Edward Albee, published by Jonathan Cape. Reproduced by permission of The Random House Group Ltd.

Extract from *Three Plays* by Alan Ayckbourn, published by Chatto & Windus. Reproduced by permission of The Random House Group Ltd.

Excerpt from *Three Plays: Absurd Person Singular, Absent Friends, Bedroom Farce* copyright © 1975 by Alan Ayckbourn. Used by permission of Grove/Atlantic, Inc. Any third party use of this material, outside of this publication, is prohibited.

Extracts from Alan Ayckbourn, *Ten Times Table*, published by Samuel French Ltd. *Ten Times Table* © 1978 Haydonning Ltd.

Extracts from Robert Bolt, *A Man For All Seasons*, by kind permission of Bloomsbury Methuen Drama, an imprint of Bloomsbury Publishing Plc. *A Man For All Seasons* © 1960 ROBERT BOLT (1973) Ltd.

Extracts from *Restoration* © Edward Bond, 1981, revised 2006, *Restoration*, by kind permission of Bloomsbury Methuen Drama, an imprint of Bloomsbury Publishing Plc.

Extracts from *The Sea* © Edward Bond, 1973, *The Sea*, by kind permission of Bloomsbury Methuen Drama, an imprint of Bloomsbury Publishing Plc.

Extracts from *Saved* © Edward Bond, 1965, *Saved*, by kind permission of Bloomsbury Methuen Drama, an imprint of Bloomsbury Publishing Plc.

Extracts from *Hobson's Choice*, 1916, by Harold Brighouse, published by Samuel French Ltd.

Extract from *Small and Tired*, 2013, by Kit Brookman, by kind permission of the author.

Extract from *Vinegar Tom* © Caryl Churchill, 1976, *Vinegar Tom*, by kind permission of Bloomsbury Methuen Drama, an imprint of Bloomsbury Publishing Plc.

Extracts from *Blithe Spirit* © Noël Coward, 1941, *Blithe Spirit*, by kind permission of Bloomsbury Methuen Drama, an imprint of Bloomsbury Publishing Plc.

Extracts from *Long Day's Journey into Night* by Eugene O'Neill, reprinted by permission of ICM Partners Copyright © [1940] by Eugene O'Neill.

Extracts from *Long Day's Journey Into Night* by Eugene O'Neill, published by Jonathan Cape. Reproduced by permission of The Random House Group Ltd.

Extracts from *Look Back in Anger*, 1956, and *Inadmissible Evidence*, 1964, © John Osborne, courtesy of The Arvon Foundation.

Extracts from *Enron*, 2009, and *The Effect*, 2012, © Lucy Prebble, by kind permission of the author.

Extracts from *The Cut* © Mark Ravenhill, 2006, *The Cut*, by kind permission of Bloomsbury Methuen Drama, an imprint of Bloomsbury Publishing Plc.

Extract from *The Fastest Clock in the Universe*, © 1992 by Philip Ridley, by kind permission of the author.

Extracts from *Equus*, 1973, and *The Royal Hunt of the Sun*, 1964, © Peter Shaffer, by kind permission of Sir Peter Shaffer, care of Macnaughton Lord Representation of 44 South Molton Street, London W1K 5RT.

Extracts from *Major Barbara*, 1905, and *Pygmalion*, 1912, by George Bernard Shaw, by kind permission of the Society of Authors, on behalf of the Bernard Shaw Estate.

Extract from *Journey's End*, 1929, © R.C. Sherriff, by kind permission of Curtis Brown Group Ltd.

Extracts from *Rutherford and Son* © Githa Sowerby, 1912, *Rutherford and Son*, by kind permission of Bloomsbury Methuen Drama, an imprint of Bloomsbury Publishing Plc.

Extract from *Wonderland*, 2014, © Beth Steel, by kind permission of the author.

Extracts from *Harper Regan* © Simon Stephens, 2008, *Harper Regan*, by kind permission of Bloomsbury Methuen Drama, an imprint of Bloomsbury Publishing Plc.

Extract from *Under Milk Wood*, 1952, © Dylan Thomas, by kind permission of Orion.

Extract from *Under Milk Wood* by Dylan Thomas, from *Under Milk Wood*, copyright ©1952 by Dylan Thomas. Reprinted by permission of New Directions Publishing Corp.

Extracts from Peter Whelan, *The Herbal Bed* (©1996) and Joseph Kesselring, *Arsenic and Old Lace* (©1941), reprinted by kind arrangement with Josef Weinberger Plays (josef-weinberger.com).

Extracts from *Cat On A Hot Tin Roof* by Tennessee Williams, from *Cat On A Hot Tin Roof*, copyright ©1954 by The University of the South. Reprinted by permission of New Directions Publishing Corp.

Dramatic Adventures in Rhetoric

A Note to the Reader

We have done our very best to ensure that this book is accurate, and that it covers the widest range of plays that we could read between us (bearing in mind how many thousands there are). However, in your reading, you may come across what you feel is a stronger example, or one which uses a device in a different way – or perhaps you know of other devices you feel it would be beneficial to include.

If so, please send your comments in an email to info@oberonbooks.com, with the subject line: Dramatic Adventures in Rhetoric. Be sure to include the quote, the character who is speaking, the play title, the playwright, the publisher, the year of publication and the page number of the playtext in which you found it.

WWW.OBERONBOOKS.COM

Follow us on www.twitter.com/@oberonbooks
& www.facebook.com/OberonBooksLondon